The Films of Michael Mann
From the Prison Wall to the Firewall

The Films of Michael Mann

From the Prison Wall to the Firewall

Deryck Swan

LIVERPOOL UNIVERSITY PRESS

First published 2023 by
Liverpool University Press
4 Cambridge Street
Liverpool
L69 7ZU

Deryck Swan has asserted the right to be identified as the editor of this book in accordance with the Copyright, Designs and Patents Act 1988.

All rights reserved. No part of this book may be reproduced, stored in a retrieval system, or transmitted, in any form or by any means, electronic, mechanical, photocopying, recording, or otherwise, without the prior written permission of the publisher.

British Library Cataloguing-in-Publication data
A British Library CIP record is available

ISBN 978-1-91132-518-5 hb

Typeset by Carnegie Book Production, Lancaster
Printed and bound by CPI Group (UK) Ltd, Croydon CR0 4YY

Front and centre, this book is dedicated to the memory of Dr Mark Brownrigg, a former and very brilliant lecturer at the University of Stirling and the University of Aberdeen who sadly died in 2010. Without his impassioned oratory and trinket box of film clips it is doubtful this book would ever have been written.

Contents

Figures		ix
Acknowledgements		xi
Preface		xiii
1	Introduction	1
2	Mann with a Movie Camera	5
3	*The Jericho Mile* and Prison Culture	19
4	*Thief* and the Criminal	39
5	*The Keep* and Stylisation	61
6	*Manhunter* and Modernism	75
7	*The Last of the Mohicans* and Professionalism	95
8	*Heat* and Los Angeles	115
9	*The Insider* and Cinematic Space	135
10	*Ali* and Recreating History	155
11	*Collateral* and Hi-Def Night	173
12	*Miami Vice* and Hi-Def Day	189
13	*Public Enemies* and the Driven Detective	203
14	*Blackhat* and Fragmentation Cinema	219
Afterword		229
Bibliography		233
Index		237

Figures

1	Jericho Mile	25
2	Jericho Mile	26
3	Thief	51
4	Thief	55
5	Keep	66
6	Keep	67
7	Manhunter	79
8	Manhunter	82
9	The Last of the Mohicans	99
10	The Last of the Mohicans	110
11	Heat	125
12	Heat	127
13	Insider	138
14	Insider	149
15	Ali	162
16	Ali	167
17	Collateral	175
18	Collateral	181
19	Miami Vice	191
20	Miami Vice	197
21	Public Enemies	205
22	Public Enemies	210
23	Blackhat	221
24	Blackhat	224

Acknowledgements

I would like to thank the (now former) editor of the *Auteur* series, John Atkinson, for his eternal patience in the writing of this book. If another is to follow, I promise to submit it in half the time.

I would also like to thank the love of my life Louise Shannon for her invaluable help with key portions of this book and for her universal encouragement throughout the final edit.

Preface

In the growing marketplace of books on the director Michael Mann, the aim of this one is to strive to emulate the methodology of the man himself. Ranging over his cinematic body of work – and, sometimes, his forays into television and, most recently, novel writing – the book will adopt an interdisciplinary approach to examine the scope of intellectual interests that his films exemplify in an attempt to mine the commonalities, themes and traits that delineate the presence of a true auteur. The book will avoid the overly academic and theoretical writing that can underpin other studies of this nature and, in doing so, may gloss over or sidestep altogether concepts that would traditionally find traction in this area of film writing; that, it is hoped, is not necessarily a bad thing.

During its investigation of Mann's filmography and the personality that flows through it, the book will supply the reader with accessible and, hopefully, new ways of thinking about his films to date, ways that will include, among myriad other things, references to Morris Louis, desert modernism, the X, Y and Z axes, West Coast prison culture, Mayor Richard Daley, Strain Theory, Mike Royko, Chicago's Auditorium building and a rarely heard-of Charles Bronson movie. The one chapter/one film approach to the book's structure means that while Mann's TV work will sometimes be set aside and some of his films may get more attention than others, less-travelled freeways of commentary and ideas will be offered as a result.

Finally, set alongside these various explorations of Mann's films will be a series of key sequence suggestions that appear at the end of each corresponding chapter. The function of each suggestion is to provide the reader with a prime example of that chapter's main themes via reference to a specific moment from the parent film. These are intended merely as stepping stones to further study, something, it is hoped, this book will encourage.

How do you tell the genuine director from the quasi-chimpanzee?

> Andrew Sarris

A director spends his life on variations of the same film.

> Jean Renoir

CHAPTER ONE

Introduction

A quick tour of the internet provides the casual reader with several links to blogs, magazine websites and published books that all, in one way or another, provide a spirited assessment of Michael Mann's career to date and why he is, clearly, not just an accomplished American director but the kind of director that François Truffaut observed as having a "certaine tendance".[1] More than just a mere stylistic inclination or thematic leaning towards a certain kind of film narrative, the "tendance" that Truffaut was alluding to meant everything that had come to define the filmmaker as a distinctive voice amid the amorphous clamour of more journeyman movie making.

Taking this idea while talking of the late film director Robert Altman in the third edition of his seminal study *A Cinema of Loneliness*, Robert Kolker writes:

> Altman's seventies films are formally and contextually of a piece, so much so that, once his style is understood it can be recognised in almost any one part of any film he makes. He stands with Kubrick as one of the few American filmmakers to confirm the fragile legitimacy of the auteur theory with such a visible expression of coherence in his work.[2]

The formal qualities that Altman exhibited across the span of his 1970s films are indeed, undoubtedly so, his own, and are so distinctive that the attenuation they suffered in later years, particularly during the 1990s in films such as *The Gingerbread Man* (1998), cannot detract from their earlier potency. A major component of Altman's success in the 1970s was the artistic and technical troupe that he managed to gather and maintain throughout that time. As Kolker observes, this group of regular collaborators provided Altman with, among other things, a form of insulation from the upheavals that the Hollywood system was experiencing at the time. They coaxed and encouraged the emergence of his formal methods during that period and helped Altman realise the distinctive soundscapes and hallucinatory zoom shots – see *M.A.S.H.* (1970), *McCabe and Mrs Miller* (1971) and *The Long Goodbye* (1973) – that would go on to immortalise his style in cinema history.

It should be clear by now that Michael Mann is another such director, a film-making auteur with that certain tendency to leave a trail of stylistic and ideological bullet casings throughout his work. The objective of this book is not to question such received wisdom but rather to analyse the relative health of this *Altmanesque* tendency across Mann's filmography, assess its potency from one film to the next, be honest about where it wanes and celebratory when it shines. The chapter headings are designed to help distil this approach into the dominant technique, idea or concern of a particular film, with what follows hopefully elucidating how that technique, idea or concern manifests itself in his work.

In order to do this, the book must try and refrain from the common mistake of taking all the films of the director in question and assuming homogeneity across the entire span of work. Yes, to be thought of as an auteur means that there are usually some identifiable and consistent determinants in your work, a set of governing principles that insulate you from exterior political, social or cultural forces that could otherwise effect a negative or, at the very least, transformative influence on your film making. Yet, as we saw with Robert Altman, established auteurs are not always guaranteed to display such traits or determinants across all their work, all of the time and with an all-encompassing consistency. Robert Kolker noted that the very idea of the auteur is a fragile one. It is open to multiple interpretations and counter-interpretations and can be clearly exemplified by those directors in some of their films but evidently not in others.

In this respect, this book might be quite different in its approach to the study of its director when compared with other notable examples. Rather than proceed from a potentially mistaken and predetermined standpoint of the kind that Kolker avoided with Altman – that all film work be shoehorned into a fixed ideological position from the outset – this book proceeds incrementally and open-mindedly, using an analytical framework to explore each of Mann's films, and sometimes his television work if and when it becomes relevant, in turn and in detail. The entire ethos of this book precludes any showboating or gun-jumping. The methodology employed here means that doubts in the mind or bumps in the road en route to such a holistic understanding of Mann's work will be actively sought out and explored; indeed, the chapter on *The Keep* (1983) will analyse just such a radical divergence. These deviations in style, content or meaning will be allowed for and, more than that, pursued fully in order to arrive at a more honest and satisfying account of this director and his work to date.

Presently, some of the closest analogues to this study are Vincent Gaine's *Existentialism and Social Engagement in the Films of Michael Mann* – a book that adopts a similar, varied approach to the focus of its chapters – and Steven Rybin's *The Cinema of Michael Mann*, a 2007 entry that Rybin himself describes as "an open-ended approach to the work of this important, and yet somehow unwieldy, director".[3] However, Rybin, later on in his book's introduction, concedes that "As I explore the shared stylistic touches and thematic tropes of these particular films, I practice a common auteurist approach: bundling the films together … and exploring the consistencies across that body of work."[4] In any examination of a director and their viability, this assessment of consistency across all their films is both essential and unavoidable. However, to be truly "open-ended", as Rybin indicates above, any such study must seek out and give weight to both the consistencies and also the anomalies in that director's body of work. Such rumination on the interplay of this dialectic can, in contradiction to the potentially forced conclusions of a number of auteur studies, actually serve to improve the understanding of a director's filmography and enhance their legitimacy.

In the main, what follows will range from 1979's *The Jericho Mile*, which here will be treated as a film rather than a TV "movie of the week", to 2015's *Blackhat*, with an Afterword that discusses Mann's pre- and post-pandemic work: directing the pilot episode of *Tokyo Vice*, writing his first novel *Heat 2* and shooting his personal magnum opus, *Ferrari*. Across the main chapters the primary aim will be to identify the key technical, cultural or ideological determinant that dominates the film under discussion and evaluate its function as another *tendency* of Mann. As the book progresses, opportunities will be taken to ask whether these different determinants are common to more than just one film and whether, cumulatively, they contribute to or detract from Mann's overall personal style. The aforementioned bumps or deviations from the norm will be folded into this analysis and will play an active part in any conclusions the book eventually makes. Woven through this process will be attempts to account for Mann's position in American cinema today, examining such aspects as his multiple roles during filming – writer, producer, assistant DOP, director – as well as his alternative roles as a producer of other directors' work, such as that of Peter Berg, Martin Scorsese, James Mangold and his own daughter, Ami Mann.

There will be discussion of Mann's intensive, research-based approach to film making, its effects on his output over the span of his career and how his approach to films is really an extension of his wish to control and modulate every aspect of his craft. As with Robert Altman, Steven Spielberg and Christopher Nolan, the book will explore the troupe of regular collaborators that Mann has gathered – Michael Waxman, Dante Spinotti, Colleen Atwood and Dov Hoenig – and how this further reinforces his desire to control the processes of film production via the administering and managing of its collaborative aspects.

Notes

1 François Truffaut, "A Certain Tendency of the French Cinema", in Scott MacKenzie (ed.), *Film Manifestos and Global Cinema Cultures: A Critical Anthology*, University of California Press, 2014, 133.
2 Robert Kolker, *A Cinema of Loneliness: Penn, Stone, Kubrick, Scorsese, Spielberg, Altman*, 3rd edn, Oxford University Press, 2000, 358.
3 Steven Rybin, *The Cinema of Michael Mann*, Lexington Books, 2007, 3.
4 Ibid., 5.

CHAPTER TWO

Mann with a Movie Camera

It's less about a fascination and more about an environment.

Michael Mann

Despite unequivocally stating that this book really deals with the *films* of Michael Mann, it is going to immediately depart from that dictum and start by discussing his work on the pilot episode of HBO's prestigious but ill-fated production *Luck* (2012), a series focusing on the various denizens of the Santa Anita racetrack in California.

This was a uniquely challenging piece of work, all the more so for being a television programme created by David Milch – a writer specialising in ultra-specific milieus and dialogue that fuses local patois by way of Shakespeare and Nadsat – and featured several determinants, both visual and aural, that gave away the creative mind behind the camera. One of the most pronounced indicators that Mann was guiding the opening minutes of the pilot show was his use of the first minute and 43 seconds of Elliot Goldenthal's "Heat", the wonderfully evocative track that Mann selected for the start of his 1995 film of the same name. As the pilot episode's pivotal horse race gets underway, Mann slows the action down, fades out the diegetic sound and brings Goldenthal's wonderful, keening guitar strings quietly into the fold. The moment is marked with a supreme sense of pathos and catharsis in a way that few contemporary American directors can do and do well.

Counter to Pauline Kael's feeling that such recycling of previous visual and aural ideas is an obvious marker of a director in decline, Mann's desire to do this, to draw attention to his continued presence, actually serves to reaffirm his authorship and augment his ability to delineate commonalities in diverse narrative material.[1] It is both a nod to his fanbase and a testament to the flexibility of his stylistic choices that such a musical selection as the "Heat" cue works as well to introduce Neil McCauley on his night train to Los Angeles as it does during a horse race many years later in an unrelated show; but this has always been Mann at his most audacious, a director who, as we shall see, makes new work by deriving ideas from his old.

Subsequent episodes of the show would go on to feature other memorable audio tracks from Mann's back catalogue in the service of similar purposes. Episode 9 uses "Nasty Letter" by Otis Taylor during another horse race, a wonderful track from the Chicago-born blues musician that Mann initially deployed during Dillinger's audacious escape from Crown Point Jail, Indiana, in *Public Enemies* (2009). This particular track has a quality to it that suggests a building determination to succeed, both here with the mounting tension of the horse race and in *Public Enemies*, where uncertainty abounds as to the likelihood of Dillinger actually escaping the jail unseen. As we make progress through his work, other examples of when and how Mann regurgitates his visual and aural cues will be considered, leading to an assessment of why they bolster his auteurship rather than undermine it.

The pilot episode of *Luck* is also highly instructive in terms of how the camera is used and what this reveals about Mann's approach to cinematic space and, by extension, narrative. Even a cursory glance at Episode 1 reveals an unbridled intimacy in the camera work through its frequent proximity to the faces of the actors and horses alike. The viewer's visual intake of the world of the Santa Anita racetrack is rigidly tethered to the inherent subjectivity of its residents, as Mann tries to approximate their internalised experience of daily life, something he has always been fascinated by but didn't really pursue visually until *Heat* (1995). A major project of Mann's since that time, what the close proximity of the camera to its subjects is doing in his work is attempting to deconstruct what he would call the *fiction of drama* and provide the audience with a visual experience as free from dramatic affectation or artifice as he can manage. For the most part *Luck* denies the viewer any sense of anchorage or suture by inducing a blistering, close-quarter array of different angles and directions via the camera. Long shots and aerial shots tend to be avoided in favour of the immediacy and verisimilitude that unmediated camera work can provide.

With *Luck* Mann clearly wants the audience inside the riders' heads, running on the racetrack with the horses and seated next to the crooks and gamblers as they bet with their lives. While this sounds like a common and all too clichéd attempt to make things look "realistic", Mann is taking things much further by having the look of *Luck* marry up with how events are organised in a narrative sense and what the viewer is denied in terms of any initial understanding. He does not want the audience to be aware that they are passively watching fictional events. Rather, he hopes that, through the deployment of these disruptive visual and aural strategies, they will become actively lost in the world he is creating – with all its trials, tribulations and textures – and, most vital of all, will feel that the world onscreen is existing concurrently with their own.

The highly mobile and uninhibited movements of the camera in *Luck* illustrate one strategy Mann has for achieving this state of audience non-awareness. He sees this approach as one method for attaining a truth-telling style, as one of his characters, Waingro, says in *Heat*, and would now probably regard more classicist forms of camera work and narrative as a betrayal of his post-millennial cinematic principles and the intelligence of the audience.[2] The most thrilling deployment of this truth-telling camera style is arguably in the show's racing sequences, which are indeed a revelation and continue the idea of deconstructing the visual presentation of drama and placing the audience inside events. The template Mann established for the horseracing sequences in the pilot was wisely retained for all subsequent episodes in Series One and, when looked at analytically, has all the flavour and veracity of the other professional endeavours that populate his film work, from safe-cracking to bank robbery to court depositions to boxing bouts. In all likelihood, the race car sequences in his upcoming *Ferrari* will continue this template.

Coinciding with this camera style, or perhaps a correlate of it, is the unmistakable narrative structure employed by *Luck*, as touched on above. Much discussed by reviewers of the pilot and the subsequent episodes, some saying it was a major plus point, others an impediment to enjoying the show, the narrative structure deployed by Mann here is bold and merciless and one of the main reasons his 2006 film *Miami Vice* was so misinterpreted in some critical quarters. Undoubtedly the show's writer David Milch had a hand in the way *Luck*'s story was conceived and told – this seems plausible given how much Milch's previous hit show, *Deadwood*, used similar narrative strategies – but its structures, beats and delicate cadences nevertheless bear the much clearer stamp of Mann and his undiminished crusade to liberate the dramatic storytelling of traditional American film making and TV.[3] The first thing one notices about the story when watching *Luck* is the complete lack of visual context in the introduction and evolution of its characters, an aspect largely due to the show's inherent *in medias res* style structure. Ostensibly present since *The Jericho Mile*, it was really 1999's *The Insider* that inaugurated Mann's progressive and experimental journey to denude the amount of exposition – both visual and through dialogue – which film narratives traditionally present to the audience. This has been a quest completely aligned with his pursuit of creating internalised audience experiences where, as with

Luck's pilot, viewers feel situated as much as possible in the environments onscreen and participate in the immediacy of the characters' situations without recourse to flashbacks or other methods of contextualisation.

The most salient and ongoing manifestation of this quest by Mann to deconstruct what is required by narrative necessity is the general absence of both classical establishing shots and expositional exchanges of dialogue in his work, those most hallowed examples of conventional American film grammar that allow an audience to locate where the film's events and its characters are situated. Several of Mann's own film commentaries testify to this unusual visual and narrative construction that has been so much the focus of his work in recent years, particularly in the opening sequences of his films, which were no doubt on his mind when he was constructing those opening moments of *Luck*'s pilot. As Mann says of the beginning of *Heat*, "there's a particular way the story tells itself that I very much wanted to try and achieve which is that you dropped into the process of what these men are doing, simulating dropping into a life almost at random so that there is no preamble".[4] Of *Collateral*'s narrative attraction to him, Mann says that

> we're seeing fractions or fractals, we're seeing a fraction that represents the whole and only what you need to know is what you're seeing ... it doesn't go back in time or give you exposition about other parts of their lives ... so in the beginning I wanted to enter these activities with kind of a torn edge.[5]

Despite being unavoidably tethered to certain aspects of the classical mode of narrative construction and presentation – cause and effect, generally clear character motivations, characters who wish to solve a set of identifiable problems, largely continuity editing – what these film commentaries point to is this alternative narrative radicalism that has clearly preoccupied Mann's work, certainly for the past fifteen years. It remains a challenging ambition of his, a gambit that seeks to revise the expectations that audiences have come to hold about film and TV storytelling. Mann frequently talks about how audiences are much brighter than they are aware of, that their subconscious processing of a film experience is far more savvy and intuitive than is given credit; whatever the ability of the amygdala, such narrative radicalism as this has certainly tested viewers' ability to distil from the elliptical fragments of information a sense of who Mann's characters are and what they are doing.

2006's *Miami Vice* is a perfect and potent crystallisation of this radicalism and likely one of the primary reasons the film fared rather less well than expected at the box office. A film that we will look at in much more detail later, *Miami Vice* is as bold as the TV series was, not only in terms of its cultural specificity (it's possible that as much nostalgia will surround the film thirty years from today as currently surrounds the TV series from the 1980s) but also in its narrative treatment of crime, detection and action. The extended opening sequence alone (the cinematic opening rather than the US DVD release featuring the offshore powerboat race) places significant demands on the audience to keep pace with events and rapidly adjust to the film's attempts to emulate real life and the way random events impact on the unsuspecting individual.

All this being said, such radicalism is far from poison to other directors. As we shall see, filmmakers such as Christopher Nolan are taking up the reins of this radicalism and invigorating old material with a mixture of ambiguity, challenge and high audience expectation. As Joseph Bevan noted in an article on Nolan in *Sight & Sound*:

> These multi-layered narratives work through visual acuity and brisk editing – and an unusual degree of trust placed in the audience to follow the story. This can involve massive compression of scenes – in the prologue of *Batman Begins*, Nolan takes us with an insistent economy from Bruce Wayne's encounter with a cave full of bats to his parents' death, acknowledging the audience's familiarity with the story while at the same time rendering it anew.[6]

Here Bevan could just as easily have been discussing any number of moments from *Miami Vice*, the sumptuous opening montage of Mann's *Ali* (2001) – a virtuoso sequence that coalesces a complex series of abstract 1960s sounds and images into something quite profound and instructive – or most of *Blackhat* (2015).

And so his narrative fragmentation, combined with the reprocessing of past aural and visual cues, are recurring determinants in his present – and likely future – projects, and aspects that will be explored further in order to see what they might yield for our purposes here. Unlike, for instance, Robert Altman's intense but relatively short-lived focus on particular soundscapes and cinematic spaces in the 1970s, Mann's narrative experiments and his reconfiguration of past ideas are but two elements of his approach that have endured, running through his canon from the Folsom prison culture of *The Jericho Mile* to the computer hacking of *Blackhat*.

It would seem then that *Luck* offers a useful and much-overlooked demonstration of who Michael Mann is today. It is a television product that maintains the complex and indelible cinematic template established by him in his films. *Luck*, just as *Tokyo Vice* would do later, ably summarises the mark of a director operating at full technical and creative strength, and for whom innovation, fragmentation and reinvention are cornerstones of his method. But to understand the genesis of this method we must turn to the Midwest of America and the Illinois state capital of Chicago.

At one point in his 2009 interview of Michael Mann for the *Guardian* newspaper's *Film Weekly* supplement, Jason Solomons is discussing the prominence of Chicago in Mann's life and work.[7] With his usual mix of erudition and exactitude Mann graciously provides Solomons with a verbal treatise about the "Brechtian" and "tough-minded" nature of Chicago, the endemic nature of crime stories to its streets and its overall wit and good humour. What's interesting is that, prior to this part of the exchange, Solomons referred to Chicago as being kind of "in the middle", ostensibly in reference to its isolated geographical location in the great American Midwest but also, perhaps in a more barbed sense, in allusion to the Illinois state capital's seeming cultural scarcity when set against the likes of New York or Los Angeles. "It's not the middle of anywhere" is Mann's succinct response before he goes on to elucidate Chicago's unique sensibility and disabuse Solomons of his odd and, more importantly, outdated impression of Mann's hometown.

Clearly, to Solomons and, by extension, a large number of people unfamiliar with the city, Chicago appeared as somehow unregarded, unassuming and, dare it be said, parochial, an almost forgotten outpost on the way West to Los Angeles. What Mann's spirited defence highlights is that it is exactly these qualities – its relative isolation, its insular demographic, its commitment to self-authorship – that permitted Chicago to acquire the distinctive authenticity that it exhibits today. Chicago is now, in the twenty-first century, a uniquely *real* American city, a place built upon hard work, preparation and pragmatism that has assiduously avoided becoming that clichéd and digestible aggregate of tourist symbology that characterises New York or Los Angeles (something that, as we shall later see, Mann would actively rail against in his presentation of these cities in *The Insider*, *Heat* and *Collateral* respectively). It is a city that seems far more credible than its contemporaries because it appears to have got there, in a sense, under its own steam and has shied away from the undue influence of others in order to craft its own unique sensibility.

As an explanatory metaphor or analogue for Michael Mann's quietly charted but steadily incremental rise to prominence, his working methods and his artistic influences, the city of Chicago is an indispensable bedfellow. Like Chicago, Mann is now a well-respected presence on the American social and cultural landscape. Both his host city and the man himself have assumed a level of integrity, quality and self-determination that is markedly different from that exuded by New York or Los Angeles and their respective cinematic chroniclers. Both the city and Mann present themselves as being autodidactic and self-formed, and they have consistently charted their own course towards the kind of contemporary prominence or pre-eminence that they now enjoy. But more than this, more than a 1-2-3 of handy analogies that can appear to be drawn between Mann and his hometown, the city of Chicago, as we shall see, is absolutely integral to understanding Mann's later work and the major influences that present themselves through his films.

Born in 1943 to parents Esther and Jack, Michael Mann was raised on The Patch in Humboldt Park, one of Chicago's many neighbourhoods for Jewish and European immigrants. At this time Chicago was a city on the verge of developing further the credibility of its reputation, both scientifically and politically. In 1942, the year before Mann's birth, Enrico Fermi had successfully conducted the world's first controlled nuclear fission reaction at the University of Chicago, a seminal moment in the Manhattan Project and the USA's larger role in the Second World War. When Mann was 12, around the time when he would be driving down Lincoln Avenue with his father talking about the Biograph and John Dillinger's untimely death, Mayor Richard Daley, that grand patriarch of the city, was inaugurating his brand of machine politics. A year later Chicago Blues was finding its feet as the likes of Cobra Records and Delmark Records were founded and the careers of Otis Rush and Roscoe Mitchell began to gain traction. Little of this would escape the attention of Mann, whose later films would often showcase his appreciation and knowledge of the radical music, politics and culture attendant to each.

Chicago was working hard to be self-sustaining and provided Mann not only with a place to grow up but with a readily accessible store of artistic expression, formidable politics and social and cultural values. The Chicagoan wellspring bequeathed Mann this trinity of value through several distinct and yet interlaced facets of the city's development that in turn gave rise to his multidisciplinary approach to film making and the dominant and determining themes in his work. The first of these was the Chicagoan architecture, specifically the very important modernist period spearheaded in the second half of the nineteenth century by Louis Sullivan, his contemporary Henry Hobson Richardson and Sullivan's student, Frank Lloyd Wright. Sullivan's revolutionary liberation of the city's architecture from stone to steel ushered in the great modernist expansion of American architecture that came to include the Carson, Pirie, Scott and Company Building and the Auditorium Building, both Chicago firsts for what quickly came to be called the skyscraper. Mann's rigorous use of architecture as an active element in the *mise en scène* of his films is, in all likelihood, a direct result of the exposure to Chicago's modernist transformation that he sought out during his early years there.

Mann's allusion to Sullivan's work in a 2004 interview with *Sight & Sound*'s Mark Olsen bespeaks the latent presence this architectural genius occupies in films such as *Thief, Manhunter, Heat, The Insider, Collateral* and *Public Enemies*:

> It's useful here to make an analogy with architecture. When steel was first introduced as a building material architects disguised the structure of their buildings to look like masonry. It wasn't until Louis Sullivan's pioneering works in Chicago in the 1890s that the aesthetics of the steel structure were allowed to be expressed.[8]

While ostensibly referring to the connection between the liberating forces of steel in architecture and high-def digital video in film making, Mann is also giving away the presence of a strong, formational force in his expressions of the urban environment and how he seeks to use architecture, namely the force of Louis Sullivan and his Chicago School style. Modernism as a mode of artistic expression and a governing philosophy in Mann's work is something that will be explored in much more detail when we come to look at films such as *Thief, Heat* and *Public Enemies*. How these films deploy modernism in order to inform both their visual presentation and moral framework is key to grasping their connection and the path they share back to Sullivan and the Chicago of the 1890s. However, as is the spirit of this book, when we come to assess *Collateral* we will find a complete inversion of the modernist ethos and a film that absolutely relies on a fragmented and postmodern view of another city central to understanding Mann's work, Los Angeles. Such is this director, someone as much characterised by homogeneity as by heterogeneity.

The second fundamental element that derives from Chicago and holds unalterable sway in Mann's films is crime and the lore of the criminal, more precisely the notion of the highly principled and rigidly self-determining criminal. In *The Cinema of Michael Mann* Rybin notes that:

> [Mann] will often state in interviews that the cops-and-robbers, criminal underworld is one he has at least a superficial personal familiarity with, a claim perhaps boosted by the fact that the director was born in the inner city of Chicago during World War II.[9]

Along with its fledgling modernist architectural forms, Chicago in the 1930s bore witness to the emergence of this new incarnation of the criminal, a criminal who was autodidactic, socially integrated, intelligent, urbane and professional. As Mann highlights in his commentary for *Public Enemies*, the notion of the criminal as being a type or subset of society ended with the rise of John Dillinger and the other Public Enemies of the 1930s. Whereas before, society regarded the criminal as being someone emblematic of moral degeneracy or imbecility, now these old patterns were being remoulded by new, modern crime figures whose allure lay in their rugged individuality and their proficiency in circumventing both the crippling economic depression of the time and the general ineptitude of the various law enforcement agencies, including the newly formed FBI. In the actions of these new criminals there is a purity of intent that, while still clearly morally wrong, could nevertheless be respected for its professionalism and skill, its strictly principled boundaries and its sublimation of all other rudimentary concerns. This modernist template introduced by the likes of Herman K. Lamm, Walter Dietrich, John Dillinger and, later, the real Neil McCauley (all products of Chicago in one way or another), would become the genome for Mann's conception and characterisation of the criminal as seen in *Thief*, *Heat*, *Collateral* or *Public Enemies*.

The characters here harken back to the blueprint set down by the real Public Enemies of Chicago in the 1930s because they, like Dillinger et al., encourage a form of deference despite the seeming immorality of their actions. As is befitting of the modernist description, these characters are ambiguous, as they shun mass consumerism but embrace technology to achieve their goal of self-expression and financial self-sufficiency. These traits and themes continued into the 1960s and 1970s when the template laid down by Dillinger and the other Public Enemies of the 1930s was reinvigorated by a new generation of Chicago thieves, men such as Frank Hohimer and John Santucci, criminals who often hailed from The Patch, the same neighbourhood that Mann grew up in. Some of the best jewel thieves of the period emerged from this area in Chicago and one of them,

Hohimer, would go on to be the entire basis of James Caan's character in *Thief*.[10]

Mann did well enough at his local high school in Chicago to attend the University of Wisconsin at Madison – to this day a progressive institution in terms of student politics, with a history of activism that includes the infamous Sterling Hall bombing of 1970 – where he studied English literature and film history. Formational events often acquire a kind of phoney retrospective significance when the individual reflects on that time in their attempts to divine some pattern to their life. With Mann, however, perhaps one of the most unlikely candidates to exhibit affectation or pretension, when he talks of seeing Georg Wilhelm Pabst's 1925 film *The Joyless Street* for the first time at Madison and its catalytic effect on his future career, you believe him. One of the earliest examples of Weimar Germany's New Objectivity movement, *The Joyless Street* saw Pabst attempt to put on screen the documentary realism that this artistic movement aspired to. Knowing the formational influence Pabst's film had on Mann, it is nearly impossible to watch any of his TV or motion picture work and not see Dennis Crockett's definition of the New Objectivity in action: "The New Objectivity is Americanism, the cult of the objective, the hard fact, and the predilection for functional work, professional conscientiousness and usefulness."[11]

From *Thief* to *Heat*, *The Jericho Mile* to *The Insider*, Mann's entire canon is most aptly characterised by its dual attention to these tenets of both fact and functional work, a wish to realise on screen the objectivity, impartiality and edginess inherent in real life. In an interview with Ken Tucker for *Entertainment Weekly*, Mann seemed to corroborate this view when he said that the "intense experiences of real people and times have a currency in them and are expressed with language that is beyond anything you can make up".[12] Mann says that upon leaving the screening of the Pabst film, he was walking down Baskin Hill on this cold winter's night and was suddenly imbued with the conviction that "this is what I must do". The persona and filmography that Mann has developed over the course of his career means that, however hokey this statement may appear to the ear, you cannot argue with the evidence and force of its execution.

By 1965 Mann was ready to begin acquiring the practical and technical skills that would go on to characterise in later years some of his best work. This aspiration coincided with the rise to prominence of America's first film schools, academic institutions that provided not only practical experience for would-be filmmakers but also significant theoretical grounding in both classical American film styles and, more importantly, European approaches as evidenced by the Nouvelle Vague. Film departments such as the New York University Tisch School of the Arts, the University of Texas Department of Radio, Television & Film and the Columbia University School of the Arts were all founded in 1965, just as films such as *Who's Afraid of Virginia Woolf* (1966) and *Bonnie and Clyde* (1967) were about to split the orthodoxy of Hollywood in two with their radicalism and boldness. However, the love of intertextuality, allusion and genre film making that emerged from this time through famed proponents such as Martin Scorsese, Peter Bogdanovich and John Cassavetes was interesting but quite antithetical to Mann's project for the future. The majority of such film schools at that time were overly concerned with the academic study of film, something Mann most likely regarded as, dare it be said, trivial when placed next to the real-world effects that Vietnam and the Civil Rights struggle were having on people's lives and contemporary culture as a whole. Mann's panacea for this would be found not in the continental US but in England, a very different environment but one not untouched by the bold social and cultural revisions currently underway.

The London International Film School seemed to offer the pragmatism and practical skill that Mann was hungering for during this time. In 1965 he made the journey to England to begin the two-year programme at the LIFS. The course equipped Mann with the technical proficiency to realise, in a very practical sense, some of the ideas swarming in his mind. His student efforts, an 8mm short called *Dead Birds* and the more accomplished *Jaunpuri*, which won some awards on both the European and Australian film circuits, are emblematic of both the energy and naivety that can often characterise the early work of fledgling filmmakers. Mann has since prohibited the public exhibition of these films because of their seeming indulgence (*Jaunpuri* is a form of melody, or raga, in Hindustani classical music) but concurrently does not regret making them in the first place. He sees them as a fundamental evolutionary step towards purging from later work those modes of affectation that can appear when a filmmaker first picks up a camera.

In 1967 Mann made his first foray into production, a move that would prove integral in helping to sustain his relative independence from studio interference in later life. Michael Mann Productions was registered as a company and the director got his first taste of professional autonomy, something he would guard as ferociously as Stanley Kubrick or Steven Spielberg. Under the auspices of his eponymous new company Mann gained some valuable work experience through the London offices of 20th Century–Fox, experience that brought into high relief the gaps in his emerging skillset. The most relevant of these was perhaps the key remit of any aspiring director, how to project-manage a large-scale film production. It was during his stint in these London studios that Mann arguably honed this skill along with the methodology and ethos of hard work that Chicago had imbued him with during those earlier years.

Mann learned that the initial approach to the behemoth task of making manageable a large-scale film production was to reduce it to its various constituent parts and address each in turn. What emerged from this deconstruction was a keen awareness of the underlying form of things, the ability to recognise the value of individual elements and rebuild something, Gestalt-style, until its overall meaning is revealed. From understanding that each actor has their own unique mode of working, to knowing how to break apart a script, to assigning individual plot points, what Mann has come to term *the action* (in short, the internal function of a scene distilled into one key word), the year and a half at Fox Studios bequeathed Mann a foundational education that would never leave him.

1968 saw the students and workers of the USA and the wider world responding to injustices endemic since the end of the Second World War. Issues of race, sex, the war in Vietnam, women's rights and the emergence of the New Left all now fell under the aegis of the countercultural movement. In 1971 Mann returned to America, fully armed with his newfound technical competency, into a quagmire of social and political tumult. South Vietnam and the US had just invaded Laos, Attica State Prison was under siege and desegregation had been made constitutional. *17 Days Down the Line* saw Mann traversing his native land from Chicago to Los Angeles during this time, ostensibly to craft a travelogue on his return from London that might test his newly acquired technical skills. Along the way, however, what this documentary also did was capture the emergent social and political dissent catalysed by the war in South East Asia. *17 Days* would become Mann's first document of social realism, an unanticipated recording of the impacts of power structures on the lives of ordinary individuals. The seeds of an eternal interest in conflict were arguably sown here as Mann bore witness to the death throes of America's, and by extension the West's, old political structures and outdated systems of control. As we will see in subsequent chapters, later films such as *The Last of the Mohicans*, *The Insider* and *Ali* would recapitulate the thesis presented in *17 Days*, albeit in augmented forms and over much more expansive tapestries. Although *17 Days* would never go on to enjoy a wide release theatrically or on home media, its impact both directly and indirectly on these other films serves to highlight one of Mann's primary and least understood interests: the reconfiguring of his past work in new forms.

The attention that *17 Days* generated during this time piqued the interest of film producer Tim Zinneman, who was looking to capitalise on the promise shown by Mann both by the documentary and also the select TV scripts he had completed for *Police Story*, *Police Woman* and *Vega$* towards the end of the 1970s. Zinnemann's offer was a project called *Straight Time*, a neo-noir prison drama with some serious credentials behind the story ideas. An adaptation of the novel *No Beast So Fierce*, the penological tour de force by former West Coast bank robber Eddie Bunker, *Straight Time* charts a career criminal's attempts to re-enter society after many years in jail. Although Mann's involvement in *Straight Time* would eventually become marginal in terms of the final credit he received or how faithful the director Ulu Grosbard and star Dustin Hoffman would be to his adaptation of the source novel, it was a seminal opportunity in the development of his larger aspirations and a true lodestone when we look analytically at his career to date.

Mann's work on *Straight Time* gave him direct access to two things that would later prove indispensable: Folsom State Prison and the novelist himself, Edward Bunker, who wrote the book while attending a writers' workshop when he was an inmate at Folsom. The confluence of these two vectors over the series of two or three months' writing for *Straight Time* saw Mann enter what he himself might term a period of graduate school education in prison culture and criminology. The specifics of this immersion at Folsom, including the insight into all the subtle details of prison behaviour that Mann would acquire and utilise, will be dealt with in much more detail in subsequent chapters; here it is sufficient to state that Mann's introduction to prison culture, specifically the West Coast prison culture of Folsom and later Chino, and the experience of meeting Bunker were formative events and must be recognised as such.

To Mann, Folsom Prison must have represented his first look at the kind of environment he has since had such a fascination with, environments populated by individuals pursuing what he would later term the *elevated experience of their lives*. Prisons, like the criminal underworld of Los Angeles or the corporate battleground of CBS News, are to Mann all milieus that allow their inhabitants to aggressively pursue an extreme form of self-determination. Mann's acquisition of the mores and structures of prison life, and his work scripting these details into something dramatic, was evidently enough to raise his profile and elevate him above the studio parapet during this time.

Barry Diller, then Head of Programming at the ABC Network and creator of the *Movie of the Week* slot that would run successfully between 1969 and 1976 – and also launch the career of one Steven Spielberg – became aware of Mann through the director's sojourn at Folsom and decided to send him a prison-themed script that he felt might be of interest. It centred on an inmate at Folsom, Rain Murphy, whose dedication to running and almost Zen-like adherence to jail-time stoicism would prove to be the catalyst for the kind of truly effervescent explosion that Mann was hungering for.

And so, in 1979, Mann directed *The Jericho Mile*, a work replete with both useful similarities and intriguing differences when sited next to his subsequent films. It is to this film that we now turn.

Notes

1 Pauline Kael, "Circles and Squares", *Film Quarterly* 16, no. 3 (April 1963): 12–26.
2 By classicist I mean the majority of American film making prior to the 1960s, when the studio system demanded certain modes of expression that included a restraint of formalism.
3 The fervour of Mann's wish to ensure that this remained the dominant project of the series, given that he would only actually direct the pilot episode, extended to a "visual syntax" folder that all subsequent episode directors were to study and follow. As reported in an article in the article "HBO Bets on Two Thoroughbreds" iby Ray Gustini in the *New York Times* on 25 January 2012, this syntax folder included "everything from shooting angles to lighting" as well as editing and scoring decisions. The same was likely true for his most recent TV work, HBO's *Tokyo Vice*.
4 See Mann's director's commentary on the Blu-ray of *Heat*.
5 See Mann's director's commentary on the Blu-ray of *Collateral*.
6 Joseph Bevan, "Christopher Nolan: Escape Artist", *Sight & Sound* 22, no. 8 (August 2012): 18.
7 http://www.theguardian.com/film/video/2009/jul/02/michael-mann-public-enemies (accessed 26 December 2022).
8 Mark Olsen, "It Happened One Night", *Sight & Sound* 14, no. 10 (October 2004): 14.
9 Steven Rybin, *The Cinema of Michael Mann*, Lexington Books, 2007, 5. Mann's father Jack was a WWII veteran who fought at the Battle of the Bulge and returned home to the United States with PTSD before the term was popularised. According to Michael, as a result of his war trauma, Jack would take him to see movies early on Sunday mornings because he found crowds too stressful.
10 See the *Thief* audio commentary on the recent Blu-ray release.
11 Dennis Crockett, *German Post-Expressionism: The Art of the Great Disorder 1918–1924*, Pennsylvania State University Press, 1999, 395.
12 http://watching-tv.ew.com/2012/01/21/michael-mann-interview-luck-hbo/ (accessed 26 December 2022).

CHAPTER THREE

The Jericho Mile and Prison Culture

> When I was in the ring at the Olympics, it was my father's words that I was hearing, not the coaches'. I never listened to what the coaches said. I would call my father and he would give me advice from prison
>
> Floyd Mayweather, Jr

In *The Jericho Mile*, Michael Mann's first cinematic entry, prison is indeed a place of sage words and life lessons. It is a film that shares some commonalities with his future work but is more interesting because of its seeming departures from the tropes that would come into play with *Thief* and related films beyond. This chapter will deal with the intriguing interplay of likeness and difference that *Jericho* offers up, and we will start with the most useful thing that it provided Mann with – Folsom Prison itself.

Ostensibly the most salient aspect of *The Jericho Mile* that recurs across a large tract of Mann's career is the idea of prison culture as a formative force in the lives of criminals. Mann's time working within the walls of Folsom Prison as a writer on *Straight Time* allowed him to acquire an intimate understanding of the culture and cadence of prison life, specifically West Coast (and, to an extent, Midwest) prison culture, as exemplified by Folsom and later by the penitentiaries of Chino, Joliet, McNeil and Stateville. It became apparent to Mann while working on *Straight Time* that Folsom and its sister institutions were of a specific kind, a breed apart where there existed a kind of counterintuitive orderliness to life inside precisely because of their hardened institutional notoriety. Because these prisons were regarded as end-of-the-line institutions, where inmates with long sentences or violent histories would end up as a last resort in their custodial lives, Mann realised that those same prisons played an often-important part in shaping the convicts' philosophies about the future and how they should conduct themselves in life. This confluence of certain breeds of criminal would result in the formation of a kind of distorted criminal graduate school, where the inmates could acquire or refine skills that would service their later careers in robbery or homicide or, in the case of Murphy in *The Jericho Mile*, running. As an extension of character and a manifestation of professionalism, the running that Murphy chooses to define himself by in *Jericho* is no different than the safe-cracking chosen by Frank in *Thief* or the bank robbery chosen by McCauley in *Heat*. All are activities learned and perfected in prison because of the way that these institutions impact on the criminal and force the mind into this very myopic pursuit of self-determination. Such a notion of prison, as something that actively promotes the kind of high-end professionalism that holds sway in much of Mann's work, is something that has its genesis in *The Jericho Mile* and its view of Folsom.

The self-determining professionalism present in Murphy through his Olympic running in *Jericho* colours his whole approach to serving out his sentence in Folsom. The film's central expression of his sagacity and stoicism perhaps shares some undercurrents with the mythos of the Chicago underworld of the 1930s and 1940s, when Mann was growing up and learning about career professionals such as Dillinger and Lamm, men dedicated to being the best at what they did. In a way, *The Jericho Mile* was Mann's first motion picture exploration of this prototype male criminal, which he would go on to investigate again and again, through the gaudy 1980s aesthetic of *Thief* and, to a lesser extent, *Manhunter*, the 1990s anti-capitalism of *Heat* and the bold 1930s recidivism of *Public Enemies* – experts all defined by a philosophy of work moulded and shaped in prison.[1] Although *Jericho* is the only Mann film where the protagonist is actually in jail (in *Public Enemies* Dillinger is in jail momentarily but only so that we can witness the thrill of him breaking out), those other entries cited above still draw upon the indelible portent of prison, a place that must be both acknowledged by the main characters as the source of their skills and repudiated as a place never to be returned to. Look again at *Heat* and the way that prison has shaped McCauley's look and behaviour – his impossibly starched shirt collar at the coffee shop meeting, the origami napkin he leaves around Eady's glass, the newspaper cuttings that hide his domestic life – or the way a forced return to Folsom hangs over his head throughout its running time, a stifling presence that threatens to nullify all his creative efforts to escape to the island paradise of Fiji and later New Zealand.

Crucially, where *The Jericho Mile* departs from this template is in its deeper characterisation of Rains Murphy, the central figure, and of Folsom itself. Murphy, unlike Frank in *Thief* or McCauley in *Heat* or Dillinger in *Public Enemies*, was not a career criminal before his incarceration and has no criminal aspirations beyond it. At the start of the film Murphy finds himself in jail for the murder of his abusive father and is doing his time in strict adherence to a dictum of self-imposed solitude that exiles him from the normal spectrum of prison experience.[2] Murphy regards his imprisonment as a justified response to the murder of his father and, through his running, gains a kind of catharsis from his experiences there. The view that Mann's criminal protagonists would later take, that prison is a necessary learning curve in the beginning and an impediment to success later on, is completely absent here, replaced instead by this almost idealistic stance that Murphy has regarding his jail time and what it can give him. Murphy is resigned to his imprisonment and has adopted a mental attitude and a physical activity to endure it.

The Folsom of *Jericho* is a place that, rather than inhibiting opportunity, provides it willingly. It is jail that affords Murphy the recognition of his true running ability. It is jail that facilitates his track time and the practice needed to qualify for his climactic Olympic bid. It is in jail that he breaks the four-minute mile record and, in doing so, transcends his past criminal deeds. These aspects point to an odd naivety in the film, a naivety that runs, perhaps deliberately, against its bid for authenticity and realism, but is nevertheless very helpful in understanding *Jericho*'s overall uniqueness in Mann's canon. Despite the seriousness of the stories found in *The Jericho Mile*, the environment of Folsom seems somewhat outlandish in what it permits Murphy to achieve, given what we know about the prison industrial complex in America today.

The film begins with a series of abstract images presenting the vagaries of experience to be found during a stint of yard time for the inmates at Folsom. One prisoner dances in time to the beat pouring from his hand-held stereo, a variant of the unmistakable sound of The Rolling Stones' "Sympathy for the Devil" emerging from both his speakers and the soundtrack itself in a playful manipulation of the diegesis of the film. Still further images show inmates playing chess, lifting weights, styling one another's hair and, in the case of Murphy and Stiles, running on the track. The discordant choice of music and the selection of these disconnected and subjective images establishes Folsom as an unknowable and highly individualised environment, a place where a clear establishing shot is never fully rendered for the benefit of the audience. This method of providing the viewer with fractions that represent the whole, of limiting the spatial understanding of a place and instead offering a smattering of disparate vignettes, is both an element crucial to understanding the politics of *The Jericho Mile* – and by extension what Murphy represents – and Mann's enduring project to deconstruct the conventional requirements of drama.

The opening sequence offers an understanding of these facets willingly, particularly a glimpse into the politics of the age and the director. The montage has a freshness to it, a feel of quintessentially 1970s radicalism that chimes with the film's larger story of an inmate going it alone and empowering himself in time with the movements of emancipation and liberation that characterised the decade as a whole. The film will maintain this note of defiance right to the celebratory closing shots when Murphy ceremonially discards his stopwatch as "Dirty" Harry Callahan did with his police badge in 1971's movie of the same name. Both are loaded gestures, acts of movie insubordination that bookend the tumultuous years in between. Indeed the very first image of *Jericho*, the inmate bopping to the beats on his hifi stereo, has a definite dissenting quality to it as the inmate loses himself in a world of music and, as a result, gives the finger to the warden and the system that holds him. It's worth recalling that Mann himself used the opportunity to attend the London International Film School in the late 1960s not only to learn how to wield a camera but also to avoid the draft for Vietnam, a conflict he, like Muhammad Ali, objected to and refused to validate by allowing his conscription. *The Jericho Mile* capitalises on this conscientious objection and can be viewed, beyond itself, as a run-through of some of the ideas and character traits that Mann would condense, most potently, into *Ali* (2001).

The shots of Murphy running in these opening minutes hint at an idea that will be quickly developed as the story takes hold, namely that this character deliberately insulates himself from the gamut of normal social experiences on the yard because of the guilt he feels for killing his father. This dedication to principled behaviour is something that, as we shall see, Mann often uses both to generate sympathy for his criminal protagonists and to separate them from the more extreme criminals who are, to all intents and purposes, the conventional "villains" of his films.[3] This allows Mann to avoid any overt moralising with regard to the criminal activity undertaken by his protagonists – specifically bank robbery and high-end burglary – because their acts are offset by the real criminals, the psychotic murderers and drug dealers who attract and deserve our judgement.[4] These creations, the psychopaths such as the Tooth Fairy in *Manhunter*, Mann's 1986 adaptation of Thomas Harris's *Red Dragon*, are rendered as the real criminals because they don't appeal to any precept of professional conduct that validates their actions and restrains their behaviour. Consider again how appealing Hannibal Lecktor is made in *Manhunter*, how thrilling the reach from his cage is, how absolved he is of his past history, when placed against the psychopathology and chaos of Tom Noonan's lunar killer. Such is the extent of the moral relativism in Mann's evocation of crime and criminology, a framework that can be frustratingly ambiguous and yet also thrilling in its manipulation of audience sympathies and loyalties.

Some of the other principal characters of *The Jericho Mile* are introduced in these opening minutes, including Dr D (played by Brian Dennehy), Folsom's resident drug king and the most *criminal* criminal of the film; Stiles (played by Richard Lawson), a key black character who here appears as Murphy's running mate and will later prove to be his counsel; and, most interestingly, the genuine Folsom convict Steve White, a white supremacist both in the film and outside it, whose character is used here by Dr D to murder Stiles when he refuses to be co-opted as a drug mule. The patina of prison life that is offered to the audience here evinces the odd notion of being both realistic and contrived at the same time. The sense of realism emerges from the identification of aspects such as the racial gang structures in Folsom, the affiliations between the powerful, the modes of personal expression that include tattooing, and the existence of a micro economy founded on the illicit distribution of drugs and pruno. Most of the montage captures these details in static shots stitched together elliptically in a manner popularised during the 1970s by the likes of William Friedkin (a fellow inner-city Chicagoan) and Costa Gavras who, in turn, borrowed from Truffaut and the late, great Godard. What's past is prologue indeed.

Counterposed against this *verité* feel is the emergence of a style that, while not palpable (this would not happen until Mann's next feature, *Thief*), nevertheless seems to impose itself on the material before us – most notably, Mann's camera dollies around the African American crew lifting weights and then Dr D and his cronies, two very obvious camera movements that undermine the candid nature of the rest of this montage. Is this the first example of the tension that exists in some of Mann's films between style and realism? Like Martin Scorsese, most evidently in his 1973 calling card *Mean Streets* with its fusion of long lens street realism and red light bar-room styling (Scorsese has always worn his love of Powell and Pressburger's *The Red Shoes* (1948) on his sleeve), Mann has often engaged in a balancing act of needing to tell narratives that are grounded in a form of street realism but that also look dreamy, even hallucinogenic, to the eye. The style imposed here by Mann, the smooth arcs around these groups of principal convicts, is not something that characterises him today – indeed it is a struggle to think of another of Mann's films that uses such a camera movement around its characters. What it does point to, however, is the emergence of direction, of the sense that there is a personality behind the events of the film, something "distinguishable", in the words of critic and theorist Andrew Sarris. What this aspect of *Jericho*'s opening sequence shows is that Mann was already peeking above the parapet of pure narrative and offering a notion of a creative agency to the savvy viewer, albeit a marginal notion at this early stage.

The final element of *Jericho*'s minor prologue worth mentioning here is its splicing in of Folsom's mural artwork, specifically the work of Willie Heron III of *Los Illegals* fame. The celebratory bleakness of Heron's famous Folsom portrait of Death, here glimpsed in disparate fragments that build towards a full reveal of the skeletal figure dressed in a black hooded cloak and bearing what looks to be a staff of lightning and Christ's crown of thorns, sums up the overall philosophy of many of these West Coast institutions. It's a kind of rigorous, violent, faith-based, tightly structured nihilism and reinforces the ultimate fate of many of their hard-line inmates – like the rest of the inmates, Murphy will likely die in Folsom despite his attempts to transcend its walls. Mann's love of street art and the inclusion of it in his films dealing with, in particular, West Coast narratives is another key element in grasping his overall attempt to express the truer racial, social and political nature of an environment. As we shall see, the environment in and around Los Angeles is equally as important to understanding his view of modernity as Chicago is to understanding his view of crime.

The *verité* feel returns as the story proper asserts itself. A journalist for the *Folsom Reporter* is interviewing the various racial groups on the yard, who are all asserting themselves as No. 1, the crew in charge of things. Mann cuts between these groups and therefore highlights the stark racial divisions that exist in Folsom and the justifications each group gives for its perceived dominance. As Mann noted in his director's commentary for *Heat*, prisons typically exhibit all the normal characteristics of open society – sexuality, gang structures, commerce – except, of course, that they're all hugely ramped up and exaggerated in jail. Here the African American group promote their vigorous weightlifting regime, while the Chicano crew stress their primacy in the handball ranks and the white supremacists, run by Dr D, show their rule over the distribution of contraband. Quite distinct from this is Murphy, who now finishes his run for the day with a final exhausting sprint, the African Americans, Chicanos and white supremacists a blur of motion as the camera follows Murphy, alone, to the finish line. Yard time is over and the inmates file indoors as the title credits appear onscreen. We glimpse the riflemen in their high towers, complete with requisite mirrored shades and stark demeanour. *The Jericho Mile*, however, is not really a prison film that deals with the tension between inmates and the guards and wardens which is so much the focus of other entries in the genre. Its drama is drawn from other sources.

THE JERICHO MILE AND PRISON CULTURE

Figure 1. Jericho Mile

While most of the prisoners now relax with either a rerun of a televised game show or a book from the library cart, Murphy cools down in his cell, trying to recover from his punishing run on the track. For Murphy his running is a form of catharsis and flagellation. He uses his track time both to escape the confines of Folsom and to punish himself for the murder of his father. Now in his cell, a space utterly bereft of personal expression or home comforts, he is utterly exhausted and paces back and forth trying to walk away the pain in his legs. Stiles's cell, by comparison, is cluttered with photos and trinkets from his former life. The juxtaposition of *mise en scène* is a little forced by Mann but effective nonetheless – it says what it needs to about Murphy's philosophy. If the *mise en scène* wasn't enough, Mann also deploys a shallow depth of field that appears to squash Murphy between the back wall of his cell and the bars that hold him, the metaphor of a caged animal there for all to see.[5] As the higher echelons of prison management begin to take notice of Murphy's running ability the film begins to spend some time in the offices of the bosses, where unusually avuncular wardens and managers actually work to organise some official running opportunities for Murphy so that his mettle might be professionally tested.

This is not the kind of altruism we have come to expect from prison movies and certainly not in the late 1970s, when cinema audiences were witnessing the sadism and indifference of the penal system in films such

THE FILMS OF MICHAEL MANN

Figure 2. Jericho Mile

as Alan Parker's *Midnight Express* (1978) and Don Siegel's *Escape from Alcatraz* (1979). Both these films deal with institutions that are so infiltrated by barbarous managers and fiendish wardens that the only way their central convicts can survive is by busting out, the act of escaping being the source of the expression *midnight express*. That both these films are based on true events, where the main characters did successfully escape their respective prisons, is perhaps testament to the manner in which the prison system was viewed by movies at this time. Despite repeated viewings we still root for Clint Eastwood's Frank and Brad Davis's Billy Hayes in their audacious escape bids, such is the power of the negative characterisation of their prisons and those in charge there. Another prison film from the 1970s that elevates the notion of escape to near parodic levels is *Breakout*, director Tom Gries's 1975 Charles Bronson vehicle about a wife who enlists the all-action star to bust her wrongly convicted husband out of jail. The histrionics of the whole thing may mask the fact that, again like *Midnight Express* and *Escape from Alcatraz*, *Breakout* is based on a true story and deploys the same repugnant prison warden characterisations (this time, Mexican wardens and guards as opposed to Turkish or American screws) in order to promote the prison break narrative that caps the movie and generate sympathy for the main character.

This feeling, however, is oddly absent from *The Jericho Mile*. You never feel as though you want Murphy to escape from Folsom, even though his whole *raison d'être* – running – is completely anathema to the notion of imprisonment and confinement. Prison is where Murphy lives and we, the audience, are just as resigned to this as he is. As Vincent Gaine notes in *Existentialism and Social Engagement in the Films of Michael Mann*, "Rain Murphy in *The Jericho Mile* understands that running the Olympic Mile will not release him from his life sentence, but he pursues his record breaking time regardless."[6] The drama of his narrative comes not from his escape attempts (which he could have mounted if he wanted to – one scene shows him being allowed outside the prison walls for an extended run) nor the brutality of the guards nor the sadism of the chief warden, but from the prison's desire to see him recognised in the face of the bureaucratic rules of the Olympic committee.

This is perhaps the source of the film's seeming naivety. Audiences correctly presume that prison is an extremely tough environment where violence, extortion, rape and racism are all facts of daily life. Of course, *The Jericho Mile* explores some of these elements – Stiles's bullying and eventual murder at the behest of Dr D, the racial divisions and antagonism of the rival crews – but they are all, in the end, transcended by Murphy's record-breaking run and the catharsis of him smashing the stopwatch at the film's end. The overall optimism of *Jericho*'s construction of both its prison environment and Murphy's character arc – and the positive or negative connotations you take from these – remain, however, a tantalising part of the film's overall appeal and its odd place in Mann's filmography. The simulated realism generated by the film's use of genuine Folsom convicts, authentic Folsom locations and its accrual of West Coast prison culture offsets the naïve optimism of its narrative. Mann was no doubt aware of the tension here, and his navigation of the two halves as the story unfolds is at times skilful and not always lacking in subtlety.

That being said, so far in the film there is little evidence, visually, that this is what would become known as a Michael Mann film. In any evaluation of the film's contribution to Mann's auterism, *Jericho* evinces a flatness in its visual construction that, while perhaps the product of more than one factor, nonetheless renders the piece as anomalous as, say, *The Keep* in some respects. In particular, the film suffers from that quintessentially 60s/70s lo-fi, blue hue common to Polaroid photography and related media of the period, and while this is not necessarily an issue in itself, when combined with working, first and foremost, within the constraints of TV, *The Jericho Mile* does not always distinguish itself visually in the way that Mann's subsequent work would. Again, this is not an attempt to detract from what strengths *Jericho* does have, merely to suggest that its relevance to Mann's future work, and this study, lies, for the most part, in its evocation of prison culture as a lifestyle choice and guiding principle.

Following the scenes where the prison management pull strings to get some state sports coaches in to visit Murphy, Stiles gets in deep with Dr D. Stiles is desperate for a conjugal visit with his wife and approaches one of D's lackeys about organising such a visit. In return, Stiles will acquire the extra sugar that D's crew need for their pruno operation to continue, following the isolation of a key former member. Stiles fails to understand the scope of D's operation and the depths of his depravity and becomes subject to coercion in the form of being set up as a mule for D's influx of contraband. By virtue of their close proximity to each other in the cells and their shared time on the track, Murphy also becomes implicated in Stiles's desperate situation and views this intrusion as a violent disruption of his regimen. A key scene exploring this dynamic follows just after the African American crew has assailed Stiles and Murphy for their involvement with Dr D. Both men are back in their cells and Murphy is initially haranguing Stiles about allowing himself to become exploited by Dr D. Mann frames the two cells frontally, allowing both a visual and thematic opposition to be established between these two men. Stiles, angered by Murphy's indifference to his plight, offers an equally angry but highly insightful analysis of Murphy's shortcomings in a manner, rare for *The Jericho Mile*, that resonates with some of Mann's future work. Thematically, this is the moment when the normally self-assured, highly disciplined protagonist is ably deconstructed by an outside party, and in the process learns a valuable truth about themselves. It's there in the diner scene in *Thief* where Tuesday Weld's character confronts Frank's criminal past; it's there when Lecktor dissects Will Graham in the mental institution in *Manhunter*; in *Heat* there are several such moments, the best of which must be the coffee shop meeting of Hanna and McCauley; and *Collateral* has its moment in the taxicab when Max pierces right to the heart of Vincent's pathology with his "there are standard parts that are supposed to be there in people and in you … aren't" speech. Visually and thematically, these moments are all of a kind, blocked so as to present the two characters in each instance as binary opposites and written so that what emerges is the acknowledgement of the key character's true self and their real reasons for being involved in crime. As a totem of existential philosophy, *The Jericho Mile* is, in this aspect, very much in step with a large part of Mann's overall body of work.

Stiles highlights that Murphy is hiding from the truth of his prison existence by denying himself normal pleasures and instead punishing himself with running and isolation. Murphy retorts that he doesn't want his time to be characterised by anything other than running, that he has no need for wives or friends or conjugal visits. As before, Murphy accepts his sentence and doesn't want to dilute the potency of it with the kind of distractions that Stiles invites. And yet the final shot of this sequence has Murphy bowing his head in a mix of realisation – what Stiles has said is accurate – and sadness. His mystique, the secret to serving out his time, has been exploded by Stiles. In the next scene Murphy is back to punishing himself, albeit witnessed by the state sports coach whom the prison warden has called in to time Murphy's run. With a mile done in 3m 59s the coach is impressed enough to invite Murphy to attend tryouts for the upcoming Olympics. Murphy reacts angrily to this offer, seeing it as an unwarranted distortion of his self-determined regime, and storms off back to his cell. At the same time Stiles has learned that the conjugal visit between him and his wife, set up by Dr D, is nothing but a ruse to get Stiles to ferry drugs into Folsom. The woman who turns up is not his wife but someone from the outside working for Dr D. Stiles refuses to be party to this scheme and, like Murphy, storms off back to his cell, leaving the woman to be taken into custody by the wardens.

The sequence that follows the two men arriving back at their cells is the last that Stiles and Murphy will have together. As Stiles, Richard Lawson has a powerful moment here as he laments how prison has stripped him of his dreams and expectations; that, in reality, nothing actually happens here because the individual never seizes the opportunities that come his or her way. This requiem for acts of self-determination and actualisation brings to mind Vincent's key scene in *Collateral*, Mann's 2004 hitman thriller, where Tom Cruise's character berates Max (Jamie Foxx) for never having really pursued his dream of owning a limo company, Island Limos. As Vincent observes of Max's inability to act: "Someday, someday my dream will come ... one night you'll wake up and discover it never happened, it's all turned around on you ... didn't happen, never will, cause you were never gonna do it anyway."

Stiles expresses similar ideas here, as he loses himself in a wash of self-pity and fear, made impotent by his inability to navigate the treacherous shoals of the prison system and realise life with his wife and daughter. But more pointedly, these ideas strike at the heart of Murphy who, only moments before, rejected the opportunity of running in the Olympics and thus realising his dream. In an attempt to purge himself of this feeling Murphy insists that Stiles must try to get himself into solitary confinement or on to a transfer as quickly as he can, these being the only means of avoiding the violent retribution that is surely heading his way from Dr D. Stiles agrees to meet Murphy on the other side of the dining area and, from there, form a plan that tries to avoid Dr D's wrath. It is here that *Jericho* generates its first sense of real danger as Mann delineates the way in which violence comes for you in prison – abruptly and without the possibility of escape. Murphy is locked in his cell by a goon posing with a library cart and, despite hollering and shouting, cannot get Stiles's attention as he makes his way to the meeting point. Mann prefaces the murder to come with several unanticipated cuts to the tattooed abdomen of Steve White, the real convict mentioned earlier who sports a swastika and white power design on his stomach and a shank behind his back. Stiles enters a sort of caged antechamber where the doors are shut and he is stabbed to death by White, the photos of his wife and new daughter clutched tightly in his hand as he slumps forward and down against the wire fencing. Murphy overcomes the makeshift lock on his cell door but arrives too late to save Stiles.

Mann's direction of this pivotal scene in the film is surprisingly restrained and perhaps even a touch moribund for those of us more accustomed to the rigorous sense of pathos that would normally accompany such a moment. There is a sentimentality to the death of Stiles that, while perfectly justified by the events that have preceded it (and seeming almost in harmony with the film's developing naivety), concurrently seems at odds with *Jericho*'s striving for realism, a realism that was so fervently pursued in the opening minutes. The musical cue that Mann brings in as Murphy rocks backward and forward in his foetal position of guilt and rage is shamelessly effective. It demarcates his point of no return, the jumping-off spot from which he will now at least recognise the idea of prison as a collective environment that can be experienced. Stiles's murder forces Murphy to make this change in his philosophy and thereby honour his only companion in Folsom by acknowledging that they did in fact have a friendship. The choice of Jimmie Haskell's music here makes this awareness of Murphy's character unavoidable, but also brings to light the real skill that Mann will soon wield in his musical accompaniments and cues. He would quickly become known for truly avant-garde selections, whether his fondness for Lisa Gerrard and Pieter Bourke's ethereal, New Age soundscapes, or for making use of established artists such as Tangerine Dream and Moby. Through his now practised use of these artists, music in general has become such an integral, intricate, irreducible and subtle part of Mann's visual storytelling that the choice of Haskell's melodramatic music for the death of Stiles in *The Jericho Mile* seems quite obtuse and even gratuitous by comparison. It tugs at the heartstrings a little too vigorously and renders what should have been a moment of poignancy into something bathetic and jarring.

THE JERICHO MILE AND PRISON CULTURE

From here Murphy realigns his priorities and informs the prison that he will run for the Olympics, but with a few conditions of his own. Murphy asks to be allowed into the "metal industries" room alone in order to "do something for Stiles". Murphy gives the warden the kind of here and now ultimatum favoured by a number of other characters in Mann's canon – decide right now, yes or no, because there is no time to wait, to ponder and then make your choice. The warden agrees and Mann's camera tracks Murphy left to right as he strides through the metal industries room, Mann even using a fast zoom to remind us that this is the 1970s. Some of Dr D's cronies are told to clear the room and Murphy is then left alone, the prison officer wandering off oblivious to what's about to happen. *Jericho*'s view of prison culture reveals its native naivety again here as Murphy is left alone to smash up the workshop in a slo-mo paroxysm of what initially looks like blind rage, but is revealed to be about something else. Murphy checks the back of each smashed tool cabinet before moving on to the next and eventually locates his quarry, the very meat of Dr D's metier, his ill-gotten drug money. Murphy is then shown on the yard with the drug money in one hand and a can of fuel to burn it in the other. From behind the wire fence bounding his perch on the prison bleachers Dr D, with just a hint of irony, says "He's gonna burn something, what's he gonna burn?" Murphy incinerates the dollar bills as Dr D realises what is happening and yells that he's "looking at a dead man". Mann cuts to a long shot of the burning pyre and then to a close-up, the burning heap becoming a kind of prison Olympic torch for the running events to come.

Murphy is now outside the walls of Folsom, doing a series of practice runs with his spikes on in a scene that forms the height of the film's optimism about the nature of prison culture. His new mentor hands Murphy a stopwatch, *the* stopwatch, with the inscription "To the Jericho Mile" on the back. He runs off down the track followed by his mentor in a slowly moving car, the quarried walls of Folsom to screen right and the desolate winds of change blowing on the soundtrack. From here Mann segues into the bureaucratic preparations of the chief warden, as he tries to navigate the catch-22 of giving a prison inmate the chance to run in the Olympics. In order to allow Murphy to qualify the prison warden agrees to build a quarter-mile track in the yard. The labour for this eventually comes from a willing racial cross-section of the prison population – a kind of penological *build it and they will come* for Folsom – the sweep from which will keep Dr D and his murderous intentions from reaching Murphy for the moment. A scene follows that tries to articulate and justify the naivety of *Jericho*'s view of prison life and Folsom's elevation of Murphy to near poster boy status. The chief warden says:

> This thing happening could mean more to convicts all over this country than 15 years of rehab programmes put together ... Murphy's the model for connecting to the outside. Backing him means a lot. Cause not connecting means staying into those games on the yard, then they hit the streets and cop out into their comic book fantasies, screw up an armed robbery, kill a few people and then they're right back in here.

There is a great deal of sense and affirmative thinking here. However, it is this kind of pro-active imprisonment, this rehabilitative methodology for the treatment of criminals, which quickly becomes conspicuous by its absence in Mann's later crime films. Consider Dennis Haysbert's character of Breedan in *Heat*. He gets paroled out of jail and takes a job working as a grill man for Bud Cort's restaurant manager, but instead of being permitted the chance to re-enter society and work for a living, Breedan is threatened by the corrupt manager, who tells Breedan that 25% of his wages will go back to him or he will bust him back to jail on a phoney charge. *Heat*, like *Thief* before it or *Public Enemies* after, shows a great deal of cynicism towards the prison system of the West Coast and the Midwest respectively. *Heat* deconstructs the rehabilitation programmes of Folsom and Chino – similar to the one Murphy is now pioneering in *The Jericho Mile* – and presents instead an alternative and, likely, more truthful picture of how prisoners are received on the outside, if they actually make it to their release date.

Despite the prison's appeals to the inmate population to help build an Olympic grade running track on the yard, the project falters as Dr D forms a picket line, ostensibly in protest at the proposed exploitation of prisoner labour. D's real motivations for the picket line are, of course, to maintain the racial hegemony of his white supremacist gang and exact revenge on Murphy for the burning of his drug money in the previous scene. This kind of bleak virulence blunts the edges of the film's earlier optimism and returns *The Jericho Mile* – albeit briefly – to a kind of realism, the realism that audiences normally ascribe to cinematic views of prison life, those of self-interest, hostility, violence, isolation and hopelessness. This mode continues as Dr D falsely suggests to Cotton (Roger E. Mosley's character) that it was the white Murphy's involvement with Stiles that eventually led to the latter's murder. Cotton directs Murphy to the laundry area and proceeds to beat him up in a protracted sequence that wears its metaphorical significance a little too obviously on its prison overalls. Beaten but not broken, Murphy is then helped to his feet by Cotton, a gesture of both solidarity (by the end of the beating

Cotton seems to acknowledge that Murphy had nothing to do with Stiles's death) and condescension (at this point Cotton is still bound to the notion of the racial hierarchy on the yard).

It is the next scene, however, that offers up a cathartic turning point in the development of Cotton's character and the film's view of the ethos of Folsom Prison. Having purged himself of his racially inflected paranoia via his ceremonial beating of Murphy, Cotton approaches the Chicano convicts on the yard – a moment set beneath the same mural of Death that opened the film – in an attempt to cement opposition to Dr D's picketing of the track-building project. The Chicanos agree to join Cotton's militia and the new, larger group assail Dr D's supremacist barricade in a violent melee of shivs, shanks, bats and bars. This riot sequence is perhaps one of the few instances in *The Jericho Mile* where a genuine feeling of threat and danger is communicated to the audience. Six convicts are hospitalised by multiple stab wounds but the point is made to Dr D – the racetrack will be built and Murphy will have his climactic run. Before the riot scene ends Mann surveys the carnage by cutting to an overhead shot of the discarded weapons and injured men in a manner redolent of Scorsese's famed overhead shot of Travis Bickle's carnage towards the end of *Taxi Driver* (1975). Although not used to suggest mental dislocation or disassociation in the way that Scorsese meant at the end of his film, this overhead survey is still meant to invoke a similar feeling of disgust and, more importantly, closure for the audience.

In the qualifying race for the Olympics, Murphy beats the other three contestants and runs a mile in 3m 52s. Mann ably captures the unifying force of the race on the usually fragmented prison population. The diegetic sounds of the crowds chanting and cheering and yelling recall the whoops and cries of the Huron war party in Mann's 1992 film *The Last of the Mohicans*, while his use of slow motion, as Murphy breaks through the finishing tape, is shamelessly effective at crystallising the triumphalism and melodrama that lies at the heart of the film. Murphy's validation is, however, short-lived as Mann imbues events with the banal reality of normal life that often plagues his characters, something Neil McCauley would refer to in *Heat* as "barbeques and ball games". Murphy is denied a place at the Olympics due to his being an inmate who shows little sign of having been "rehabilitated", in the words of the Olympic board member. Dr Bill Janowski (Geoffrey Lewis) replies by saying that such a term "is no longer current", pointing towards an understanding that Folsom Prison, at least as it exists within the confines of the film, should be viewed not as an institution bent on "correcting" Murphy but instead as providing him with ann opportunity worthy of his latent talent. This kind of notion again suggests the naivety that courses through *The Jericho Mile*, a feeling that is by now obviously being intentionally cultivated by Mann. In this sense, *The Jericho Mile* may have more in common tonally with Frank Darabont's ultimately celebratory *The Shawshank Redemption* (1994) than it does with other prison films of the 1970s or 1980s.

The climactic sequence of *The Jericho Mile* provides the viewer with a welcome reprieve from what might be termed the dour optimism of its narrative up to this point. Having been forced to accept the Olympic board's decision, Murphy returns to his state of penal acceptance, of serving out his sentence in accordance with his self-imposed dictum. As the momentum of the Olympic bid begins to fade, the old racial structures and divisions reassert themselves as the heightened reality of prison life comes, once again, into play. The African Americans resume lifting weights, the Chicano convicts return to their handball and Dr D's white supremacist crew are back peddling drugs and creating a false sense of purpose on the bleachers. There's something oddly reassuring about this given the chaos and upset to the established order that Murphy's Olympic bid seemed to cause. Murphy is hurting though. When all hope of a true atonement for him seems lost, Mann reintroduces that strange little convict character from the opening minutes of the film – the radical and revolutionary inmate with a stereo who is still bopping to the sounds of his music – and thus posits the idea that something good may still happen.

This little cameo character serves a very similar narrative function as the man with the green radio does in Mann's 2001 epic *Ali*, the muscular biopic about the irreverent boxer's decade-long journey to the Rumble in the Jungle. In that film the man with the green radio also appears twice during the film's running time. The first instance is when Ali is running through the backstreet slums of Kinshasa and witnesses the man among the crowds that have gathered next to the hand-drawn murals of Ali smashing the tsetse flies and tanks. The second is when, nearly beaten by George Foreman during the climactic Rumble bout, Ali looks to the crowd, once again spots the man with the radio and is imbued with an invincible spirit that allows him to come back and win the fight. The reappearance of the convict with the hifi in *The Jericho Mile* is most certainly an analogue or precursor to this idea. He's back again, invoking the radical spirit of the 1970s and the insurrectionary idealism that, as in *Ali*, says that an individual can speak truth to power and win the battle against the established order.

Murphy is out on the track once more, aware that the Olympic race is taking place very soon but equally aware of the need to return to his old life. Mann cuts to the man with the hifi, who seems to be jiving both to music and the radio commentary from the Olympic pre-event, such is the playful nature of Mann's diegetic sound design. The commentator proclaims "Frank Davies blew everybody away with a time of 3m 50.6s in the mile ... and is the number one miler in the States", the sound overlapping with several cuts to other prisoners, finally ending up at Murphy's cell. Mann reminds us of the extent of Murphy's entrapment in Folsom by cutting to this shot of him in his cell, a shot that's very similar in its composition to an earlier shot where Murphy was buttressed and barricaded by the walls and bars of his fate. Murphy is viewed here much in the same way as he was subsequent to Stiles's murder, both events – his friend's killing and his rejection from the Olympics – serving as markers of inner change. Murphy is blocked between the bars of the cell door, back to the audience and head down in a posture of solemnity like some reversed version of Aaron Shikler's famous portrait of JFK. Imbued with the desire to prove his worth he grabs his running shoes and heads to the track for one last time, the moment signposted by the return of the Stones' "Sympathy for the Devil" on the soundtrack.

Murphy runs his mile and beats Davies's time of 3m 50.6s. The prison unites around him and Mann captures Murphy's victory in another splurge of glorious slow motion, the runner crossing the finish line with arms outstretched in a gesture that seems to say, "I did it, now do with me what you will." Murphy knows he has beaten Davies's time but the other prisoners rally around him to check the numbers. Murphy then launches his stopwatch high into the azure sky, eventually causing it to smash against the perimeter wall into several pieces. There is an obvious aspect to the symbolism here that perhaps masks the underlying ambiguity of Murphy's climactic actions. Does he smash the stopwatch because he has achieved the ultimate validation in his life and is happy to discard it or because the stopwatch has been the source of a deviation from his rigid doctrine of self-flagellation for the murder of his father? Does he return to the track at the end to prove to himself that he is the best or to atone for his inability to prevent the murder of Stiles? Is it enough that the only recognition Murphy will get for his winning time is from Folsom itself and not the outside world? There is both a positive and negative connotation to the action of smashing the watch that renders these questions at once troubling and fascinating in the pursuit of a closed reading of *The Jericho Mile*.

There is, then, much to admire in Mann's inaugural run. It is a film of some quality, no doubt, and certainly punches above its weight in terms of narrative ambition and its striving for verisimilitude, particularly in its deployment of real Folsom locations. The film's view of prison culture is interesting and useful in a limited way when we consider the importance of this theme in some of Mann's future work. It presents some of the character archetypes and traits that will later feed into the figures of Frank in *Thief*, McCauley in *Heat* and Dillinger in *Public Enemies*, and is notable for its use of real Folsom convicts in some of the key roles. Nevertheless, and in spite of its Emmy Award-winning success, *The Jericho Mile* must be considered a minor component in Mann's overall portfolio when factored into this book's assessment of his auteurism. From the perspective outlined above, it can be concluded that the film is not an indispensable progenitor of Mann's related future projects – in the way that his next film would be – due to its lack of two things: an overt technical presence (on the part of Mann) and those wonderful narrative opportunities from which emerge the pathos and sense of modern, existential alienation that characterise his best efforts.

In some ways *The Jericho Mile* is like Steven Spielberg's *Duel* (1971) in that both were highly impressive TV movie debuts that nevertheless bear few of the hallmarks that would later characterise both directors. There is a cynicism and flat linearity to *Duel*'s tale of an everyman pursued by the murderous truck that, slight elements of *Jaws* aside, would quickly wane as Spielberg's more genuine traits and tropes began to gain traction. With *The Jericho Mile*, instead of *Duel*'s cynicism, there is a melodramatic naivety to its view of prison culture and the opportunities given to Murphy that seems at odds with what would soon constitute a large part of Mann's MO, namely his much more morally neutral to negative view of the penal system and its ability to "rehabilitate". It is interesting to consider then that the cynicism that characterises *Duel* would become Mann's typical view in some of his key films, whereas the naive optimism of *The Jericho Mile* would quickly pass to Spielberg and colour much of his work until *Schindler's List* (1993).

The Jericho Mile is, at most, a valiant attempt to perhaps open up the form of prison drama endemic to the 1970s. It is also the source of one or two of Mann's enduring narrative traits when looked at from the perspective of 2023. And yet it must remain a marginal work when folded into our assessment of Michael Mann as an auteur. Though technically competent, it is not in possession of a demonstrable or distinguishable personality and certainly seems devoid of an obvious interior meaning that could be thought of as common or unique to Mann. Its made-for-TV origins might be responsible for the film lacking a demonstrable Mann stamp, while any attempt to suggest that its interior meaning is common to the rest of Mann's work falls away

The Jericho Mile and Prison Culture

when you closely examine the film's naive view of prison culture and its characterisation of Murphy.

> **Key scene suggestion for prison culture – the opening montage of Folsom, its murals and its racial segregation on the yard.**

Notes

1 *Collateral*, although dealing with a criminal, is the exception here because Vincent is not an ex-con but a morally ambiguous remnant of the post-Cold War private security industry. In the film's striving for allegory it is death and not imprisonment that must meet Vincent at the film's end.
2 The idea of the negative manifestation of the father is something that Mann would repeat and modify in *Heat* (1995), *Ali* (2001), *Collateral* (2004) and *Public Enemies* (2009): in *Heat* McCauley's father is an absent figure in his life; in *Collateral* Vincent jokes that he killed his father when he was a boy before then revealing the truth that he died of liver disease, probably from alcoholism; in *Ali* Muhammad's father is a weak figure who worships a "blond haired, blue-eyed Jesus" and then descends into alcoholism along with Bundini Brown; and in *Public Enemies* Dillinger openly admits to Billie Frechette that his father beat him when he was young because he didn't know any better. The exceptions might be *Thief* and *The Insider*; in *Thief*, Okla (Willie Nelson) is a pseudo-father figure and mentor to Frank, and in *The Insider* Jeffrey Wigand talks fondly of his own father, a mechanical engineer and "the most ingenious man I ever knew".
3 Think of Dr D in *The Jericho Mile*, Leo in *Thief*, the Tooth Fairy in *Manhunter*, Waingro in *Heat* and Baby Face Nelson in *Public Enemies* as examples of this extreme pathology that helps render the main criminal more appealing.
4 As Steven Rybin notes in *The Cinema of Michael Mann*, "Caan's character in the film clearly states that he doesn't perform home invasions" (43), an admission that somewhat ameliorates the crimes that he does commit during the text of the film.

5 Mann would use a similar approach in the climactic scenes of his magnum opus *Heat* where an extremely shallow depth of field helps condense the film's multifarious narrative down into a simple but beautifully blocked gunfight between two men.
6 Vincent Gaine, *Existentialism and Social Engagement in the Films of Michael Mann*, Palgrave Macmillan, 2011, 3.

CHAPTER FOUR

Thief and the Criminal

> What it really is, is first you see something and you like it, and then it's a mystery, and you go into the mystery and that's what's interesting. And the test of criticism is: can you make a case for it?
>
> Andrew Sarris

If *The Jericho Mile* is about the punishment aspect of Dostoyevsky's famous book then Michael Mann's first legitimate foray into cinema is without doubt about the crime. *Thief*, Mann's 1981 follow-up to *The Jericho Mile*, appears as a natural bedfellow to that TV movie in that it seems to form a kind of bookend or continuation of Murphy's jail time story in Folsom. *Thief* is, however, more notable for its sometimes radical departure from the template of *The Jericho Mile* and how it both inaugurated a very definite sense of style, something that would go on to flourish in *The Keep* and *Manhunter*, and prompted the beginning of the debate about whether Mann is just an empty stylist or if the style is a product of something deeper. The core of this debate was catalysed at the time of the film's release by esteemed critics such as Vincent Canby and Pauline Kael, who noted, respectively, that the film is "pretty enough to be framed and hung on a wall, where, of course, good movies don't belong" and "all highfalutin hype ... a great big trailer for itself".[1] The very particular style of *Thief*, aspects of which we would now consider quintessentially "eighties", is unavoidable and must form part of any assessment of the film and its project. This will be the case here as the chapter holds aloft and deconstructs the film's most interesting instances of stylisation and the possible motivations behind them. What must be cautiously remembered here, however, is that the danger with any critical assessment of *Thief*, or Mann's subsequent two films, can be the tendency to keep falling back on an analysis of its style, an emphasis that can be much to the detriment of the film's other strengths and ambiguities.

What this chapter will focus on, aside from the import of style in *Thief*, is the film's more important rendering of both crime and the character of the criminal, as Mann saw them in 1981 at the very beginning of his motion picture career. As we shall see, one of the most intriguing things about *Thief* is the way in which it legitimises the criminal activities of Frank (the late James Caan's character) through a fascination with showing the audience *how* he commits his crimes. There is a love of procedure in *Thief* that is so rigorous that the jewel heists and robbery sequences assume a kind of reverence or liturgical quality that completely nullifies their immorality (the same quality that the hacking sequences in Mann's *Blackhat* also strive for and sometimes achieve).

Thief qualifies its criminal activities such as high-end robbery as acceptable, even respectable, because of the inherent skill required on the part of the robber to pull off the scores.[2] The payoffs from the robberies in the film are frequently huge, with the accrual of wealth being one of Frank's primary motivations – along with the very rapid crafting of a life for himself, post-prison – and the source of his ultimate weakness. In its love of money, wealth-as-status and Western materialism, the film, in many ways, pre-empted the emerging yuppie culture of the 1980s with its rigidly business-like central character and his portfolio of bars, car dealerships, cash and diamonds. On the surface of things *Thief*'s main character seems so obsessed with acquiring a lavish material security in his life that it borders on the ridiculous. His is indeed the American Dream writ large, detailed and blueprinted right down to the prison collage he keeps in his wallet that shows the entire matrix of his life's meaning and aspirations. As we shall see, *Thief*'s view of crime is one that seems to validate yuppie criminal activity as long as it's concerned with upward social mobility and the accrual of wealth from even wealthier yuppie criminals. In the current period of recession, inflation and financial desperation for many, *Thief* and its Marxist ethos of wealth redistribution and worker control may be more timely now than ever before.

Thief begins in the rain. Over the United Artists logo we hear the unmistakable sound of raindrops spattering on the pavement. The sound design immediately establishes a kind of sealed environment where the rain generates the notion of the city as an enclosed space or, in Mann's words, "a three-dimensional machine" to which the characters are indelibly tethered.[3] The film's first image is of a car starting up and its lights coming on. It's dark, night time, and we cannot quite glimpse the driver and passenger in the vehicle. A lavish electronic composition by Tangerine Dream rises on the soundtrack and instantly infuses the opening scene with a fugue-like quality. The viewer's awareness of the cutting and the disparate events of each shot seem to fade away as Tangerine's New Age score gives the scene an unmistakable sense of homogeneity, of intent and common purpose, of distinct events being pulled together to reveal a singular intention.[4] Mann also captures the realistic dimensionality of his characters' environment in these opening moments, a quality that seemed lacking in *The Jericho Mile* with all its shallow-depth-of-field running shots and tight prison cell close-ups. As the car drives off down a city avenue we see a perfectly balanced shot filmed with a very long lens that, as Mann noted earlier, really offers a sense of the three dimensions of the city, where colonnades of streetlights are reflected on the glossy black tarmac of the roads. Mann then cuts to a shot which pans vertically down through the night and the rain, first past a very bright light source that reinforces the high artifice of the film precisely because of its glaring artificiality, and then past the angular and elongated forms of fire escapes and balcony railings. This is neo-noir meets Escher and his zany work *Relativity*, with its impossible staircases and physics-defying angles.

The car from earlier is now parked in an alleyway, lights off, the driver monitoring the police radio band. The love of procedure is apparent as Mann's camera lingers on the blinking red lights of the scanner, the driver making tiny adjustments to the reception. Another cut and we see a second man working at a junction box. Mann's camera pans down the miles of cables and circuits and electrics as the second man rewires them and watches the effects on a bank of amp meters. Another cut and we meet Frank as he lifts a huge magnetic drill to the face of a vault door (something Christopher Nolan would borrow for the opening of *The Dark Knight* (2008)), his goggles and overalls making him look like a coal miner, steelworker or a warped version of Dwight Schultz's Oppenheimer from Roland Joffe's *Fat Man and Little Boy*.

Frank begins to drill a hole right through the outer door of the vault, slivers of metal forming a cloud around the drill bit. Mann wants to capture how physically demanding this kind of robbery is, how technically proficient the robber is and how skilled a crew needs to be to successfully pull it off. Via these ideas and characterisations Mann manages to legitimate, in the space of a few minutes' screen time, Frank's criminal actions. He is clearly skilled at what he does and this immediately qualifies him as worthy of our respect. The businesses and corporations that he steals from remain faceless throughout the film, helping to reinforce their image as unknowable totalitarian entities totally removed from Frank's experience of the street. This extended opening sequence is also remarkable for its bravery in focusing on the minute procedural details of breaking into a vault. Mann absolutely limits the visual exposition and use of explanatory dialogue – as he did in the beginning of *The Jericho Mile* – and instead offers this aforementioned fugue where the audience is denied an overall picture of who these men are and why they are breaking into this vault. Instead, what's being prized here is the process, the method, the doing of the thing itself. This is the direct, centred intelligence of high-functioning individuals and their effect on their environment.

Mann's camera is now mounted on the drill itself and is looking along its long axis as more pieces of shrapnel come flying out of the hole in the door. The montage of shots renders the robbery as a surgical procedure, where tiny decisions or changes can have a massive and cumulative effect on the outcome. We even get the safe-cracking version of a surgical endoscopy as Mann's camera peers directly into the hole Frank has drilled in the door, thus taking his desire to bring the audience into an internalised understanding of events to an extreme degree (2015's *Blackhat* uses a similar camera shot, this time of a USB stick being inserted into a PC port). Frank then prises open the inner doors of the vault and sifts through the bounty in search of diamonds, a high-value prize that's easy to front in a sale. Some five and a half minutes of screen time have now elapsed since the beginning of the film, all devoted to the thrill of procedure, the love of seeing skill and professionalism onscreen. Frank and his two accomplices pack up their gear and slip away from the scene of the crime.

En route back to their lockup – during which time we get some gorgeous and consciously noiresque shots of Chicago's Lower Wacker Drive that communicate an industrial foreboding – they wash off of any physical evidence that might point to the commission of the crime, switching cars and changing clothes in the process. There is a definite signature to *Thief*'s opening robbery, an attempt to generate a specific style that correlates very strongly with the narrative events onscreen. Mann's use of the Tangerine Dream track "Igneous" in these opening minutes now seems a choice synonymous with the cultism of the 1980s aesthetic. However, at the time in 1981 the electronic and synthesised film score was in its infancy largely due to the enduring popularity of the late seventies return to classical and orchestral scoring, the most successful of which surely remains John Williams's soundtrack for the *Star Wars* trilogy. With this in mind, it can be argued that the style and cultural aesthetic established in the opening robbery of *Thief*, via its choice of music and *mise en scène*, was actually as perceptive a reflection of its time as Mann's *Miami Vice* (2006) would be twenty-five years later. As *Miami Vice* did for the early post-millennial years, *Thief* very accurately perceived what would quickly become the dominant aesthetic of its time – neon credits, electronic score, yuppie narrative, stonewashed denim – and used it to complement the events onscreen. Such is the cultural specificity of some of Mann's work that, as alluded to earlier, thirty years from now *Miami Vice* will no doubt appear as "dated" as *Thief* does today. This is by no means a criticism.

It is now daytime and Frank is striding through his car lot. Mann shoots him with another long lens as he moves towards us, walking between the bumpers of cars, issuing orders to his mechanics and workers offscreen to the left (our never seeing the people whom Frank addresses in this shot gives it a contrived feeling, as if Mann is trying that little bit too hard to characterise Frank as the alpha male).[5] This is the legitimate, business portfolio side to Frank's life, a front that gives off the appearance of a regular existence; this is the 1980s after all, and seeming to be a yuppie is better than not being one at all. It's interesting that by the time *Heat* graced our screens in 1995 this affectation of a criminal having a legitimate side to their life had been dispensed with entirely. Neil McCauley's existence is completely given over to crime in that film, and for reasons, as we shall see, that differ dramatically to Frank's.

Frank collects a newspaper and makes a phone call from his dealership office before heading to a meeting with The Man, a bizarre cameo by Hal Frank, to see if he can fence the diamonds he stole the night before. This meeting in a diner serves two narrative purposes that will prove significant to Frank's criminal trajectory later in the film. First, via an interstitial cut away to her, as Frank talks business with The Man, his love interest Jessie (Tuesday Weld) is introduced to us, a waitress in the diner who will have considerable bearing on Frank's future. The second element introduced here is Frank's reluctance to meet with outside players. The Man foolishly suggests that Frank meet with some "stand up guys" or put his hard-earned money on the street in a high-risk attempt to increase his profits. Frank's reaction to these suggestions bristles with the normally clamped-down fury that will also erupt later from McCauley in *Heat*, Vincent in *Collateral* and Dillinger in *Public Enemies*, when pedestrian irritations or threats to their criminal philosophy loom. Frank retorts, "If I wanna meet people I'll go to a fuckin' country club … my money goes in the bank, you put your money on the street!"[6]

The potentially negative and superficial characterisation of Frank that *Thief* offers the audience – as a kind of detached, anomalous, working-class yuppie criminal – is ameliorated by the film's subsequent use of scenes such as this one. Mann was clearly conscious of moulding a character who, although a career criminal whose motivation in life is to acquire a kind of stolen material security, is nevertheless respected by the audience because of the specifics of his crimes. Mann deftly avoids rendering a negative judgement on Frank's criminal activities because his crimes are shown to be corporate, principled, professional and – most important of all – uninterested in the traditionally psychotic pursuits of assault, abduction or homicide. These, as we have seen, are left to the traditional antagonists of Mann's work. From what we have surveyed so far, those antagonists would be Dr D in *The Jericho Mile* and the upcoming Leo in *Thief*, characters whose criminality is inherently psychotic, predicated on murder and, therefore, morally reprehensible.[7]

The details and vagaries of Frank's seemingly gallant criminality arose not from Mann's typewriter but from a real-world source – a Chicagoan jewel thief named John Seybold, who more commonly went by his pen name, Frank Hohimer.[8] Hohimer's infamy reached its apotheosis in 1973 when the *Chicago Sun-Times* ran a story that directly implicated him in the murder of Valerie Percy, a Lake Michigan woman who was found beaten to death in her home sometime in late 1966. Leo Rugendorf, a former associate of Hohimer, told the *Times* that Hohimer had said, "They'll get me for the Valerie Percy murder. The girl woke up and I hit her on top of the head with a pistol."[9] Hohimer was never convicted of the murder due to lack of evidence (at one point Ted Kaczynski – the Unabomber – was a suspect),[10] but he was at that time in jail anyway, serving a thirty-year sentence at Ford Madison for a string of high-end burglaries in the Chicago area. It was during his time at Madison that Hohimer penned his memoirs, *The Home Invaders: Confessions of a Cat Burglar*. The confluence of these two events, Hohimer being hoisted back into the public consciousness via the *Sun-Times*'s article and the writing of his memoirs, ultimately led to *Thief* and Mann's conception of the character of Frank. Mann secured the rights to *The Home Invaders* and began extracting from it all the useful details, or what Mann would call "soft" info, that would eventually lend *Thief* much of its technical credibility and industrial milieu.

Mann would very quickly plane off the fact that, for instance, Hohimer burgled, not just the corporate domains of high-rise towers and metal depositories, but domestic homes as well during his time as part of a group of high-end thieves operating in Chicago. Despite the rigour of Mann's wish to inculcate a reality-based style of film making, even he knew that to distil a movie character out of a real-life burglar and possible murderer was risky. Mann therefore modulated the criminality of his muse for *Thief*, retaining what he responded to most in Hohimer, his technical skill and adherence to professionalism.[11]

Frank returns to his office on the car lot to attend to some more paperwork. His secretary stays too long at his desk and Frank waves her

THIEF AND THE CRIMINAL

away. He then rises and walks out of frame. Outside, he strolls to a private space on the edge of the car lot. Mann signals Frank's exit from the point of view of the mechanics working in the shop, a car to the left and right of frame, bonnets raised and wheel bolts being tightened. Thirty years later, Nicholas Winding Refn would borrow this framing arrangement for the early garage scenes in 2011's *Drive*, a film that owes more than a passing debt to Mann's work and his view of, in particular, Los Angeles. Frank takes a seat on a crash barrier in front of a blue fence and handles a document of immense importance to him, just as Will Graham will do in *Manhunter* (1986), sitting on the driftwood with Crawford (Dennis Farina) looking at the family murder scene that prompts the rest of the story. The document here is a letter from Okla (Willie Nelson), Frank's jail time mentor – and a rare positive father figure in Mann's films – who is still in prison serving out a long custodial sentence. In the letter Okla begs Frank to go and visit him in jail. Frank acknowledges the urgency of this and takes out his padded wallet to review his photo collage, something he made while he himself was in jail. According to Mann this collage is a veritable artefact of prison life, not just a visual metaphor for what Frank will later discard when things spiral out of control. Something that a number of real convicts make on the inside, the collage is a distillation of the most important and personal aspects of the convict's life. It's a visual record of enduring people and personal ambitions for life upon release that also serves to eliminate everything ephemeral and inconsequential for its owner.

However, although in the text of the film Frank's collage suggests that his aspirations are purely about family and emotional security, the reality is perhaps more complex. The lingering shot on Frank's wallet just prior to him removing the collage, a wallet loaded with credit and debit cards, suggests he may have parallel or dual motivations at work. Is Frank not also a criminal intent on financial upward mobility? It's arguable that this drive assumes as much prominence in the film as his pursuit of love and family; remember that his intent to be wealthy could be considered the reason he destroys his life with Jessie and his adopted child.

In the next scene Frank goes to his bar to call Barry, his partner. He wants to know if the cash payment for the diamonds he stole at the start of the film has been delivered by The Man. Barry tells Frank that The Man is dead, having been thrown from a balcony with Frank's money on his person. Angry and out of pocket, Frank goes to see the middleman in an attempt to collect his money. This is Frank manifesting his authority, exerting his sense of criminal entitlement and what Robert Kolker terms his ideological certitude.[12] Frank is attempting to steal back money that, in turn, has been stolen from him that, in turn, he earned from stealing diamonds. There's a satisfying brio to this scene as Frank disabuses the weasel-like middleman (played by Tom Signorelli) of the notion that he could just take money from him. Again, Frank's disciplined professionalism elicits audience sympathy for his character, ensuring that, although he is a criminal, he remains the protagonist in the minds of the viewers.

There's a liberalism and fairness to Frank's criminality here that, at least on the surface and as expressed in Mann's fiction, can be traced back to the romanticism and even-handedness of John Dillinger and Herbert K. Lamm via Frank Hohimer and John Santucci. Put simply, Frank just wants what's owed to him. When the middleman attempts to blow Frank off, Frank erupts into the lethal automaton of Mann's alter ego. While Caan is not quite as successful in conveying the thinly veiled threat and menace that, say, De Niro captures as McCauley in *Heat*, there is a satisfying aspect to this scene. Frank holds his gun and moves in the same way that McCauley does when he's threatening the corrupt money launderer Van Zant (William Fichtner) in *Heat*. Here Mann blocks the scene so that Frank is illuminated against the large office window, the quintessentially Chicagoan Halsted Street canal bridge visible outside as in a Hopper painting. Furthermore, Frank's directness as a criminal is translated not just via the precision of his actions here but also through the speech patterns he has cultivated for himself. According to Mann's director's commentary on *Thief*, Frank's avoidance of contractions in his speech is a remnant of his prison days where survival was predicated on the clear, precise and articulate dissemination of information. Frank's thinking goes something like this: in order to safeguard your life in a dangerous environment like jail you need to take the time to speak clearly so as to avoid confusion, avert time-wasting and sidestep any violent consequences. A counterintuitive notion certainly, but when you consider this idea and Caan's delivery here, the singularity of his purpose and the dedication to his chosen profession helps elevate Frank's criminality beyond street-level thuggery, gangland chaos or Mafia bravado and into something like the warrior nobility of ancient feudalism.

In the next few scenes all the dice are loaded by a series of fateful decisions and errors of judgement. Frank visits Okla in jail and, in the film's most touching scene, agrees to get him out before he dies from angina. In these moments, Willie Nelson's eyes communicate a bond stronger than anything Frank will establish with Jessie or his criminal associates on the outside.

Frank then meets with Leo (Robert Prosky in his first film role) and gets his money from the opening diamond heist. Leo suggests to Frank that he should come to work for him. Frank is initially reluctant but the pull of the financial rewards eventually proves too much for him. Leo sees this yuppie weakness in Frank and sets about exploiting it to the fullest, disarming Frank with the promise of legal representation and big cash payouts. Mann contrasts the tight, fraternal close-ups of the previous scene with Okla with long shots here, as Leo baits Frank and sets the trap. There's real painting with light here as distant streetlights are drawn out in watery vertical lines across the slick tarmac of the dockside, bioluminescent strips organised in rows like one of Morris Louis's giant modernist canvases. Frank then heads to his date with Jessie (for which he is now late), the streetlights flowing over the bonnet of his car, as they did in *Taxi Driver* (1976), as Mighty Joe Young plays over the soundtrack.

This sequence sees Mann returning to that pseudo-*verité* feel he sought to capture in the opening moments of *The Jericho Mile*. There's lots of cutting to abstract images and panning shots, like the hands of the guitarist playing in the club where Jessie languishes or the drummer moving frenetically, as much professionals with their tools as Frank is during a robbery. When Frank arrives in the car park he's viewed from a distance, a clear picture of him obscured by crowds and parts of buildings. There's an attempt to convey the notion of found footage here, a lovely little "accidental" documentary snippet in a film that is more aptly characterised by its foregrounding of artifice and its feeling of deliberate design.

After some protest Frank convinces Jessie to accompany him to a nearby diner where, in a pivotal scene and Caan's favourite from his career, he lays out his life story and his hopes for the future. Mann blocks things simply for the scene with most shots being individual midshots of either Frank or Jessie, intercut with an occasional wider shot of them both sitting at the table with a freeway beyond the windows, the car lights again blobby and out of focus. Frank's prison patois – or prisonese – here is a delight to listen to and, although their philosophies of communication are diametrically opposed, exhibits a love of street language, cadence and timing in the way that Jonny Boy's famous monologue does in *Mean Streets* (1973), when De Niro's character explains at length why he's so depressed.

Although Frank's communication style is entirely predicated on precision and a lack of contraction and Jonny Boy's is filled with nothing but contraction and obfuscation, the two scenes foreground a love of language and the truths it speaks about character. The crucial theme to be divined from this scene, then, hinges on Frank's line when he says, "I have run out of time … I can't work fast enough to catch up and I can't run fast enough to catch up." Frank is here referring to the fact that because he spent so many of his younger years in prison – he stole $40, a misdemeanour very similar to John Dillinger's first crime – he missed his chance to acquire the material security most people have accrued by his age. This is Mann invoking the *fin-de-siècle* fatedness of William Holden in *The Wild Bunch* (1969) or Lee Marvin in *Monte Walsh* (1970) or John Dillinger shortly before his death, the sense of men approaching the end of their time and becoming living anachronisms. And like Dillinger, Frank doesn't know each day whether he will live, die or get rearrested, such is the extent of his wish to live what's left of his life while he can.

Of course, in this important diner scene Frank is also appealing to Jessie to be with him, but, as we know by now, this is not the motivating factor behind his criminal activity. Frank steals because of the paucity of regular opportunity in his ex-con life. In this sense *Thief* advocates the Strain Theory of criminology suggests that "mainstream culture, especially in the United States, is saturated with dreams of opportunity, freedom and prosperity", as Merton put it, "the American Dream":

> Most people buy into this dream and it becomes a powerful cultural and psychological motivation. Therefore, if the social structure of opportunities is unequal and prevents the majority from realizing the dream, some of them will turn to illegitimate means (crime) in order to realize it.[13]

In the context of this view of the criminal, Frank commits crimes because the material existence that his environment and society suggest he should have is not available to him via any other means. Frank's crimes are not motivated by vengeance or an unhinged pathology but rather by the pursuit of the materialistic yuppie life model that he feels he must have. His interest in this lifestyle is so fervent that at one point he lists to Jessie, as a point of pride, all that he has so far acquired through his criminal activities, as if to legitimate his illegitimate profession: "I wear $150 slacks, I wear silk shirts, I wear $800 suits, I wear a gold watch, I wear a perfect D flawless 3 carat ring, I change cars like other guys change their fuckin' shoes." Like Dillinger before him, Frank enjoys the fruits of his labour as soon as he can. He parades his criminal wealth like a white-collar crook because he knows time is not on his side. As Depp's Dillinger says in *Public Enemies*, "[I want] everything, right now." By the end of the diner scene Jessie has agreed to be with Frank, after he offers her a genuinely emotional appeal through both his wallet collage and his sheer honesty.

With the conclusion of this element of the domestic story, *Thief* switches back to its criminal mode as Frank and his crew, now led by the strangely avuncular Leo, head to Los Angeles to scope out the site of the film's audacious robbery sequence. *Thief* is firmly back at its procedural best as Frank, following his reconnoitre of the Los Angeles building, visits a metallurgist to design and build the tool necessary to crack the safe. In its procedural mode, *Thief* has the confidence to delineate the process of crime and trust that the audience will invest in its evocation of the technical aspects of things like safe-cracking – "Swedish cold roll 247", "titanium/copper alloy" and so forth.

In the next scene *Thief* displays its cynicism and scepticism of the criminal justice system, a viewpoint, as we have seen, notably absent from and in contradiction to *The Jericho Mile* but one that would be actively developed by Mann in *Heat*, *Collateral* and *Public Enemies*. The judge overseeing Okla's case is bribed by Frank's attorney to parole Okla early, in return for $6000. Frank is astonished at how easy the bribe was and gives the attorney a cash payment. This scepticism of big city power owes a debt, at least in part, to Chicago figures such as Mike Royko, the famous *Daily News*, *Sun-Times* and *Tribune* journalist who wrote witty exposés of city corruption and abuses of power, most notably of Mayor Daley's stranglehold on the Illinois state capital in the best-selling book *Boss*. Throughout his career Royko railed against the kind of corruption and machine politics that had come to characterise Chicago. *Thief* criticises the Chicago justice system by normalising the bribery of Okla's judge, showing how well-worn its patterns and procedures are. Both the judge and Okla's attorney have a code for communicating how much money will be required for Okla's early release. It was this sense of normalisation that so angered and motivated Royko, the expectation that because it's Chicago anyone can be bought and paid for.

The discrete storylines propel events forward as Frank and Jessie are denied the chance to adopt a child. In this powerful scene Frank assails the insanity of denying a state-raised child (as he was) the opportunity of a caring home because of his prison history. Mann captures the couple's pain in the next shot with a slow zoom outward as Frank and Jessie sit on their patio furniture staring at the fire, their mutual sense of agency steadily shrinking away like the undertaker's at the start of *The Godfather* (1972). Like the good angel on Frank's shoulder that he still purports to be at this point, Leo comes to Frank's aid and offers to provide him and Jessie with the child they were denied by the city's social services. This scene, which takes place in Frank's bar, is the sealing of the Faustian pact that Frank has unwittingly made with Leo. Frank's attempt to inform Jessie of the good news is thwarted by her news that Okla is in hospital and critically ill. Moments later Okla does indeed die, Frank losing his father just as he becomes one himself.

In the next scene Jessie collects their new child and the two go to dinner at a Japanese restaurant. Michael Paul Chan is Frank's waiter for the evening, an actor who connects *Thief* to Mann's last film of the 1990s, *The Insider*, in which he plays Norman the cameraman, a character deployed by Mann to make Pacino's Lowell Bergman appear more proficient. Here, however, Chan is given a smaller role but in an integral scene, where he shares in Frank's only real moment of domestic unification.

At the restaurant Mann brings together all the key tangents of Frank's prison collage and, for a moment, he seems complete. Through Frank's advocacy of his unique brand of criminal activity and the yuppie lifestyle it has afforded him, he has managed to acquire the emotional life he believes he needs. However, as the film will detail in the coming scenes, this restaurant scene is the apex of the rollercoaster, the high vantage point to which Frank's life will never again ascend. This portent is sown in the restaurant itself. Despite the hopeful nature of the scene – a family having dinner together – and its accompanying non-diegetic synthesised scoring by Tangerine Dream, Mann blocks and shoots the scene in a way that suggests both the unity achieved and the separation still to come. Barricaded by the walls of their booth, Frank and Jessie are enclosed in the same space but, nevertheless, rendered incomplete. For the most part we only see their heads and shoulders because Mann's camera shoots over the top of the booth, only occasionally cutting to a wider two shot that allows us to glimpse the characters' whole selves. For the most part they are dislocated and fragmentary despite the unification that the narrative suggests.

Like *Heat* after it, *Thief*'s narrative now turns towards the series of doom-laden decisions and events that will ultimately lead to the central character's simultaneous destruction and liberation. Frank now has the custom-made burning bar for his capstone Los Angeles robbery, along with the password for deactivating the alarm system. Corrupt Chicago police detectives, unsuccessful in their earlier attempts to coerce him as part of their protection racket, subsequently arrest and beat him up as punishment for his earlier rebuttal of their offer. This scene further cements *Thief*'s advocacy of its brand of crime over the venal, corrupt and ineffective police and penal systems of the Midwest. Frank's chosen lifestyle, the bribery of the judge during Okla's hearing and the Chicago PD's attempted coercion – and beating – of Frank all hold aloft *Thief*'s contempt for the established power structures of the time. In this regard *Thief* is a counterpoint to *The Jericho Mile*'s optimism about the rehabilitative systems of police and society. It was also a catalyst for the deepening exploration of this cynicism in Mann's films to come.

THIEF AND THE CRIMINAL

Figure 3. Thief

Before Frank can successfully take down the robbery in Los Angeles he must escape the Chicago PD's incessant surveillance of him. Following the police beating, two units follow Frank. Urizzi (Santucci), in the lead car, is incensed by Frank's continued refusal to cooperate with them and is now absolutely intent on catching him in the act. Frank knows this and ditches the transponder that the Chicago PD low-jacked his car with among some luggage waiting to be loaded on to a bus destined for De Moines. This is a beautiful sequence, filled with the emerging style of *Thief* that could by now be most aptly described as, in the words of author Woody Haut, *neon noir*.[14] The night-time streets of Chicago in *Thief* are gaudy and bruised with luminescent signage, an existential netherworld the way New York was in *Taxi Driver* or Los Angeles was in *Hardcore* (1979), except here the villains are police and not pimps. The luminosity of *Thief*'s night-time scenery is also important for understanding Mann's view of Los Angeles in *Collateral*, a crime film that also uses noir stylistics and a similar colour palette in its evocation of nocturnal urbanity.[15] *Thief* is, by this point in its running time, in possession of a clear and demonstrable style and texture, a signature of sorts that seems to be emerging as a product of the film's narrative choices, in a way that *The Jericho Mile*'s story and context made impossible. Is it then the arena of the city and the actual display of procedure – the protagonist performing, so to speak – that has permitted Mann to wield something authorial and uniquely *his* with *Thief*? And does the film owe its love of procedure, its alienated central character (who is deeply suspicious of the established power systems of the city) and its

51

haughty production design of neon modernist lines to Mann's emergent vision in the early 1980s, or, maybe, to Jules Dassin, the French director Jean-Pierre Melville and the style of the *cinema du look*?

Despite Mann's incessant proclamation that his films are derived from real life and not from other cinema, *Thief*'s style is best understood as a product of both Mann's emergent vision *and*, like all great art, key aspects of that which went before. With *Thief*, Mann's narrative concerns, along with those elements of character and architecture derived from the modernist aspects of Chicago's twentieth-century history, find their first real and significant expression. The confluence of Frank's criminal characterisation – stemming from the template of Herbert K. Lamm – and the modernist encryption of his city – the liberated steel architecture of Louis Sullivan and the concrete of Lower Wacker – supplants *The Jericho Mile* as the film that gives birth to something quintessentially Mannesque. Where these elements fuse with *Thief*'s debts to the existential procedure of Dassin's *Rififi* (1955) and Melville's *Le Samourai* (1967), and the 1980s visual style of the *cinema du look*, you have a film that, in the words of Andrew Sarris, "looks and moves ... the way a director thinks and feels".[16]

Through its near silent, sweaty and stoic robbery of a Parisian jewellery shop, *Rififi* provides a cinematic context for understanding *Thief*'s insistence on allowing the mechanics of robbery to play out in their entirety. Like *Rififi*, *Thief* insists on the audience understanding how difficult, physically demanding and time-consuming orchestrating and carrying out a robbery can be. Despite Mann's insistence to the contrary, *Rififi* is a likely cinematic precedent for *Thief*'s bold focus on the action of crime as well as its consequences. With Melville's *Le Samourai*, the dues *Thief* must pay are connected to Alain Delon's portrayal of Costello, the Bushido hitman who lives by a strict set of guidelines and is a strong fictional progenitor of Frank in *Thief*. In the film, Costello reaches a point where he knows he cannot win and is pursued, like Frank, by both the police and his employer. He tells his girlfriend that things will be OK, similar to the assurance that Frank gives Jessie before sending her away forever, and then enters into a climactic purge of his situation, knowing full well that he might not survive. The existential awareness of these two men, the sense that they will uphold their worldviews irrespective of the outcome, is a potent force in *Le Samourai* and *Thief* that, while guilty of perhaps generating the sense of contrivance that stains each film on occasion, nevertheless provides the high tragedy of their respective endings.

The final aspect of this trinity, the film's heralding of the *cinema du look* (a short-lived stylistic movement in France in the 1980s led by Luc Besson, Jean-Jacques Beineix and Leos Carax), may go some way to contextualising Mann's stylistic choices in *Thief* beyond the fact that the 1980s was a high point for style or a "cinema of surfaces", in the words of Jürgen Müller and Steffen Haubner. Writing of the *cinema du look*, Müller and Haubner state:

> France witnessed a kind of rapprochement between Hollywood and the European tradition. The cinema du look pioneered by Jean-Jacques Beineix and Luc Besson marked the arrival of design as an autonomous mode of cinematic expression. This artificial "neon cinema" was an attempt by the younger generation to create original myths and to make a clean break...[17]

In its mannerist visual conception of Chicago as a rain-slicked, neon-hued netherworld, *Thief* appropriates many of the traits laid down by Besson and Beineix in France. Where most of the American films of 1981 and 1982 were invoking traditional genre templates (action – *Raiders of the Lost Ark*, *Das Boot*; gothic horror – *An American Werewolf in London*, *The Howling*; or fantasy – *Time Bandits*, *Clash of the Titans*, *Tarzan the Ape Man*, *Excalibur*), *Thief* was exemplifying the more critical and slippery aesthetic of the 1980s *cinema du look*, an aesthetic Ridley Scott would defend when he said "sometimes the design is the statement".[18]

Ostensibly Scott was responding to accusations that *Blade Runner* (1982), a film now regarded as a triumph of design and ambition, was a hollow exercise in style. However, Scott, himself a graphic designer and artist, was in a larger sense supporting the notion of design in any film as a valid entity in itself and not just an adjunct of film's more general creative impulses. *Thief*'s design, more than just another proponent of the contemporaneous 1980s look (which, of course, it now is), actually serves to validate Müller and Haubner's view of the *cinema du look* as "an autonomous mode of cinematic expression". Talking of *Thief*, they continue:

> Michael Mann's *Thief* demonstrates how a character's entire inner life can be conveyed by means of lighting effects ... Practically the entire film takes place on wet streets in darkness. Many scenes play against a background of display window glass, where reflections of the interiors merge with the light from the street ... Mann drives this home by conjuring up a diffuse limbo, in which the borders between the internal and the external worlds fluctuate and blur.[19]

As noted near the beginning of the chapter, the stylisation in *Thief* is perceptive in its 1980s specificity and, maybe, even predictive of the wider aesthetic to come, such as that later espoused by *Miami Vice* the TV show. But more than this, when the influence of the *cinema du look* is invoked, this same style actually enters into the narrative of *Thief* itself and, as Müller and Haubner note above, becomes a criterion of Frank's characterisation and the overall thematic landscape of the film.

Thief's central robbery arrives at nearly 1hr 20m and is instructive here as it acts as a distillation of both the film's Bressonian/Dassinian sensibility and its debt to the look of those French films that paraded style as substance. Frank and his crew have broken into a Los Angeles tower from the roof and now prepare to melt off a huge safe door with their custom burning bar. Mann's notion of robbery as a liturgical event is no purer than it is here. His camera tracks all the labour, sweat, procedure, planning and literal fireworks of the crime, the entire cutting away of the safe door done without recourse to dialogue, just like *Rififi*. Sparks immolate the moment in a ceremonial fire and further render Frank's criminality as something worthy, even beautiful. Is this Mann using style to, in the words of Müller and Haubner, "create original myths", to generate a fresh mythos around the criminal act? As half the safe door falls away, Frank's associate climbs inside to retrieve the diamonds while Frank, in a wonderfully candid moment, is viewed in midshot by Mann taking a seat and smoking a cigarette. Caan's expression here is one of true exaltation and relief as he looks on with satisfaction at his accomplishments, the actor having actually wielded the tools and cut open the safe at Mann's behest. For Frank, however, opening the safe also means opening the door to the totality of Leo's exploitation and sadism.

Leo betrays Frank and only pays him a fraction of his agreed reward for the diamond robbery. It soon becomes clear that Leo has engineered his working relationship with Frank so that he effectively owns Frank's life. Leo helped with Frank's house purchase, the adoption of his son, his police problems and, now, has invested the majority of Frank's pay for the diamond heist in a shopping mall. Leo, however, in his sadistic attempts to own Frank, has now come up against the rigid doctrine of self-determination that Frank so assiduously adheres to. Frank demands the remainder of his money within 24 hours or, as he says to Leo, "You'll be wearing your ass for a hat." After his ultimatum to Leo, Frank is back on the street, his sense of agency dissolving and merging with the objective circumstances of the exterior world. As Müller and Haubner highlighted earlier, this loss of agency, this decentralisation of the modern male criminal, is signified by the neon lights of the street. As Frank drives away into the night, Mann cuts to an overhead shot of the bonnet of Frank's car. The reflected neon streetlights and signs of Chicago seem to

THIEF AND THE CRIMINAL

Figure 4. Thief

literally spill into Frank's world, gliding as they do over his car like some viral miasma spewing forth from the outside. As Frank pulls up at his car lot – the street sign reads "Western" and we are indeed headed for a showdown – Mann intercuts this with Leo's henchmen beating up Barry (Belushi's character) at the back of the dealership.

Barry momentarily escapes the clutches of Leo's cronies and lunges out of the building to alert Frank to the danger, only to be shot and killed by Carl – Dennis Farina's first film role – in one of the few instances of slow-motion photography in all of Mann's films. The death of Barry looks so anachronistic now and seems completely anathema to Mann's normally reality-based cinematic project. This slow-motion shot, and the one that will shortly accompany Leo's death, adds melodrama and expressionism to an event – a shooting – that would later be treated with a kind of dissociative realism by Mann. Of course, this is the point in a film grounded in the expressionistic flourishes of the *cinema du look*, where subjective viewpoints and ideas take precedence over objective reality.[20]

The resultant paroxysm of violence that caps the film, as Frank extricates himself from Leo's clutches and disappears into the night, returns to the use of slow-motion photography that demarcated Barry's death at the dealership. Frank has sent his wife and child away and returned to his true and natural state, the criminal automaton, the principled high-end thief whose motivation in life, which had been latent in recent scenes due to the arrival of Jessie and their son, is now made manifest again with brutal efficiency. Frank's original path to wealth, which included the legitimate bar and car dealership, is now tainted with Leo's extortion. Before Frank pursues Leo and his remaining cronies, he rids himself of his legit businesses by incinerating them like he did with the safe door in Los Angeles. These moments, although not grounded in the same religious brimstone and hellfire, nevertheless assume a biblical grandeur in the way that similar moments of destruction do in Martin Scorsese's *Goodfellas* (1990), namely when Henry Hill blows up the car lot and runs towards the camera. In *Thief* we don't get the Godardian freeze frame but the colour temperature of the fire is exactly the same – bright white, like the searing flames of hell. That slo-mo is also here, rendering the explosions as hallucinatory clouds of fire and debris, slowing things down to the speed that Frank perceives things, deliberately and precisely. When Frank finally blows up his car dealership, the cars are like the demon vehicle from John Carpenter's *Christine* (1983), fire spewing from the side windows like horns on the devil. To cap the significance of all this, Frank takes one last look at his collage before dropping it on to the tarmac of the car lot to burn with the rest of his life.

When the climactic shootout does arrive Mann blocks the scene like a scary movie sequence. It's all corners, doors and tight framing as Frank zeroes in on his prey. When Attaglia is first attacked it's at the fridge in the kitchen, as in another Carpenter film, *Halloween* (1978), where the bogeyman is lurking in the shadows ready to strike at the boyfriend. Here Prosky's Leo cuts a rather pathetic figure, a great contrast from his earlier scene in the chemical works where he tells Frank that he now owns him and that he'll feed his wife and daughter to Wimpy customers if he doesn't comply. With his velour tracksuit and bulging belly, Leo comes out from hiding, as Neil McCauley will do at the end of *Heat*, and raises his gun. Frank, quicker on the draw, shoots him first. Leo's slow-motion fall, the blood falling from his wounds, the flailing and writhing once he's down, would border on the ridiculous if it wasn't for the fact that this moment, like much else in *Thief*, is drawn from an expressive but insular source. It's not meant to feel objectively realistic but is rather characterised by Frank's view of events. His sheer bloodlust, his desire to end Leo's hold over him, means that Leo's death looks ridiculous and stylistically inflated as it would appear to Frank in his fantasies. Outside on the lawn Frank then shoots Carl, who comes bounding through the hedge, and finally kills Attaglia. Between these deaths Frank reloads his gun, the empty clip dropping to the ground with all the slow-motion bravado of the gunslinger in Robert Rodriguez's *Desperado* (1995). Frank takes a shot to the chest but still manages to kill Carl who has partially resurrected himself. Mann films Carl's death as John Woo would, repeating the shot of him falling to the ground several times to protract the moment and reinforce the notion that it's from Frank's view of the world that we often see things in *Thief*.[21] The film ends as Frank rises from the ground, injured, and walks off into the night having both won and lost everything, an ambiguity that Mann will use more than once in his career.

The ending of *Thief* draws on so many genre markers other than crime that it becomes almost a pastiche in its closing minutes. For the most part though, the film is singular in its vision and is, looking back, certainly in possession of a directorial signature. In many ways *Thief* establishes a series of determinants where *The Jericho Mile* did not. As noted previously, this may have had something to do with *Jericho*'s TV roots and related constraints. More likely, however, is the notion that *Thief*'s relative success as the first Michael Mann film (according to this book's designation) is down to the source idea, the genesis drawn from Hohimer's work as a jewel thief and his criminal lineage back to Dillinger, Lamm and the modernist ideas of Chicago in the 1930s.

Yes, *Thief* appropriates several key stylistic approaches, namely the work of Le Melville and Dassin and the movement of the *cinema du look*, and these are undoubtedly important in explaining how the film operates. Presiding over these aspects, though, is *Thief*'s importance as the progenitor of the criminal type, a template that Mann would remain deeply interested in for years to come. Hohimer's memoirs gave Mann the algorithm that helped him connect the professionalism and intelligence of Dillinger and Lamm with the modern, urban environment of Chicago – and later Atlanta and the city of Los Angeles – towards the end of the twentieth century.

It is *Thief*'s stylisation, however, and not its criminal template that carries us forward to Mann's next film, the frustratingly divergent *The Keep*.

> **Key scene suggestion for the criminal – the liturgy of the main safe-cracking sequence in Los Angeles.**

The Films of Michael Mann

Notes

1   See Vincent Fanby, *"Thief"*, *New York Times*, 27 March 1981, 12, quoted in Steven Rybin, *The Cinema of Michael Mann*, Lexington Books, 2007, 44; and Pauline Kael, *Taking It All In*, Marion Boyars, 1986, 188.
2   As Pauline Kael noted in her 1981 review of the film published originally in the *New Yorker*, "[Frank is] a hard labourer and he's pure – he's spiritually cleansed by his dedication to his craft"; reprinted in Kael, *Taking It All In*, 187.
3   See Mann's director's commentary on the Blu-ray of *Thief*.
4   The 2011 film *Drive* would also capitalise on this style of opening to great effect, here using the track "Tick of the Clock" by The Chromatics to layer on to events a fantastic sense of intention and noir-ish purpose.
5   *Thief* evinces several instances of similar contrivance that perhaps undermine Nick James's statements that "*Thief* is the closest of Mann's features to verité" and that the film "also shares the funky urban grain of such 1970s underworld movies as *Mean Streets* (1973) and *The French Connection* (1971)". See Nick James, *Heat*, BFI Publishing, 2002, 20.
6   The dynamics of this scene are replicated almost exactly in *Heat* when Neil McCauley meets Nate (Jon Voight's character).
7   Frank does of course kill people in *Thief*. He eventually kills Leo and some of his cronies, but this is only in response to Leo's violent extortion of Frank and the threats Leo makes towards Frank's new family. These murders are not part of Frank's career criminality but, instead, are a result of Leo's psychotic nature.
8   Despite this, *Thief* does have startling similarities to other notable crime films including Bresson's *Pickpocket* (1959). When Roger Ebert spoke of that film's main character and his connections to the novel *Crime and Punishment* he could have instead been talking about Frank in *Thief*: "Bresson's Michel, like Dostoyevsky's hero Raskolnikov, needs money in order to realize his dreams, and sees no reason why some lacklustre ordinary person should not be forced to supply it. The reasoning is immoral, but the characters claim special privileges above and beyond common morality. Michel, like the hero of *Crime and Punishment*, has a 'good woman' in his life, who trusts he will be able to redeem himself." See https://www.rogerebert.com/reviews/great-movie-pickpocket-1959 (accessed 26 December 2022).
9   See Robert McCoppin and Glenn Wall, "Newly Disclosed Account Surfaces in 1966 Valerie Percy Murder Case", Chicago Tribune, 14 June 2011, https://www.chicagotribune.com/news/ct-xpm-2011-06-14-ct-met-percy-murder-20110614-story.html (accessed 23 February 2023).
10   A character dealt with tangentially by Mann in his 1999 film *The Insider*.
11   The home invasion narrative so skilfully avoided in *Thief* would find later expression in Mann's novel prequel/sequel *Heat 2* and the character of Otis Wardell, a serial rapist and burglar.

12 Robert Kolker, *A Cinema of Loneliness: Penn, Stone, Kubrick, Scorsese, Spielberg, Altman*, 3rd edn, Oxford University Press, 2000.
13 Robert Merton, *Social Theory and Social Structure*, Free Press, 1957, 205; as discussed at https://www.santoshraut.com/forensic/criminology.htm (accessed 22 February 2023).
14 See Woody Haut, *Neon Noir: Contemporary American Crime Fiction*, Serpent's Tail, 1999.
15 Rybin, *The Cinema of Michael Mann*, 54.
16 Andrew Sarris, "Notes on the Auteur Theory" (1962), in Leo Braudy and Marshall Cohen (eds), *Film Theory and Criticism*, Oxford University Press, 2004, 452.
17 Jürgen Müller and Steffen Haubner, "Aesthetics of Film in the Eighties", in *Best Movies of the 80s*, Taschen, 2006, 10.
18 Ibid., 11.
19 Ibid.
20 This notion would be repeated through a complex *mise en scène* in *The Keep* and *Manhunter*.
21 The John Woo reference would reappear in Mann's *Heat* and *Blackhat*. When Pacino's character shoots dead Cheritto (Tom Sizemore) in *Heat*, Mann repeats the shot of Pacino shouldering his rifle prior to taking the shot, just as Woo loved to do with Chow Yun-Fat in *Hard Boiled* (1982) or *A Better Tomorrow* (1986). In *Blackhat*, it's there in the shot repetitions when Hathaway swings away at a bank of hard drives with an axe inside the Chinese nuclear power station.

CHAPTER FIVE

The Keep and Stylisation

> The captain has a lot of help running the ship ... but he's still the captain.
>
> Billy Wilder

Was *The Keep*, Mann's 1983 financial folly, an instance of the captain not seeing the iceberg ahead? Or was Mann, as some of his interviews around the time of the film's release seem to suggest, trying something a bit more radical, a film that prioritised the visual and the experiential before all else? If we take the latter explanation to be the case, *The Keep* is a film that continues and augments those stylistic aspects of *Thief* that pointed towards the *cinema du look* (the use of expressionistic lighting, the synthesised score, the slow-motion photography and the pastiche of genre markers) while also consciously leaving behind those Dassinian notions of street, crime and character that Mann had traded in up until now. If the former explanation is the truth, if the film was indeed a huge misstep away from the cinematic milieu that Mann had just begun to cultivate, then *The Keep* still deserves inclusion here by dint of its sheer strangeness, its bizarre narrative construction and its distracting visual design. In reality, *The Keep* is both of these things.

As an industry product, *The Keep* lost over $3,000,000 at the box office amid, for one reason, stiff competition from other releases of that year such as *Return of the Jedi*, *Scarface*, *Terms of Endearment* and *Trading Places*. In its genre hybridity of WWII/horror/fantasy elements, *The Keep* also occupies a place in a scant and largely unsuccessful sub-genre that, *Pan's Labyrinth* (2006) aside, has usually been characterised by hokey and exploitative elements. One need look no further than Jesus Franco's *Oasis of the Zombies* and Jean Rollin's *Zombie Lake*, both released in 1981, as evidence of these elements at their most extreme. Though not strictly the same – these two films present the Nazis as the sole villains whereas in *The Keep* the Nazis are part of a larger, ambiguous evil that may or may not include Molasar, the film's central monster – the one commonality that unites all three films (and *Pan's Labyrinth* with its Spanish Francoists) is the way they situate fascism within this larger framework of horror, fable and the supernatural. The Franco and Rollin films, and to an extent *The Keep*, pit unsuspecting protagonists against undead remnants of an evil ideology, the evil having been perpetuated through the ages until the events of each film, where the main characters must purge it once and forever. The majority of films in this sub-genre then draw upon these narrative elements, situating them within the aforementioned mysticism, folklore and occultism that so preoccupied the fascist war machine – specifically divisions of the Nazi party – during the Second World War.

With all that being said, *The Keep* is perhaps something more. It is a film in definite possession of some truly beguiling aspects, aspects that, if we permit Mann his indulgences, point towards something experimental, maybe even radical, in its intent. The film's effort to generate what Mann termed a "relativistic universe" – something based on the fantasy of a dream, the idea of a constructed environment of the mind (an idea *Blade Runner* and, much later, Christopher Nolan's *Inception* are entirely predicated on) – was a fledgling idea in American cinema in 1983. In this respect *The Keep* is ludicrous as a horror film situated in a real historical context. Despite Mann's insistence that the uniforms, weapons and haircuts of the film be authentic, the thick layering up of what might be termed the film's visual somnambulism means that *The Keep* is, its attention to Nazi period detail notwithstanding, completely disconnected from any reality. If, then, we are to devote a chapter to *The Keep* it must be thought of in these terms, as Mann's curate's egg, a film that tries desperately (and succeeds spectacularly in places) to be part of the cinema of surfaces that *Thief* pre-empted, while also suffering from some intractable lapses in aspects such as narrative construction.

Unlike *Oasis of the Zombies* and *Zombie Lake*, *The Keep* has a degree of literary pedigree behind it. Mann's film is based on F. Paul Wilson's 1981 novel of the same name, a book that appeared on the *New York Times* bestseller list and was very successful as a horror story. This success led to the book coming to the attention of Hawk Koch and Gene Kirkwood, producers who had had a successful few years with films such as *Rocky* (1976) and *Gorky Park* (1983). By the time *The Keep* was entering its pre-production stage Mann had also worked extensively in television, fulfilling the roles of director, screenwriter and producer on such series as *Bronk*, *Starsky & Hutch*, *Police Story* and *Vega$*. *The Jericho Mile* also originally emerged from this environment, one that was, as has been well documented elsewhere, having a seriously pernicious effect on cinema attendances at the time. Almost as a counter-offensive against this

THE KEEP AND STYLISATION

change in audience viewing habits, Mann's immediate take on Wilson's source material was to bring to the fore its potential as a visual fable, as something that was in keeping with other select and successful films of the early 1980s that, in the words of Müller and Haubner, were part of the decade's "dream machine".[1]

Mann begins *The Keep* with a vertical pan shot that's akin to the one early on in *Thief* where the camera tracks down between two buildings and into a consciously noirish alleyway in Chicago. Here the camera roves down through a grey cloudbank to reveal the oppressive image of military trucks moving through green countryside. The visuals combine with an insistent and echoing cue by Tangerine Dream to produce something that approximates those great shots of trucks driving in William Friedkin's *Sorcerer* (1977), a film also scored by Tangerine Dream and in possession of a similar, dreamy quality. The trucks carry what eventually seems to be a group of excommunicated Nazi soldiers led, for the moment, by Jürgen Prochnow's Captain Klaus Woermann. They arrive in a small village high in a pass in the Carpathian Alps with orders to hold the area indefinitely. Mann returns to the slow-motion photography of *Thief* to underscore the threat the soldiers pose as they are seen arriving by the villagers, their trucks indicative of Robert Kolker's idea of "death mechanised". The village itself is like a Disneyland set or the seaside resort in Robert Altman's *Popeye* (1980), something that convinces from the front but doesn't bear the scrutiny of too many close-ups. The close-ups here are of Woermann's blue eyes, as Mann cuts between them and the slow-motion imagery of villagers pulling their children back into their homes and the local priest, Fonescu – a very different Robert Prosky – surveying the outsiders with scepticism and anger. The other great, oppressive image here after the arrival of the trucks is the road bridge into the keep itself. Woermann's troops stop at the foot of the bridge and Mann places his camera in the back seat of the truck for an over-the-shoulder shot of the bridge leading up to the dark maw of the keep entrance. This image will be returned to again and again, particularly as the first deaths take place, the overhead lighting that the soldiers foolishly install swinging in the wind, casting shadows and ratcheting tension.

Mann's obfuscation of clear narrative checkpoints, perhaps in his attempt to generate a story that mimics the disjointed structure of dreams and fantasy tales, means that it's worth explaining the story now so that we can then consider specific sites of interest later. Once the Wehrmacht have arrived they glibly set up camp in the keep and begin plundering the silver crosses installed in its walls. This unleashes the evil within, an entity named Molasar, who kills the soldiers one by one. The awakening of this ancient evil also alerts a man called Glaeken (Scott Glenn) who, like Dick Hallorann in Stanley Kubrick's *The Shining* (1980), is compelled to travel to the source of this beckoning and confront the evil there. In the interim Woermann calls for reinforcements both to swell his diminished ranks and find the source of the murders of his men. Major Kaempffer arrives, played by a young Gabriel Byrne, a far more sadistic soldier who, in *The Keep*, assumes the role of the psychotic force of nature that was fulfilled by Dr D in *The Jericho Mile* and Robert Prosky in *Thief*. The major randomly kills some villagers to mark his arrival before consulting the village priest, Prosky, regarding who could help to answer the riddle of the keep. The priest points to Dr Theodore Cuza (Ian McKellen), a Jewish expert on local history and the occult who is currently imprisoned in a Nazi concentration camp with his daughter Eva (Alberta Watson). In fact the priest has only suggested Cuza to the major in order to liberate him and his daughter from the concentration camp and secure their freedom. Cuza, with some swift legerdemain of his own, begins playing both the major and the more sympathetic Woermann as he pretends to decode the keep's messages and give them what they want. Eventually, Cuza encounters Molasar but manages to broker a deal with the entity that will give him eternal life in return for the release of a far greater demon from the keep. Glaeken then arrives at the village to confront Molasar and return its evil to the sanctuary of the keep. In doing so, he becomes romantically involved with Eva, Cuza's daughter. The film culminates in a battle between Glaeken's largely good character and Molasar's evil one for the soul of all humanity. Good wins out but at the cost of Glaeken's life, an ambiguous ending perhaps not in keeping with the fairytale's traditional conclusion.

The narrative meanderings of *The Keep* point to both the difficulties of successfully adapting a novel and the risks of making what's left work when your film is really interested in something else. *The Keep*'s failures are largely – but not exclusively – the result of its narrative inconsistencies, the way in which, as the synopsis above demonstrates, the story keeps introducing additional acts while ignoring things such as realistic character motivation or effective exposition.[2] As with all things in this film, however, there is a caveat to what might on the surface appear to be its failings and weaknesses. As suggested earlier, with *The Keep* Mann may have wanted to disregard or marginalise the story logic in favour of presenting something intensely visual, something that melds the 1980s *cinema du look* aesthetic of *Thief* and the *memento mori* and *danse macabre* art movements of the 1300s and 1400s, movements that embodied the universality of death, regardless of your station, through their architecture of bones, pillaging, avarice and darkness. Indeed, near the beginning of the film, when Woermann's men are dismounting from their trucks, a fresco can be glimpsed on the chapel wall of saints with bright yellow halos. Yet like those *memento mori* frescoes – such as the one at the Sv. Trojica Holy Trinity church in Hrastovlje, Slovenia – the image is always disrupted by the harbingers of death. Here, the arrival of Nazi soldiers and their vehicle represents just such a harbinger.

The dreamy, relativistic universe of *The Keep* and its aesthetic of appearances takes further hold when Woermann first enters the keep itself. Viewed from the outside as one large precipitous wall, the inside of the keep defies its physical limitations and proves to be a gargantuan space of exaggerated X/Y axes, shadows and Escheresque staircases. The influence of German Expressionism is evident in Mann, who is an admirer of F.W. Murnau, a director strongly linked to the expressionist movement in German cinema in the 1920s. This expressionist link to *The Keep* is all the more timely and rewarding when you consider two thematic aspects of the film: the first is that many scholars believed that German Expressionism, with its high symbolism of peril and its fantastical architecture, perceived the coming onslaught of Nazi fascism in the 1930s; the second is that the prominent actor and director of the Nazi propaganda apparatus Paul Wegener, secretly an anti-fascist who worked covertly to destabilise Hitler's authority, was obsessed with the Jewish notion of the Golem, the avenging entity brought into being to wreak havoc. In *The Keep* both of these elements are fused by Mann when he has the Nazi evil of the film purged by an even greater, medieval villainy that resides within an expressionistic architecture of threat.

Of course, all this must be folded into the unique visual sensibility that Mann brings to *The Keep*, one that is fantastically demonstrated during the first night-watch sequence. The soldier on duty is startled first by the overhead light, with its metal shade, scraping on the stonework of the outer wall as the wind gusts by in clouds of dry ice masquerading as fog. Mann then cuts to the same frontal image of the keep entrance and captures a wonderful sense of symmetry and formal foreboding by having the soldier, with his back to the darkness, framed by the steadily rising sides of the keep structure. A kind of atonal non-diegetic synthesised note is heard that incorporates what sounds like tubular bells and a malevolent hissing noise, providing a complex viewing experience that has less to do with storytelling than the *cinema pur* movement of Henri Chomette.[3] Inside the keep one of the silver crosses begins to glow, attracting the attention of the soldier on guard. This points to an ambiguity in the film. Rather than plundering the keep for its riches outright (as would have been commensurate with Nazi villainy), it is the demon in the keep

THE FILMS OF MICHAEL MANN

Figure 5. Keep

that prompts the events of the film by first teasing the soldiers with this illuminated silver cross. The non-diegetic high note of more conventional movie horror gives way to Tangerine Dream's next big cue, an anachronistic and oddly reassuring composition that is perhaps the best piece of scoring in *The Keep*.

As the soldier walks in slow motion towards his doom a strong backlight emanates from the cross and refracts in the camera lens. Once viewed as a sign of poor cinematography, the refraction here is befitting of *The Keep*'s knowing aesthetic of twinkle and sparkle, or what Mark Cousins would call "bauble" – the notion of cinema as decoration.[4] As the soldier removes the alluring cross and peers into the tunnel behind it Mann gives us a virtuoso camera move that shows the sheer extent of space within the keep. It's a showy moment and, as a special effect, the most successful in a film that was marred by the sudden death of its lead effects technician, Wally Veevers, only weeks into production. Veevers had previously worked on such films as *Dr. Strangelove* (1964), *2001: A Space Odyssey* (1968), *The Rocky Horror Picture Show* (1975) and *Superman* (1978), and it is tantalising to consider what might have become of *The Keep*'s effects work had he lived. The virtuoso camera pulls back and back and back, scouring over the rocky floor of a gargantuan chasm that sits behind the main keep building until a white phantasm appears and flies off back towards the tunnel and the soldiers outside. The dark power is unleashed and the soldier and his companion are brutally killed but in a way that sidesteps bloodletting and gore in favour of bodily destruction.[5] Like the tracking used in Martin Scorsese's famed nightclub shot in *Goodfellas* (1990), this huge *reverse* tracking shot in *The Keep* is Mann drawing attention to his technique, almost as if he's saying to the audience

66

THE KEEP AND STYLISATION

Figure 6. Keep

"Look what I can do." In keeping with the film's aesthetic of appearances, this shot signifies the presence of the camera just as the lens refraction did minutes earlier. This is not a convention that Mann would continue in his future work.

The Keep continues in this vein as it mixes together macabre medievalism with German Expressionism and the bauble of the 1980s dream machine aesthetic. Another striking example of this fusion is the scene where Cuza's daughter is being attacked by two Nazi soldiers in the keep. As they attempt to rape her the first manifestation of Molasar arrives, first as an invisible presence that causes the soldiers' heads to explode as in *Scanners* (1981), and then as a bodily form shrouded in lustrous billows of fluffy smoke and backlit with an electric blue hue. This, accompanied by a choral musical track, creates a visual moment that is quite beautiful and ethereal in its characterisation of Molasar as a golem or Frankenstein's monster or King Kong, rescuing the fair lady from human evil. *The Keep*'s aesthetic of appearances often treads a fine line between profundity and absurdity and this moment is no different. The apparition of Molasar returns Eva to Cuza's room, where he sits preparing his fake notes on the keep for the major. Now the clouds part a little and Molasar's red eyes appear as the entity addresses Cuza with, of all things, an English-speaking voice. The conceit of *The Keep* fails here, something its relativistic universe needs to uphold if the audience is to willingly leave behind reality for its world of fairytale physics. The previously amorphous being of Molasar has now gathered shape and a personality as it gradually rebuilds itself in order to fulfil its mandate of destruction. Now the demon entity touches Cuza and cures him of his scleroderma. By this point in *The Keep*, as Molasar is accruing its body, Jürgen Prochnow's Woermann is being disassembled, his facade of fascist allegiance falling away as he comes round to helping Cuza and Ava escape the clutches of the major.

Before this happens Ava meets Glaeken as he arrives at the pass and settles into one of the houses in the village outside the keep. As soon as the two see each other a kinetic attraction is formed and one of the most elliptical passages of the film begins, a sequence that many critics of *The Keep* seized on as an example of Mann's poor direction and the rushed editing job the studio performed after he turned in his original three-hour cut. After talking in the bedroom Glaeken has rented (during which time there is a reverse shot that shows Eva in a mirror reflection but not Glaeken, pointing to the fact that he is a ghost or phantasm himself), there is a cut and Eva is then in bed, alone. She rises and surveys the room and Glaeken's belongings before moving to the window. A dissolve and Eva and Glaeken are then at the top of a hill, the pink sky of dusk in the distance like the blood to come. Another dissolve and the two are back in the rented room where they make love in a tangle of limbs like Doré's drawing of the spider woman from Dante's *Divine Comedy*. Just as the spatial orientation of the keep was distorted by Mann during Woermann's arrival, with high-angle shots that also looked like low-angle ones, here he does the same with Eva and Glaeken's moment of intimacy. His camera looks straight down from the ceiling space on the two lovers but the rug they lie on, with its horizontal line patterning, makes it seem as though they are climbing the wall of the room, again reinforcing the idea of some horrible mesh of the spider woman from Dante and the creature from John Carpenter's *The Thing*.

This sequence also proves interesting for other reasons. First, it's the most protracted display of human intimacy in all of Mann's films to date. Similar to Martin Scorsese in this respect, Mann tends not to focus on sex in his films and, when he does, the moments tend to be infused with other qualities – the disorientating angles in *The Keep*, the bold use of colour in *Manhunter*, a feeling of distance in *Heat*, focus pulls and hi-def imagery in *Ali*, humour and rock scoring in *Miami Vice* and elliptical editing in *Public Enemies* – that give the scenes a sense of detachment.

The second interesting aspect of this entire sequence is its editorial construction and the feeling of otherworldliness this generates. As highlighted by the brief synopsis of the sequence above, this union of Glaeken and Eva could be viewed as one of *The Keep*'s most potent displays of studio interference or shot-from-the-hip film making due to the complete elision of logical storytelling. Is, for instance, the sequence a demonstration of the unfinished script Mann was using during production? In Taschen's lovely 2006 appraisal of the director, Mann

THE KEEP AND STYLISATION

notes "*The Keep* was really hard because I did something I'd swore I'd never do again. And that is that I went into pre-production without a completed screenplay."[6] This sequence could certainly be viewed as an example of the chronological chaos that can ensue when shooting is being conducted alongside script rewrites, additions or omissions.

One could, however, put forward an alternative reading of the sequence, one that is supported by a similar sequence of editorial disjunction in Mann's *Public Enemies*. In that roving, hand-held look at the last years of John Dillinger's life there is a love scene between Dillinger and Billie Frechette that Mann approaches in a similarly elliptical and, more crucially, dreamy fashion. In the director's commentary he notes, "In fact I wanted the unification of this Morphean sensibility … the scene here is kind of deconstructed to get at a very candid statement about who she [Billie] is…"[7] Watching this scene in *Public Enemies* there is indeed something Morphean or dreamy about the moment that connects it with Eva and Glaeken's union in *The Keep*. If *The Keep* is about appearances, about the aesthetic of the visual rather than the literary, then such a reading of this love scene helps support the view that in order for the film's "relativistic universe" to be successful it must employ the structure of dreams, just as the love scene in *Public Enemies* does. Despite the fact that *Public Enemies* is about the existential reality of its characters, this elliptical moment of intimacy works because it speaks about Dillinger's and Billie's internal world, their world of dreams and fears, a world *The Keep* is entirely based upon (as Glaeken says to Eva at the end of the scene, "go to sleep … and dream"). In short *The Keep* must trade in the kind of deception that Eva and Glaeken's love scene demonstrates if it is to be worthy of Mann's wish for it to be a fairytale for adults.

The boundary lines between reality and fantasy continue to be blurred as *The Keep* moves towards its supernatural reckoning. Another kind of blurring is also taking place now, a tension between the film's success as a standalone piece of visual cinema (of which, as we have seen, there are definite examples) and its usefulness in a study such as this, which is trying to connect – in an honest way – Mann's films.

By the hour mark it is hard to divine any sense of Mann's presence or directorial signature beyond those more esoteric instances that are discussed above. *The Keep*, in many ways, erodes whatever unique sensibility Mann had cultivated with *Thief*, those aspects not just chiefly concerned with imagery and that slippery term *style* but with things like the criminal character template of Hohimer and Dillinger, the view of modernist architecture as an expression of alienation, the cynical view of the criminal justice system and the love of profession and procedure.

THE FILMS OF MICHAEL MANN

Although, in this sense, *The Jericho Mile*'s usefulness was also marginal in establishing Mann's template, it was at least situated within a milieu that has remained important to understanding some of his best characters and their skills. *The Keep* lacks even this and, despite its strengths as a visual fairytale with rewarding references to German art – just look at the architecture of the keep and its similarities to the German-built Flak Tower in Vienna, with its protuberances like the keep's crosses, to see what I mean – and the medieval macabre, to force through a view that says *The Keep* is as indispensable as *Heat* is to understanding Mann as a filmmaker would be obviously wrong. *The Keep* is the least useful and consequently most intriguing addition to Mann's body of work and so deserves a chapter in this book if only to delineate that very idea.

A series of scenes now appear that serve to further obfuscate *The Keep*'s fairytale of nightmare. The priest goes to talk with Cuza in the keep, passing a soldier on post at the main entrance who shakes uncontrollably as if not in possession of his own body. Has Molasar infected him also? If so, like Eva and Glaeken's climb to the top of the hill, it is not something we get to see in the film. The priest meets with Cuza – who's viewed in shadow like the arriving exorcist in William Friedkin's 1973 horror, both experts in the occult who get too close to the evil they try to combat – and immediately senses Molasar's presence. Tangerine Dream's score at this point becomes like György Ligeti's haunting work in *2001: A Space Odyssey* when the astronauts arrive at the monolith on the moon, all ghostly voices and sounds of wailing. Like *2001*'s journey into the metaphysical, *The Keep* now heads towards an arena of the elemental, all mist and diabolical *mise en scène*, as Hades might appear. Glaeken is shot repeatedly and thrown into the canyon by the keep after he tries to escape the custody of the remaining Nazi soldiers. He bleeds green like the alien in *Predator* (1987), so we know he's probably not really dead. Next, the major shoots Woermann dead when he discovers his anti-fascist leanings. The major leaves Woermann's body but takes the cross Woermann was given by the priest for protection. The major emerges into the main chamber of the keep to find it shrouded in mist, crumpled and charred heaps of Nazis and equipment strewn everywhere. The spatial limitations of the keep are now completely abandoned by Mann as his *mise en scène* and camera manipulate the environment, similar to what happens in the architecture of dreams and nightmares. Dislocated screams emanate from the dark ether and once knowable shapes become chimerae of the deep as Mann descends into the conventions of horror. The film is now moving from its abstractions of terror to the more familiar bogeyman tropes of *Halloween* (1978) or *Friday the 13th* (1980).

THE KEEP AND STYLISATION

Feeney, the author of Taschen's *Michael Mann*, considered an alternative possibility that might have saved *The Keep* from its second half histrionics. He proposed making the entity of Molasar part of Cuza's character, a Jekyll and Hyde duality that would have negated the need for complex prosthetics and special effects work. By rendering Molasar as an aspect of another character's psychology, Mann might have preserved the sense of abstraction that works so well in the first thirty minutes of the film. This was, however, the era of *The Thing*, *Star Wars* and *Videodrome*, films that exemplified the high art potential of puppetry and physical effects work in science fiction cinema. *The Keep* had to keep pace with this and the result was the muscular, Nietzschean and frankly silly figure that now appears. Mann should have given the effects job to Rob Bottin.

Molasar saps the major of his life force and drags his lifeless body off into the mists. Cuza locates the talisman deep in the chasm that sits behind the keep, the vital relic that permits Molasar to leave the keep and enter the world forever. Mann spends minutes tracking Cuza's valiant climb back to the keep with the talisman in hand, even going so far as to include a bizarrely triumphant piece of scoring that is strongly reminiscent of Philip Glass's score for *Koyaanisqatsi* (1982). Cuza unites with Eva and Molasar in the keep but soon realises Molasar's duplicity when he is ordered to kill Eva in a show of loyalty. Cuza throws away the talisman only for Glaeken, who now returns with a greatly inflated set of trapezius muscles, to reattach it to a staff he has been guarding since his arrival in the village. Glaeken now summons power from the staff and projects it out to the silver crosses that pockmark the walls of the keep. This, in turn, forms a beam of light that sends Molasar back to his prison below. Glaeken is then drawn into the depths of the keep himself, obviously the yin to Molasar's yang. The final image of *The Keep* is a freeze frame of Eva as she looks back into the keep, the site of Molasar's great evil but also her now lost love Glaeken. The choice to end the film here leaves things on a more ambiguous note than is usual for Mann. Molasar was not a force for good in the film; yes, the entity wanted to destroy the evil that the Nazis represented, but it also wanted to be unleashed on the world at large, somewhat negating the idea that my enemy's enemy is my friend. At the end Cuza has his eternal life taken from him by Molasar, punishment for spotting the entity's ruse and refusing to help it further, and so is re-stricken by his scleroderma with only days to live. Glaeken is now trapped in the keep with Molasar because the talisman, the key to Molasar's escape, was exhausted by Glaeken in his battle with the entity. Eva is Little Red Riding Hood at the end of that famous fairytale. The wolf has been vanquished but Red Riding Hood's innocence is now gone, replaced by the knowledge that the woodcutter must now reside with the beast forever.

The Keep is a very curious addition to Mann's body of work. In many ways it is more significant, stylistically and in the scope of its ambition, than either *The Jericho Mile* or *Thief* and yet, at the same time, it is the least useful film so far in terms of the determinants it offers us. It is marred by an often bizarrely constructed narrative that, while successful in places at generating a dream-like architecture, nevertheless steals from the film any potential for pathos or catharsis. What *The Keep* does provide in place of these aspects is a rigorous and frequently beautiful visual aesthetic that reminds us of the growing technical skills of the man behind the camera.

With *Manhunter*, the film we turn to next, what we find is an entry in Mann's filmography that offers both a revision of the specific visual stylisation introduced in *Thief* and developed in *The Keep* and the first real sense of a recurring directorial signature, something tangible and consistent that feels quintessentially Mannesque.

> Key scene suggestion for stylisation – the dream sequence featuring Glaeken and Eva.

Notes

1 Jürgen Müller and Steffen Haubner, "Aesthetics of Film in the Eighties", in *Best Movies of the 80s*, Taschen, 2006, 10.
2 As Steve Rybin notes in his chapter on *The Keep*, "Mann's film version, at its most interesting, avoids describing events through exposition and instead evokes their meaning through intricate aesthetic designs". Steven Rybin, *The Cinema of Michael Mann*, Lexington Books, 2007, 64.
3 Ian Aitken, *European Film Theory and Cinema: A Critical Introduction*, Indiana University Press, 2002.
4 Mark Cousins, *The Story of Film: An Odyssey*, documentary, More4, various episodes; first screened September 2011.
5 The production sketches for the film support this view of violence as

The Keep and Stylisation

destruction rather than gore, with Nazi soldiers appearing to dematerialise or turn to dust. See Duncan Feeney, *Michael Mann*, Taschen, 2006, 46–47.
6   Ibid.
7   See the director's commentary track on the Blu-ray edition of *Public Enemies*.

CHAPTER SIX

Manhunter and Modernism

> It's a struggle finding the language for each film. It's also one of the most exciting parts and, admittedly, I do it intensely.
>
> Michael Mann

If Mann did one thing with his next film, 1986's *Manhunter*, it was to provide audiences with a new visual and narrative language for the police procedural and the serial killer movie. Prior to the film's release terms such as serial killer and FBI profiler were not part of the common vernacular and rarely appeared in films dealing with these kinds of stories. Cinema had dealt with the aberrant behaviour of the serial killer before, but rarely was the science of finding them and the psychosis motivating them given such credence. Fritz Lang's *M* (1931) is one of the earliest examples of cinema and the serial killer, in this instance a child murderer (Peter Lorre) who is living in Berlin and whose character was perhaps based on the real 1920s Vampire of Düsseldorf. Graham Greene famously summed up *M*'s love of binary opposites when he said that the film was like "looking through the eye-piece of a microscope, through which the tangled mind is exposed, laid flat on the slide: love and lust; nobility and perversity, hatred of itself and despair jumping at you from the jelly".[1] *M* succeeds as a moving character study of the psychotic mind and was bold for its time, not only for its innovative use of sound but for encouraging audiences to sympathise with the killer Beckert. Lang uses the idea of the binary mind (something popularised forty-five years earlier by Robert Louis Stevenson's novel *Dr Jekyll and Mr Hyde*) to bring to light Beckert's mania, even going so far as to have Beckert say in the closing minutes of the film that he is constantly plagued by his "other self" chasing him. The cinematic idea of the serial killer as a bodily war of selves had been formed, something that would become a central tenet of *Manhunter*.

Of even greater relevance to *Manhunter* is the great game-changer of the 1960s, *Psycho* (1960). As a child, the director Alfred Hitchcock was a fan of Victorian literature and read both Stevenson's *Dr Jekyll and Mr Hyde* (1896), a text with undeniable influence on *M*, and Oscar Wilde's *The Picture of Dorian Gray* (1891) during his formative years. Their central conceits – the Freudian notion of the personality schism – would prove to be the foundational aspect of *Psycho*, Hitchcock's best film about a serial killer. In attempting to understand *Manhunter*, *Psycho* is instructive for several reasons. The first is in the way the film took the idea of the killer with the personality schism, which here came from Stevenson via Lang, and placed him in what we now consider to be a quintessentially American horror milieu, a closed environment in the desert badlands. Unlike Berlin in *M*, which was used by Lang to more or less passively reinforce the loss of its children, the motel and the house on the hill in *Psycho* are active participants in Norman Bates's madness, environments that reflect his state of mind back at the audience in a self-reflexive way that was quite new in 1960. *Psycho* gives its killer an American geography and uses its intricate *mise en scène* and stylisation to delineate his mania, an aspect integral to *Manhunter* and something that critics of the film at the time of its release incorrectly perceived as merely style for style's sake.

In the battle between the two warring factions of Norman's psyche, *Psycho* also opened up the form of film violence – this is the second aspect integral to understanding *Manhunter*. *Psycho* perceived and expressed screen violence in a way never done before, and several of today's most prominent scholars consider much of the bloodletting that soaks contemporary cinema as having its roots in this film's violent frankness. Robert Kolker writes:

> In its nameless and inexplicable horror, *Psycho* looks ... forward to a new history of film violence, which it has never been able to have represented too much ... *Psycho* in particular is the source not only of many formal strategies but of the blood that has flowed in so much recent film.[2]

In its story of a man who assumes the clothing and hair of his long-dead mother to kill residents staying in his family motel, *Psycho* appropriated the sense of disgust and absurdity that surrounded the real-life crimes of killers Ed Gein and Albert De Salvo, both figures who operated around the time of *Psycho*'s production and release. The general inability to understand the horrible crimes of these two men is, to a degree, captured in *Psycho* by the film's formal strategies and its choice of setting. *Psycho*'s evil is made all the more opaque and abstract because it is removed from the communal environment of the city and dumped in the desert, left alone to mutate and be warped by time and isolation. The film is much more of an attempt to grapple with the sense of absurdity that comes with murder, the physical and mental void that killing generates. Indeed, the emptiness that surrounds Norman Bates throughout the film is brought to an extreme degree near the end when he has been institutionalised. Norman sits on a chair against the blank wall of the asylum, clothed in a blanket with a cup at his feet, and Hitchcock frames the shot so that there is a large amount of empty space to screen right. The shot eventually tightens in on Bates for the famous image of him smirking with his mother's skeletal teeth superimposed over his own. Yet the most astonishing part of this whole sequence is not this tricksy superimposition but that bold use of negative space to screen right, deployed as an expression of Bates's now completely evacuated mental state.

Although *Manhunter*'s geography and *mise en scène* are, in many ways, the complete opposite of *Psycho*'s – *Manhunter* is exclusively urban, with a deliberately cluttered *mise en scène* for the killer – its baseline strategy of conveying Dollarhyde's madness primarily through its visual construction is the same approach that Hitchcock used in 1960 and, indeed, before: "Much as, say, Hitchcock's *North by Northwest* (1959) uses the lines of renaissance perspective as a consistent visual motif, so Hannibal Lecktor's prison bars are echoed throughout the design scheme, usually through adroit use of modernist architecture."[3]

So *Manhunter* has some clear debts. To *Psycho* it owes both the borrowing and augmentation of what could be termed psycho-geography, the idea that the mania of a serial killer can be essayed via a complex *mise en scène*. To Hitchcock's film, *Manhunter* also owes its conception and expression of screen violence, not just in its frankness or in the way it has an interest in the leavings of a violent crime scene but also in how violence is used by the film to bring down to ground level the vaunted ambitions of its characters. And to *M*, although this idea is also present in *Psycho*, *Manhunter*'s debt is more about the uptake of this notion of the serial killer as a divided soul, a character whose life is lived at the behest of two warring factions within their psyche. Although we are never encouraged to empathise with Dollarhyde as we are with Beckert in *M*, he is still shown to have a split personality of sorts that hints towards the possibility of a good life or, at the very least, one not predicated upon murder. Where these debts fuse with Mann's rigorous methodology of research and the fledgling popularity of crime forensics on screen, you have *Manhunter*, a film with an old-fashioned serial killer and a thoroughly modern approach to finding him.

The Films of Michael Mann

Manhunter begins in a state of abject terror. Its first image and the subsequent minute or so are even more decontextualised than those of *The Jericho Mile*, *Thief* or *The Keep*. This lack of anchorage, coupled with the film's initial horror genre mode of address and the eerie Carpenter-esque music by The Reds, makes for an arresting opening and a marked tonal shift in Mann's film making. The first image of *Manhunter* is of the lights and roof of a black truck. It is a supremely abstract composition but one that is also very threatening in its seeming pointlessness. The camera tracks left and then cuts to a point-of-view shot of someone ascending a set of carpeted stairs, torchlight illuminating a discarded trainer on one step and then a stuffed penguin further up. The torchlight is roving from side to side to indicate human motion. Is Mann implicating us in an act of some kind in the way John Carpenter did in the opening scene of *Halloween* or, more importantly here, the way Hitchcock repeatedly does in *Psycho*? A minor-key note appears on the soundtrack, an unmistakable leitmotif for evil, threat and death, and Mann holds it long enough to firmly establish the thorough grounding of psychological horror that *Manhunter* will reside in. The subjective point of view is maintained as we track past a child's bedroom, along a wall and into another bedroom. From the stuffed penguin earlier and the shot of the child's bedroom, we intuit that this threatening presence is now in the parents' room. The torch is now pointed directly at the woman in the bed. She stirs and then wakes, raising her head to the source of the light. A series of percussive beats erupt on to the soundtrack and the scene cuts to black before the title card "Manhunter" appears on the screen in poisonous green lettering.

Aside from establishing *Manhunter*'s important tone of psychological horror, this prologue is important in founding a concrete and perhaps indispensable determinant of some of Mann's best work, the dual sense of abstraction and modernism. Although 1981's *Thief* was a film with some thoroughly modern – and modernist – sensibilities, it lacked the potent sense of desolation, emptiness and the clear foregrounding of modernist ideals that *Manhunter* – and later *Heat*, *The Insider* and *Public Enemies* – display so well. These opening minutes of the film both yield the desolation and emptiness of this trio and pave the way for the thoroughly modern, technologically proficient and coolly urban hunt for a killer. Through their rigorous decontextualisation and abstract forms, glimpses, shapes and shadows, *Manhunter*'s opening minutes present the mind of its psychopath as a fragmented expression of its *mise en scène* and sound design, just as Hitchcock's *Psycho* did so well in 1960 (indeed, the very images of the prologue are from Dollarhyde's 8mm camera, a perverted p.o.v. home video shot by the killer himself for the purposes of a deranged

Manhunter and Modernism

Figure 7. Manhunter

posterity). Following the title card, Mann shifts from black to a deep azure blue. Things are still abstract, with no shapes or texture to help us decide what we are glimpsing. We are back to the opening of *The Keep*, where the camera panned down through a sky to eventually reveal something we could recognise, the arrival of the Nazi convoy at the village.

Here a wispy cloud slips past, highlighting that it's the blue of the sky somewhere. The camera finally settles on the horizon. In the foreground two men sit at opposite ends of a large piece of driftwood on a Floridian beach. Dennis Farina's Jack Crawford is on the right and William Peterson's Will Graham is on the left. The composition of the shot and the blocking of the two characters is Mann's first real use of what would go on to become his celluloid binary shot, an image that features two men, sometimes friends, sometimes enemies, engaged together in a conflict. Just as the binary shot opens *Manhunter*, it closes *The Last of the Mohicans* (where Chingachgook kills Magua), forms the central showpiece of *Heat* (when Hanna and McCauley have coffee) and shows the antagonism between Bergman and Wigand in *The Insider* (when the two are in the Japanese restaurant).[4] Crawford is trying to get Graham, a former and quite brilliant FBI profiler, to come out of retirement and take on one last case, the hunt for a lunar serial killer known as the Tooth Fairy. As the men chat Mann breaks up the formalism of the binary shot with tighter medium close-ups and a cutaway to Crawford's hand as he slides two evidence photos along the driftwood log towards Graham. It's a highly theatrical shot and gesture but also hints at the strong fraternal bond between these two men, just as would be the case in *Heat*, *The Insider* and, to a lesser degree, *Collateral* and *Miami Vice*. In spite of the clear bond between Graham and his wife Molly and their son, emptiness pervades Graham's home life. Mann renders things as safe but staid and static at the same time: an empty turtle pen on the beach not yet finished; an empty and coldly symmetrical dining room; the featureless void of the Gulf of Mexico at sunset; the searing blue moonlight of Graham and Molly's bedroom where, despite appearances, sadness takes precedence over passion. Graham's domestic arena is safe but banal, just like Hanna's in *Heat*, and Mann very quickly ushers Graham back into the dynamic horrors of his work.

In Atlanta Graham arrives at the house of the family from the film's prologue, the latest victims of our killer. His police escort tries to be friendly but Graham can't stop looking at the house and the horrors awaiting him inside. He enters the way the killer did according to the police report and steadily proceeds upstairs. Mann frames and lights the scene in the same way as earlier so as to forge the psychic link between Graham and his prey. Graham passes the children's room and enters the master bedroom. Mann shoots Graham from above looking down on the doorway, just as he did when the Nazis arrived at their place of horror in *The Keep*. In *Manhunter* this is also about making this moment more oblique by providing odd camera angles, obfuscating things until the shock reveal. Graham flicks on the lights and, in a crash cut of editing, the room, previously quite dark, is now a starkly bright netherworld of white and red, the white codifying the modern living space, the red, arterial spray and pools of collected blood from the horrible murders. Mann abstracts the horror of the act by showing us what Justine Hanna in *Heat* referred to as the "detritus" of the crime, here the blood left by the killer and the subsequent police response team's taped body outlines on the carpet. Along with Graham's forensic testimony into his Dictaphone, the audience is left to use this detritus to imagine what took place here, to empathetically piece together the narrative of the killer and the exact nature of the crime. Indeed, it is through Graham's first grand forensic oration here – where he intuits the fundamentals of the crime scene – that *Manhunter* foregrounds, along with its abstraction of murder, its love of a modern, highly contemporaneous and professional language, a key Mann determinant:

> Intruder entered through kitchen sliding door, used a glass cutter anchored to a suction cup. His entry was skilful. All the prints are smooth gloves. Blonde hair, strong, size 12 shoe imprint. Blood AB+ type from saliva on glass from licking the suction cup. Why didn't he care that he left saliva on the glass? It was hot out that night so inside the house must have felt cool to him. Intruder cut Charles Leeds' throat as he was rising then shot Mrs Leeds. Bullet

entered right of her navel but lodged in her lumbar spine but she died of strangulation. Moderate elevation of serotonin and marked increase of free histamine level from gunshot wound indicates she lived at least five minutes after she was shot. All her other injuries are post-mortem.

Part of the way through Graham's reading of this crime scene Mann cuts to a close-up of the autopsy report that he's carrying, showing a tabulation of the murders in a detailed but standardised way. This shot brings the audience closer to an internalised experience of the FBI process but also serves to highlight its limitations in finding a seemingly motiveless killer such as Dollarhyde. It will take the dynamic, unscripted and potentially dangerous intuitive processes of Graham's mind to connect these standard forensic details and make the empathetic leap towards Dollarhyde's true identity and why he is targeting families like the one found murdered here. The oration is nevertheless a cool evocation of *Manhunter's* pioneering forensics language. Just as Mann would deploy the modern and contemporaneous tongue of journalese in *The Insider*, a film that's every bit as in love with language as it is with litigation, so *Manhunter* seeks to impress its audience by virtue of its professional vocabulary as well as its modernist abstraction.

To go further still, by this point 12 minutes into the film, the establishing of these components – horror, psychology and the language of procedure – qualifies *Manhunter* as a possible example of the *giallo* genre, a genre that has come to include, most notably, *Psycho* but also Michael Powell's *Peeping Tom* (1960). A description of the *giallo* genre that appeared in the letters section of *Sight & Sound* goes some way to corroborating this idea:

> Rather giallo ... is a type of procedural thriller with visceral horror elements that has very specific generic traits: a black-gloved killer; fetishised murder set pieces; an investigation; glamorous affluent characters; a modern, metropolitan setting; psychological themes; and a preoccupation with style, beauty and surface.[5]

While aspects of this description might strain to fit with *Manhunter's* vision – glamorous and affluent characters being the most obvious example – those that remain do, in one way or another, quite aptly summarise the film's blend of procedural realism and stylistic flair, a dynamic also to be found in *Thief* and much of Mann's subsequent work. Certainly the notions of an investigation, a modern and metropolitan

The Films of Michael Mann

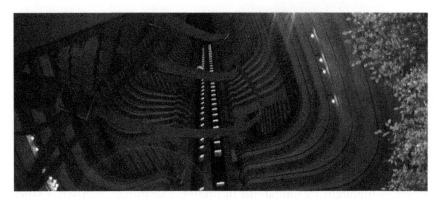

Figure 8. Manhunter

setting, psychological themes and a preoccupation with style, beauty and surface are aspects that arguably lie at the very heart of *Manhunter* and its enduring appeal. And when *Manhunter* veers away from its *giallo* tendencies it enters into another European sub-genre, the Italian *Poliziotteschi* movement with its insistence on forensic science and police procedure beloved by the likes of Ed McBain and Joseph Wambaugh. These aspects of style, beauty, surface, forensics and procedure coalesce in the next sequence of the film.

Finished with the standard crime scene reading at the house, Graham heads to his hotel room, weary from the rigours of being back at work (he is not fully operational yet and won't be until after his meeting with the film's seductive bogeyman, Hannibal Lecktor). He gets into the elevator in his hotel, the Marriot Marquis in Atlanta, and leans back against the handrail, shot from a low angle by Mann. Ostensibly such low-angle shots are used to confer power and authority on an individual – think of Welles's seminal use of low-angle photography in *Citizen Kane* (1941) – but in this scene, Mann is more interested in the stylistic opportunities and ideas presented by the strongly vertical hotel atrium behind Graham. Designed by John Calvin Portman Jr (who also designed the Westin Bonaventure Hotel in Los Angeles, a building that will prove integral to the upcoming chapter on *Heat*), this Atlanta hotel is a triumph of modernist architecture that presents an empty, inward-looking but technologically impressive space to visitors and residents. For *Manhunter* the hotel offers the viewer an example of the film's characteristic emptiness and abstraction via this towering and bulbous interior tunnel. To stress this notion Mann cuts out to an extreme long shot of Graham's elevator as it rides up the interior wall of this seemingly exterior space, the hotel lights refracting on the camera lens and creating the impression of looking through a glossy surface or prism. It's a moment reminiscent of another great modernist abstraction from four years earlier, Ridley Scott's *Blade Runner* (1982), arguably the film that prompted the 1980s' cinematic obsession with style and surface as active participants in the language of film.[6] *Manhunter* is filled with such architectural inserts and interior stylistic events, moments that are folded into the fabric of the film by Mann so that they become part of its modernist language of detection and forward movement. When Mann and *Manhunter* are at their best this language can reflect back urban beauty, abstract emptiness or, as we shall see when Dollarhyde makes his formal appearance, a form of psychological terror that actually warps the physical dimensions of buildings themselves.

In his hotel room Graham begins to study up close the home videos of the family during happier times. Frustrated after a few moments he moves to the other side of the room and phones his wife Molly, who is back in Florida. She's asleep but Graham gets the reassurance he needs – "I love you too baby", she declares and they hang up. Graham then returns to his spot in front of the TV, somehow imbued now with a steely determination to intuit the next level of information about Dollarhyde. The scene towards the climax of *Heat*, where Hanna leaves his wife Justine at the hospital to deal with the domestic arena while he makes a final push to capture McCauley, shares this scene's sense of ideological certainty, of a central character so committed to the centrality of their profession that they push aside all other considerations in the pursuit of their goal, including, if necessary, their family.

As Graham moves both physically and psychologically away from Molly and his son, Mann shoots him from behind the TV monitor that he is using to view the home video, thereby breaking our view of the footage and demarcating Graham's movement towards the film's killer. Graham's eyes take on a new form as he aggressively engages in a mock conversation with Dollarhyde in order to arrive at an answer as to why talcum powder was found at the murder scene when none was located in the family's bathroom. Via first a home video camera and now the video copy and an Atlanta PD television monitor, Graham intuits that the killer, in a moment of uncharacteristic abandon, had removed his surgical gloves to first touch Mrs Leeds and then open the bodies' eyes so that they could "see" him and thereby assume the role of an audience. In a seminal manner that pre-empted contemporary procedural shows such *Crime Scene Investigation* (also starring William Petersen) and *Silent Witness*, *Manhunter* in general, and in this hotel scene in particular, renders in high relief the importance of modern technology in the pursuit of murderers and serial killers. Although *Manhunter*'s thrills are often derived from experiencing Graham's intuitive capabilities and deductive reasoning, it is the film's presentation of a modernist technological apparatus that facilitates such intuitive leaps and ultimately cements the case against Dollarhyde. As Steve Rybin notes in *The Cinema of Michael Mann*, "Graham is able to deduce Dollarhyde's motivations, and the mediated sensual experiences that drive his desires, by himself employing technology which aids and extends the human capabilities of vision."[7]

I would argue that, more than Rybin's contention that the technological apparatus of *Manhunter* is concerned with improving Graham's ability to "see" the motives of the killer – although this is an accurate assessment – it is more overtly an expression of Mann's love of modernism. He is enthralled by that which is most contemporary in a given time-period, by its bold innovations, pioneering outliers and radical disruptors, regardless of whether that time-period is post-millennial Los Angeles, eighteenth-century upstate New York or, as in *Manhunter*, Atlanta in 1986.[8] *Manhunter* abounds in scenes that exemplify this modernist language, a language that Graham uses again and again as an antidote to the horrors of Dollarhyde's medieval, William Blake-inspired deviancy. Indeed, a possible reading of *Manhunter* is that of a story about the triumph of modernism (Graham, the FBI) over medievalism (Dollarhyde and Blake) and its associated thinking. Just as Dillinger perishes in *Public Enemies* because of his anachronistic refusal to keep pace with modernism (the truly streamlined version of which emerged in the 1930s), so Dollarhyde suffers the same fate in *Manhunter* because he cannot anticipate Graham's fusing of modernism and an empathy for killers. This empathy that Graham has, this willingness to project himself into the minds of those he wishes to stop, leads next to an important scene where Graham returns to visit Dr Lecktor, a former psychiatrist and cannibalistic murderer now incarcerated in a mental institution in Baltimore.

Graham's scene with Lecktor is interesting in that, alongside providing the audience with another pre-digital binary opposite composition, it shows just how rigorous *Manhunter*'s modernist aesthetic actually is. Unlike Jonathan Demme's strategy in *The Silence of the Lambs* (1990) in which Lecter (note the difference in spelling) is introduced along more conventionally Gothic lines, with a classic bogeyman reveal – where the camera pans towards his window and finds him standing motionless – this scene in *Manhunter* begins from *within* Lecktor's cell in a totally different kind of prison environment. We see from a low-angle shot the extensive bars of Lecktor's pen, followed by Graham being permitted entry by one of the guards. From this initial perspective it is Graham who is imprisoned as he moves to take his seat by the door. The audience immediately notices the uniform whiteness of the cell, a whiteness very similar to the Leeds's master bedroom at the start of the film before it was besmirched with arterial spray by Dollarhyde. Mann has noted that the colour of Lecktor's cell was a very deliberate choice, an attempt to craft a thoroughly modernist setting that grates up against Lecktor's baroque and Edwardian personality.[9] Whether this polarity is actually noticeable when watching the film is neither here nor there; the cell is obviously modernist. It almost approaches one of Piet Mondrian's modernist compositions, with their starkly white areas and strongly linear divisions, and is a definite counterpoint to the basement world of Lecter's cell in *The Silence of the Lambs*.[10] Lecktor's cell in *Manhunter* supports a modernist reading of the film because it takes the architectural ideas, clean lines and sterile spaces of the other key scenes up to this point and literally paints them on the walls of this environment; it is as much an example of the modernist psycho-geography of *Manhunter* as Dollarhyde's house will later prove to be at the film's climax.

Graham talks with Lecktor, ostensibly to acquire his help in the murder investigations but really to re-engage with the psychopathic mindset, of which Lecktor is the most accomplished exemplar in the world of *Manhunter*. As Lecktor surveys the case file Mann cuts to a point-of-view shot of Graham surveying the cell. A drippy, dreamy, synthesised cue quietly rises on the soundtrack as Graham takes in first Lecktor's washbasin – complete with an odd pink hue in a largely whitewashed room that resembles those bursts of colour in Mondrian's otherwise starkly monochromatic modernist compositions – and then his collection of psychiatric journals and writing materials (including the blue highlighter pen that will play such a key part in Lecktor's upcoming ruse to acquire Graham's home address). Suddenly Lecktor rouses Graham from his fugue state with an explanation of Dollarhyde's behaviour and likely habits at the murder scenes of both families, an explanation that mirrors Graham's oration in the bedroom of the Leeds's house in its coolly modernist and detached quality:

> This is a very shy boy Will. What were the yards like? Because my dear Will if this pilgrim imagines he has a relationship with the moon, he might go outside to look at it. Have you ever seen blood in the moonlight Will? It appears quite black. If one were nude it would be better to have privacy for this sort of thing.

This is where *Manhunter* can be seen to excel over and above films such as *M* and *Psycho*. As well as presenting the archetype of a killer with a split personality and crafting a rigorous psycho-geography that reflects back on itself the horror of murder, *Manhunter* generates from its source material an adventure thoroughly grounded in modernism, a term that helps to contextualise the alliance between Graham and Lecktor.

Graham's empathetic strategy of trying to think like a serial killer and Lecktor's almost forensic reading of a crime scene brings the two characters together, rendering them almost interchangeable, and dissolves the conventional barriers between good and evil. Speaking of modernism, Theodore Adorno wrote, "[modernism] expresses the idea of harmony negatively by embodying the contradictions, pure and uncompromised, in its innermost structure".[11] Graham and Lecktor are the embodiment of the contradiction that Adorno spoke of, two potential but polarised aspects of a single idea that create a disharmony at the centre of, in this case, a film. This idea would be recapitulated in *Heat*, *The Insider*, *Collateral* and *Miami Vice*, but in *Manhunter* it is at its most amplified and magnetic. Tantalisingly, the director's cut of the film takes this disharmony one step further and includes a pre-credits scene at the end where Graham, battered and cut from his fight with Dollarhyde, visits the family the killer was targeting next. It's a scene fraught with ambiguity and, with its lingering shots of his contorted face, seems to suggest that Graham has swum too much in Dollarhyde's mindset and has now almost become like him, someone obsessed with the act of being seen as a means of validation.

Despite the radicalism of its violence and *mise en scène*, and the debt that *Manhunter* owes to both of its aspects, *Psycho* goes nowhere near this kind of relativistic morality. Hitchcock's film cleaves closely to a typical view of the detective protagonist and their unshakeable decency. Arbogast is a good guy whose quest to restore the moral order gets him killed by the aberrant Norman Bates.[12] *Manhunter*, by contrast, is a modernist work because, among other things, it dissolves such categories of understanding and provides its main protagonist with the potential to become a killer himself.

Before examining the modernist *mise en scène* of *Manhunter*'s climactic sequence, one scene worth considering in our exploration of modernism as a key determinant of Mann's work is the forensics analysis scene at Quantico. After Graham's visit to Lecktor and Lecktor's subsequent acquisition of Graham's home address in Florida – achieved in no small part via the blue highlighter pen glimpsed earlier – the officials at the institution search Lecktor's cell for evidence of communication with Dollarhyde. One warden finds a note from Dollarhyde written on toilet paper and takes it straight to Dr Chilton, the director of the institution. While on the phone to Jack Crawford and Will Graham, Chilton reads the note aloud, using a letter opener to move the note and keep his place. This scene and what follows is one of the most thrilling sequences in *Manhunter*, a beautifully edited, blocked, acted and lit depiction of the attempt by the forensics experts at Quantico to lift either a fingerprint, fibre or DNA sample from the note. The sequence revels not only in a thoroughly modernist *mise en scène* but also in the newly emergent language of forensics technology, a modernist language predicated on speed, movement and, most important of all, information. These qualities found some traction in *Thief* but were bound up in a larger examination of 1980s yuppie politics that diluted their appeal; in *Manhunter* half the film's thesis of detection is based on these, the other being Graham's intuitive empathy.

As Chilton reads out the note to Graham and Crawford over the phone, we see that his office is an extension of Lecktor's cell and the opening murder scene. White colours (walls, desk, light, stapler, desk tidy, phone), clean lines, bright look, a star of light by Chilton's head, this is a house of modernism built upon the shaky foundations of murder. As Chilton (Benjamin Hendrickson) reads the note we notice the actor's delivery style – precise, clear, articulate, modern. He wields his letter opener like a conductor's baton. In its resemblance to a knife blade, the letter opener intimates the precision and violence of Dollarhyde's campaign of terror and murder as it literally points towards his thoughts on what he is becoming. Mann intercuts Chilton's reading of the note with two other people and locations, Crawford in his office and Graham leaning on the roof of a patrol car, spaces also very much viewed along modernist lines and linked together via modern telephonic technology. Crawford's office is also white but with a black desk and black lamp – possibly hinting at his opposition to Chilton (in Thomas Harris's source novel *Red Dragon* Chilton is quite obnoxious) – and has added details such as what looks like a piece of modernist artwork on the wall behind him and a glass, cube-shaped prism with a vacuum sphere at its centre that sits on an adjacent table.

The artwork – which could also just be a bulletin board – works well in the modernist context as it appears to be a large piece of torn white paper mounted on to a larger white frame. Abstract, unorthodox, confrontational and certainly breaking conventional aesthetic boundaries, this unexplained item works best when viewed as this, as a piece of contemporary art in a film all about the modern. When we look at the cube-shaped prism, foregrounded by Mann in three separate shots as this scene plays out (suggesting a significance beyond the simple placement of a prop), any modernist reading of *Manhunter* would then point us towards the object being totemic of something like the modernist movement Cubism.

This may seem like a step too far in a detailed assessment of Mann's minutiae, but wait. The last of the three shots of the cube prism is much more tightly framed on the object. Viewed from this angle Crawford is now "inside" the prism as it lies between the camera and the man himself. This weird refraction of the image, this distortion of our viewpoint, this manipulation of space, is something akin to what Mark Cousins termed "movie cubism" in an article he wrote for *Sight & Sound*. Talking of *Psycho* and Marion's untimely death, Cousins writes, "But in the shower scene they [Hitchcock and editor George Tomasini] switch, for a short period, to portraiture editing. Their short shots accumulate ... not in time exactly, more in space."[13] Although the shower scene in *Psycho* is comprised of numerous shots whereas this image in *Manhunter* uses just one, the desire on the part of the respective directors to fragment the audience's view of the character onscreen and warp the space through which we see them is one and the same. Like the many Marions we see in the shower sequence in *Psycho*, as Crawford leaves his office we see five or six versions of him in the prism. If Cubism is concerned with anything it is the abstraction of a thing and the depiction of that thing in multiple ways.[14]

The Lecktor/Dollarhyde note is brought to Quantico via helicopter and the various forensics specialists there go to work. There is no greater distillation of *Manhunter*'s modernist themes of information, technology and detection than in the sequence that follows. Mann guides us through the various forensics departments at Quantico – hair and fibres, latent prints, ink and handwriting analysis – taking the screen time (while concurrently suggesting the extreme time constraints of the characters onscreen – they have four hours to analyse the note and return it to Lecktor's cell before he is likely to get suspicious) to detail how professionals working in this most modern of sciences go about generating a language of information and evidence.

Mann blocks the three stages of forensic analysis with colour – pink for hair and fibres (the same pink as glimpsed in Lecktor's cell as Graham gazed and dreamed during his visit to the institution), blue for latent prints and red for ink and handwriting – and frames his shots to carefully maximise the bulk and heft of cutting-edge equipment used by these individuals. The blue sequence, when Jimmy Price (played by Dan Butler, who would later play an entirely difference character, Roden, in *The Silence of the Lambs*) studies the note for print evidence, is in thrall to the deep blue laser light used for conducting a spectral analysis of the paper. Mann's camera seeks out the bolts of light and reflecting prisms (more prisms) that direct the light towards the note and the leavings of its writer,

Manhunter and Modernism

and reveals to us how Graham's empathy for the killer is augmented and improved upon by modern technology.

In the final red sequence, this application of technology as an extension of Graham's intuitive skills is given a thrilling stage as Bill Smitrovich's Bowman unearths fragments of Dollarhyde's handwriting that Lecktor had attempted to blot out using a felt tip marker. Bowman utters, "You're so sly but so am I", as he circumvents Lecktor's attempts at subterfuge and reveals the tops of three Ts and an R, which Crawford works out correctly to be a reference to the *National Tattler* newspaper. The lead-up to this reveal is masterful as Bowman runs through a series of spectral filters in order to (literally) bring to light the contents of the missing portion of the note. Although the *Tattler* evidence does not lead directly to the arrest of Dollarhyde, it is nevertheless instrumental in baiting him later on when a false story is concocted by Graham and printed by the *Tattler* that suggests, among other things, that Dollarhyde might have been sexually abused by his mother as a child.

Between the forensics sequence at Quantico and the climactic showdown at Dollarhyde's house there are a number of other scenes that, while being narratively and aesthetically important, also serve to repeat and modify the modernist themes the film has established up to this point. With that in mind, we turn now to the climax of the film.

At 1hr 40 mins we find ourselves at Dollarhyde's isolated house on the shores of the Cape Fear river. The design of the house carries the heavy influence of modernist architect William Lescaze, a pioneer of the futurist movement in US cities such as Philadelphia. By this point Dollarhyde has kidnapped a blind woman, Reba (Joan Allen), whom he used to work with at the film-processing plant, the place where he acquired the home video footage of the families he has since murdered. Dollarhyde is infatuated with this woman but has known her only briefly, an obsessive characterisation that Mann took from Dennis Wayne Wallace, the paranoid schizophrenic serial killer he researched prior to filming. Reba moves around Dollarhyde's sitting room in an attempt to locate herself in her surroundings. Mann and production designer Mel Bourne present a masterful psycho-geography here, modernistic and destabilising in its use of canted lines and odd colour mixes to get at the troubled and delusional mental state that Dollarhyde resides in. Like *Psycho* before it, *Manhunter* largely intimates its evil and horror rather than gratuitously exposing it. The modernist *mise en scène* of *Manhunter*'s climax supports such a view and it is worth analysing in detail.

The first interior view of Dollarhyde's house is of a series of vacuum tubes linked together in a kind of matrix. This is again a debt to Wallace, whose delusional architecture was largely predicated along the modernist lines of technology and communication. He believed that the spark inside the tubes held the key to unlocking his true personality and, as such, surrounded himself with them and other technological artefacts that might have allowed him to attain this higher understanding. The camera pans upwards as Reba rises from her chair and tries to feel her way around. There is a photograph of the moon on the far wall, large enough in its resolution to see the various impact craters and lines of ejecta. Wallace was also obsessive about alien landscapes and the promise they held of enlightenment and resolution. Reba continues to try and locate herself, all the while passing by abstract paintings above the fireplace and the main window of the house which, bizarrely, sits in its frame at an acute angle to the building itself. Reba backs herself up to the window, its dissecting vertical and horizontal planes resembling prison bars to keep the outside world away or the Red Dragon caged. Dollarhyde enters from frame right and passes another extra-terrestrial image, a huge wall hanging of what is again the moon but looks more like the Martian landscape, a distinctly red hue suggestive of blood and rust – biology and metallurgy mixing like a knife piercing flesh.

Like Beckert in Lang's *M*, Dollarhyde is now clearly wrestling with the two dominant but opposing aspects of his psyche. He loves Reba (or at least he thinks he does) but has a need to kill her and therefore protect his identity. Here he is trying to stay away from her, and Mann blocks him so that he appears encumbered by furniture, unable to reach Reba who is still against the window. Iron Butterfly's "In A Gadda Da Vida" rages on the soundtrack and smothers the visuals with its psychedelic noise, the song yet another reference to Dennis Wayne Wallace who felt that it was *his* song. Reba passes by Dollarhyde's TV, which is jumping between frames and suggesting the unhinged mania of its owner, but Mann then cuts away to Graham and Crawford who are on a Learjet. Graham is on the phone to police officers as they search the Missouri Department of Revenue database for Dollarhyde's driver's licence. As *Manhunter* reaches its conclusion Mann is bringing together the abstract and pathological horror of Dollarhyde with the conflicting modernity and technology of both his own house and that of Graham, forming a kind of dialectic out of which only one can survive. A printout comes through to the Learjet and Graham instantly and intuitively knows it's his man. Cutting back to Reba at the house, the murderous aspect of Dollarhyde's psyche has won out and he smashes his bathroom mirror to produce a shard. He grabs Reba and takes her to the kitchen to kill her. Holding Reba with one hand, Dollarhyde smashes more glass into small pieces, preparing the mirrors for Reba's eyes so he can be seen and feel validated by her. Mann is now cutting between this and Graham speeding towards Dollarhyde's house in a convoy of patrol cars.

The climactic confluence of Graham's modernity and Dollarhyde's medievalism is now brought into high relief. As Dollarhyde prepares to kill Reba we really sense the way in which Mann is offsetting the baroque personality of Dollarhyde with the ultra-modernist *mise en scène* of his house (just as he did with Lecktor and Lecktor's cell) and the modernist methodology of Graham. Dollarhyde has arranged his murder scene in a highly theatrical and organised way with Reba lying on the kitchen table. Dollarhyde brings Reba's neck up to his blade and then pauses, still wrestling with the duality of his nature. He sees his reflection in the shard as Graham comes crashing through the front windows, correcting their destabilising acute angles as he does so. Dollarhyde slashes at Graham's face, scarring him just as Norman does to Arbogast in *Psycho* and Beckert symbolically does to himself in *M*, pulling his middle fingers down his cheeks and creating mock scars. In a series of staccato edits and over-cranking, Mann ups the disorientation and tension as Dollarhyde grabs his shotgun and kills the other cops as they try to enter the house, Graham still unconscious on the kitchen floor.

Here Dollarhyde resembles the Terminator in James Cameron's original 1984 film, a shotgun in one hand, killing police officers with cold indifference. Dollarhyde returns to kill Graham but Graham shoots him down in a highly theatrical fashion that shadows what Reba's death would have looked like had she not been saved by Graham. The manner in which Mann views Dollarhyde's death also mirrors the explosive ending of *Thief* where Frank's retribution is presented in a series of repeat edits, slow-motion photography and highly theatrical staging. Dollarhyde's death is as baroque as his, or Lecktor's, personality. In the film's only real overt reference to the medieval Red Dragon that inspired his crimes, Dollarhyde lies dead on the floor, arranged with his arms outstretched and his blood pooling beneath them like reptilian red wings.

Four films in and *Manhunter* presents us with only the second convincing iteration of a quintessentially Michael Mann film. Though it is a work that borrows from the films before it and indeed continues some of the ideas presented therein, *Manhunter* breaks new ground in Mann's canon in the way that it more fully expresses the burgeoning auterism of its director. It is a confident film that beautifully marries a strongly modernist sensibility – its architecture, artistic references, environment, *mise en scène* and narrative language – with aspects of the *giallo* and *Poliziotteschi* sub-genres. Its scenes have a characteristic emptiness about them that more than hints at the feelings of existential loneliness endemic to some aspects of the modernist aesthetic, an idea that Mann would return to, most notably in *Public Enemies*.

Despite its box-office failure, *Manhunter* has since become an important touchstone for both the dramatisation of forensics work (*C.S.I.*, *Silent Witness* etc) and the cinematic genesis of the characters of Will Graham and Hannibal Lecktor. Mann's next film, *The Last of the Mohicans*, would prove to be equally as culturally and artistically significant; it would also be a massive box-office success.

> **Key scene suggestion for modernism – the forensic analysis scene where Graham and the team work under pressure to study the note fragment found in Lecktor's cell.**

Notes

1 Stephen D. Youngkin, *The Lost One: A Life of Peter Lorre*, University Press of Kentucky, 2005, 118.
2 Robert Kolker, *A Cinema of Loneliness: Penn, Stone, Kubrick, Scorsese, Spielberg, Altman*, 3rd edn, Oxford University Press, 2000, 18.
3 Nick James, "No Smoking Gun", *Sight & Sound* 10, no. 3 (March 2000): 16.
4 Mann's use of the binary shot seems to have ended with his uptake of the digital camera. From *Ali* onwards, Mann's formalism, his use of symmetrical forms, his balance and composition, changed radically as if he himself was liberated by the possibilities and increased freedoms of the digital medium.
5 James Blackford, "Letters from Readers", *Sight & Sound* 22, no. 11 (November 2012): 76.
6 The specific moment that comes to mind in *Blade Runner* is Roy Batty's elevator ride to see Tyrell.
7 Steven Rybin, *The Cinema of Michael Mann*, Lexington Books, 2007, 84.
8 Mann's next film, *The Last of the Mohicans*, literalises this modernist idea of forward movement in its opening sequence as the three main characters are introduced already running.

9   See Mann's director's commentary on the Blu-ray of *Manhunter*.
10 Other contrasts include the fact that in *Manhunter* Lecktor's cell is up high on the top floor of the institution whereas in *The Silence of the Lambs* it's in the gloomy basement.
11 Theodor Adorno, *Prisms*, The MIT Press, 1981, 32.
12 It's interesting to note that, just prior to his death, Arbogast is slashed across the face by the killer, just as Graham is at the end of *Manhunter*.
13 Mark Cousins, "Still Life with Attitude", *Sight & Sound* 23, no. 3 (March 2013): 17.
14 The Czech modernist architect Pavel Janak actually wrote an article entitled "The Prism and The Pyramid" which advocated dynamic architectural compositions and the destabilising of traditional right-angled buildings.

CHAPTER SEVEN

The Last of the Mohicans and Professionalism

> Daniel [Day Lewis] and I did a training regime that resulted in that conceptual reorientation, as well as picking up all the physical skills and, equally important, the attitude that the physical skills generate.
>
> Michael Mann

Although *Thief* pursued the notion of skill and professionalism via its main protagonist Frank, it was a professionalism viewed from the unreliable perspective of a criminal caught in the three-dimensional trap of urban Chicago and therefore not universal. As Mann notes:

> I didn't approach this movie [*The Last of the Mohicans*] the way I approached *Thief*, where I was so excited by the world Frank lives in and the way he sees his world that I made the physical world of the film appear as though it is perceived through Frank's brain.[1]

Frank is a professional safe-cracker no doubt, but his is a professionalism acquired in response to his desire to pursue the dominant yuppie lifestyle of the 1980s. This makes *Thief* a character study where professionalism is viewed along the very narrow, corruptible and highly specific lines of diamond robbery. Frank's professionalism is a lifestyle choice rather than a universal, historical and environmental necessity predicated upon the need for survival.

Mann's first film of the 1990s, *The Last of the Mohicans*, took *Thief*'s singular view of professionalism and opened it up, universalising it by placing it within a much larger historical context in which the main characters are forced into being professional as a response to exterior forces. As Mann's quote above highlights, *Mohicans* generalised or objectified the conception of professionalism in *Thief*, rendering it a globalised character trait that completely reorients the perception of the individual.

Mann's wish to make (or remake, or readapt, depending on your preference)[2] *The Last of the Mohicans* can probably be pinned down to two reasons, one grounded in personal experience, the other a wish to offer a corrective to the literature of the period. George B. Seitz's 1936 adaptation of James Fenimore Cooper's 1826 novel was the first movie Mann recalls seeing as a young filmgoer in or around 1949, and although the film offers some questionable characterisations and representations, the screenplay on which it was based was, Mann felt, good in itself and superior in many ways to Cooper's original novel. Seitz's film captured the sense of constant motion and activity that was no doubt a prerequisite for survival on the American frontier in the 1750s (with Randolph Scott's Hawkeye frequently entering or exiting scenes on foot and at speed), while avoiding the racial hierarchy – natives at the bottom, whites at the top – that mars Cooper's book. This notion of physical activity, of a life lived through movement, would germinate in Mann's mind over the years before presenting itself as a kind of dominating characteristic of his take on the story (as we shall see, his *Mohicans* film begins and ends with running, a corollary of the professionalism of Hawkeye). Mann notes: "I had an image … of running and movement and it occurred to me in 1991 … it's been with you your whole life and it just never occurred to me, why not make *The Last of the Mohicans*?"[3]

Aside from this desire to recapture the excitement of what was probably his first movie experience, Mann's wish to film *The Last of the Mohicans* was also at least partially motivated by a more mature disposition to counter the racism and imperialist supremacy promulgated by Cooper's novel (and, to a degree, white psychology in general at the time). At least within the confines of cinematic expression, Mann clearly wanted to give back to the indigenous peoples of the American frontier period the qualities of racial pride and self-worth that Cooper's take on those times had stripped from them. Of Cooper's novel, Mann states: "[I] read the book, the novel is horrible. It's just a terrible piece of writing by James Fenimore Cooper and it is also politically evil because it is highly revisionist."[4] He comments in an interview with Graham Fuller:

> Cooper believed in static hierarchies, a kind of political harmony of the spheres: If people and classes stay in place, there's a harmony; if they don't, there are problems. In Cooper, Hawkeye is constantly apologizing or reassuring total strangers that he's not of mixed blood! "Hi, I'm Hawkeye, how are you? I'm not of mixed blood."

So the whole notion of races crossing, of miscegenation, of people moving into different classes, was anathema to Cooper.[5]

As our tour of the film will show, where Mann's desire to capture the physical excitement of frontier existence fuses with his more mature corrective to Cooper's racism we find the rebranding of the Hawkeye character, now – in 1991 – a highly trained ambassador for the Native American peoples. This corrective was exemplified further in an article in *Sight & Sound* where John Harkness notes:

> In Mann's hands, *The Last of the Mohicans* is less a blueprint for the rejection of white civilisation than an attempt to give us in the 1990s a new birth of a white culture that respects the individuality of other cultures, at least to the point where we can regret their destruction. If Cooper's Natty Bumppo [Cooper's original name for the character of Hawkeye] leads to Eastwood's William Munny, then Mann's Nathaniel Poe [Hawkeye] leads to (and emerges from) Little Big Man and Lieutenant John Dunbar in *Dances With Wolves*.[6]

The notion of a conscious professionalism at the heart of *The Last of the Mohicans* is first and foremost characterised by that sense of motion and physicality that Mann remembered so clearly from the 1936 version of the film he saw in 16mm in a neighbourhood church basement in Chicago. Like *Thief* (down into the alley) and *The Keep* (down into the mountain pass) and *Manhunter* (down to the beach) before it, *Mohicans'* key opening camera movement is a descent from above, a fall down into the environment of the film from an external position "up there", the viewer being dropped into the narrative as if at random. "I wanted you", Mann explains, "to feel that you were falling into one of these hollows, to drop into it as if you were dropped into a wilderness forest."[7]

It's 1757 and we alight from the downward camera move into the dense forests of what is now upstate New York. At the time, however, this was the leading edge of the Euro-American westward expansion, the liminal zone between what Mann refers to as the *future and the past*. Emerging from the dense foliage are Hawkeye (Daniel Day Lewis), Uncas (Eric Schweig) and Chingachgook (Russell Means), three hunters slicing through this primeval forest either in pursuit of or flight from something. Mann chooses to hold back the answer to this query until the end of the sequence, instead electing to draw out and foreground the skill and proficiency of these characters' movements, their process and their relationship to the environment around them. This is achieved not only through the evident physical training of the characters themselves – and, by extension, the actors portraying them – but also through the editing rhythms and sound design that Mann establishes at the start of the film. Professionalism is self-reflexive in *Mohicans*, in the sense that the professionalism of the characters is reflected by the precision of the film's construction, its aesthetic design, its verisimilitude and the research-based methodology of the director, something that had, by this point in his career, evolved massively.

As we witness the three introductory characters moving through this environment, Mann lays bare the fundamentals of their professionalism, the accoutrements of survival and action. The camera swoops down past a fallen log and Hawkeye speeds towards it, a long rifle in his right hand and a small hatchet bound to his back. Trevor Jones's score renders the movement of Hawkeye here with urgency and the sense of time running short, thus creating the implicit understanding that, even though we have yet to see a quarry, we know that Hawkeye and the other two characters are chasing something rather than being chased. Dante Spinotti's lighting of this sequence further adds to the feeling of urgency and to the characterisation of this forest environment as both hostile and beautiful. Shafts of light break the canopy above and dissect the shots of Hawkeye and his men, producing a spatial environment that appears jagged and splintered, a lethal obstacle course that must be navigated with professionalism. Shots now bring Uncas into the fold as he too runs through spaces and down slopes, eventually joining Hawkeye in a two shot. Bringing up the back is Chingachgook, the older father figure moving uphill towards the others. We cut back to Hawkeye and Uncas who now run side by side, Hawkeye naked from the waist up, allowing the audience to both understand the physical effort required to traverse this environment and witness the musculature and tribal geography of his body. These images of our characters are constituted from a broad mix of crane shots, tracking shots, long shots, close-up shots and shots that employ both deep and shallow depths of field, such is Mann's wish to render the American frontier as a once harmonious place that has now become heterogeneous, in light of both who has arrived and who is yet to come (English, Scottish, Irish, Dutch and French Huguenot imperialists). Like Spinotti's jagged lighting of the forest floor, Mann's cacophony of shot choices in this opening sequence splinters the world of Hawkeye into a very hostile assault course.

The sequence closes with Hawkeye bringing his long rifle up and taking aim at a deer. Mann has his camera positioned close to the muzzle of the

The Last of the Mohicans and Professionalism

Figure 9. The Last of the Mohicans

rifle as Hawkeye brings it to bear on his target in a way that's very similar to Hanna (Al Pacino) in *Heat*, when he shoots Cheritto after the botched bank robbery. Mann's camera pulls focus down the length of Hawkeye's rifle, from back to front, as Jones's score reaches its high note. Hawkeye shoots and the deer is felled, tumbling over a drop and coming to rest. Mann then cuts back to Hawkeye and captures his poise and perhaps his feeling of ennui, that listlessness that follows intense professional activity. It is there too in that moment in *Heat*; after Hanna shoots Cheritto dead, Mann cuts back from Cheritto falling to the ground to Hanna raising the barrel of his gun and breathing, a man of professionalism composing himself, resigning himself to inaction once more.

The sheer extent of the professional training that Daniel Day Lewis undertook for this film at the behest of Mann illustrates why *The Last of the Mohicans* is the strongest exponent of the notion of professionalism at this stage in Mann's filmography. While it is true that James Caan had to undergo some significant training in preparation for his role as Frank in *Thief* and William Petersen worked closely with the Chicago Police Department Violent Crimes Unit and the FBI Violent Crimes Unit in preparation for the role of Will Graham in *Manhunter*, neither of their respective regimes approach the curriculum designed for Lewis in *Mohicans*. Beginning at the Many Hawks Special Operations Center in Pittsview, Alabama, Lewis began an extensive programme that took him from an understanding of contemporary weapon use (M16s, shotguns, handguns), armed combat and survival skills back to the related proficiencies of the 1750s. By the time Lewis had completed this regression, under the eye of Fort Bragg Colonel David Webster, he was fully competent in the handling of eighteenth-century edged weapons, the maintenance and reloading of a long rifle with black powder while running, and the tracking of both animals and humans via the reading of mud prints. In many ways Lewis had become like the professional survivalist Daniel Boone, the noted eighteenth-century frontiersman who was clearly one of Mann's templates for his revised version of Hawkeye. The various skillsets and survival competencies that Lewis acquired during his training at Pittsview would feed directly into his characterisation of Hawkeye and, by extension, the film's representation of the Huron, Mohawk and Abenakis tribes. This reclamation of the sovereignty and capability of the Native American peoples by Mann, this corrective to what Mann terms the "gross oversimplification ... of the noble savages" in Cooper's book, flows first and foremost from the professionalism that Lewis imbued Hawkeye with via this training programme.

Over the course of the next few scenes the various warring factions and political interests are introduced by Mann in his attempt to depict the tumultuous backdrop to Hawkeye, Uncas and Chingachgook's movements along the frontier. These introductions, which follow from the primary introduction of Hawkeye and his men, bolster the film's revised interpretation of the Native American peoples because they show the imperialist parties – be they English or French – to be, at best, unprofessional, at worst, incompetent. As John Harkness noted above, this strategy enjoyed a flurry of popularity in the early 1990s as certain filmmakers such as Kevin Costner and Clint Eastwood sought to reorient the balance of representation between whites and indigenous populations (or, in the case of *Unforgiven* (1992), African Americans) and establish much more faithful characterisations where they were long overdue. Although by the mid-2010s this move away from a fictionalised white superiority and professionalism had reached a state of justifiably deliberate exaggeration – consider any of the white American characters in Quentin Tarantino's *Django Unchained* (horribly racist, permanently inebriated, mentally incapacitated or just plain psychotic) – in 1992 Mann deftly handles the mechanism in order to give back to the Native Americans the professionalism that American fiction had often stripped from them.

The main white character to receive attention at the start of *Mohicans* is Major Duncan Heyward (Steven Waddington), an important character used by Mann to exemplify the arrogant incompetence of the British imperial war machine and its colonial project. Heyward arrives at the way station of the ineffectual General Webb and is soon after despatched by him to Fort William Henry, charged with safely escorting to that beleaguered outpost the two daughters of its watchman, Colonel Munro. Heyward's most telling mistake upon his arrival at General Webb's quarters is the way in which he addresses Magua, the Huron warrior who is ostensibly working in alliance with the English army as a scout and local advisor. Magua's marginalisation in this scene by Heyward – something that Magua tactically allows and to which he will violently respond in a subsequent scene – is further complemented by Mann's and Dante Spinotti's lighting of the scene, which has Magua hidden in darkness at the back of the room despite the sunny weather outside. As Mann notes in the commentary on the film, before the advent of electric lighting, indoor spaces such as this were characterised by pools of light and darkness due to the obviously limited nature of the candles and oil-fed lanterns used. In this regard the scene recalls the interior moments of Kubrick's *Barry Lyndon* (1975) and his pioneering use of super-fast 50mm lenses, lenses that boasted such huge apertures that they allowed Kubrick to realistically recreate "the huddle and glow of a pre-electrical age".[8] Heyward exits Webb's quarters and makes straight for Cora Munro (Madeleine Stowe), the elder daughter of Colonel Munro and the woman he wishes to take as his wife. The two take tea outside in a highly formalised fashion, sitting at a table sipping from china cups, attired in period dress, the picture of gentility and imperialist decorum.

Heyward tries to make his case for marriage but Cora is resistant, psychologically aware of his limitations and her own boundless ambitions for her life in the New World. The background to this very mannered courtship is the wilderness of the Algonquian forest, the old-growth cathedral of life, energy and spontaneity that presents a stark opposition to Heyward's imperialist project and the society he advocates. It's an obvious metaphor but not one that Mann dwells on. After the establishing shot of the two at the table, the trees blowing in the background, he cuts into a series of medium close-ups as Heyward's advances are rebuffed by Cora. Like his truly wonderful, expensive and detailed recreation of the Biograph Theatre on Lincoln Avenue in Chicago for the climax of *Public Enemies*, the wilderness vs. civilisation metaphor here in *Mohicans* is posed to the audience but then sidelined in favour of the dramatic potential of the story. For all his supposed stylistic excess and action beats, Mann can be a very restrained and subtle storyteller, aware of how artifice should be used in the service of a story's drama rather than as a fairground attraction to entice people in.[9]

Cora and Heyward taking tea, the despatching of Heyward to Fort William Henry and the opening deer hunt with Hawkeye and his men all help form Mann's introductory remarks on the historical corrective he wishes to offer audiences with *The Last of the Mohicans*. The emergence of a new balance, of highly professional American natives versus ineffectual imperialist aggressors, is struck in these opening scenes, and what remains is for the film to zero in on and augment these new weightings in Mann's now customary style.

Hawkeye's usefulness as the conduit of professionalism in *Mohicans* is made manifest in the next key scene where Heyward, Cora and Alice are betrayed by their "scout" Magua, en route to Fort William Henry. The combat sequence that emerges from Magua's betrayal and the subsequent speedy rescue of Cora and Alice exemplifies not only the professionalism that lies at the heart of the vast majority of Mann's protagonists but also that of the director himself. Outside of the training regime Mann constructed for Daniel Day Lewis and the other primary actors, Mann also initiated a boot camp programme for around 75 additional male actors who would become the infantry in the film, rerouted flights over the film's exterior locations so as to avoid contrails in the sky, closed nearby state highways so that cars were not visible in the distance, studied an eighteenth-century sabre-fighting manual, built the fort of Fort William Henry and the homestead out of lumber hewn from the surrounding forest, consulted extensively with the Smithsonian Institute on the look of the Huron, Mohawk and Abenakis aesthetic, used *The Death of Wolfe* by Benjamin West (1770) as a vital reference point for Indigenous tattooing customs and, finally, became proficient in the economic accomplishments and political systems of the tribespeople via books such as *The Oregon Trail: Sketches of Prairie and Rocky Mountain Life* by Francis Parkman and the writings of Louis Antoine de Bougainville, the aide-de-camp of Montcalm. Of this last point Mann has noted that many of the Indigenous tribes of the period operated bicameral political legislatures that were at least the equal of anything the white settlers had established by this point. Mann also highlights that, contrary to the incompetent and insular stereotype popularised by Cooper during the period, the tribes of the American frontier in the 1750s "probably controlled 75% of the world's fur trade, as both merchants of fur, middlemen for other tribes and also trappers".[10]

This reflexivity between the professionalism of the film's characterisations and the film's director is not a facet unique to Mann or *Mohicans*. What is unique is the devotion that Mann has exhibited across the span of his filmography, both to date and by the midpoint of his career that *Mohicans* marked in 1992. By the early 1990s Mann had become one of the few directors working in American film to adopt such a rigorous, research-based film-making style, a style that directly correlated with the huge gaps between his projects during which he would be compulsively engrossed in the subject matter of his next film.[11] Of this methodology

Mann has observed, somewhat contradictorily, that "as a director you immerse into the totality of the event of the movie"[12] but that "the amount of time I take between projects is not a method, it's an irritant, it's frustrating to me".[13] The relationship Mann shares with his protagonists is of this ilk, drawn from the process of taking the time to be proficient at what you do, learning the skills and the craft through a process of total immersion until you become the best runner, safe-cracker, bank robber or frontiersman alive. He continues:

> The most important thing for me personally ... that affected the way I make film, which is relative, is only significant to me, it's not a prescription for anybody else ... is an interdisciplinary approach, meaning that I was drawn to use all the tools at my command.[14]

Here Mann alludes to his complete immersion in the film-making process, an approach that sees him fulfilling not just a directorial role but also, across his career, that of screenwriter, producer, cinematographer, editor and actor.[15] If this chapter is about anything, it's about this determinant, the consistent expression of a director's professional methodology through the actions and lifestyles of his characters onscreen.

Magua's betrayal of Heyward, Cora and Alice is total and he and his brothers kill several of Heyward's military escorts before Hawkeye's triumphant arrival. The English are here shown to be weak because of their linear and predictable fighting style, which involves maintaining a solid group, crouching and firing their long rifles in an attempt to suppress any oncoming attack. By contrast, Mann blocks the Huron attackers in such a way as to make clear their more professional style, which is predicated on quick adaptation and dynamic bursts of parry and blow. In his book *The Cinema of Michael Mann*, author Steven Rybin incorrectly attributes this new weighting, not to Mann's wish to offer a corrective to Cooper's original bias, but to a

> lack of respect for the ability of the British to make war: a counterpoint persists throughout *Mohicans* whereby the controlled and assured movements of the army's ritualised procedures (such as their march into the forest at the beginning of the film, when Cora and Alice head toward Fort William Henry) are contrasted with the inability of that same army to defend themselves against attack...[16]

While *Mohicans* does at times seem dismissive of the British Army, Mann made clear during his publicity tour for the film that his intention was always first and foremost to redress what he saw as the thus far poor representation of frontier tribal people in cinema and in Cooper's original *Leatherstocking Tales* series, rather than offer any overtly critical analysis of the British. Yes, a consequence of that redress might be a less than favourable view of the British Army, but such a view is a secondary result of the film's true focus, not its primary aim.

As the sequence plays out we note a degree of reflexivity here too, this time in the way that Mann stages this first real combat sequence. In both its sound design and editing rhythms the scene captures something thrilling in its efficiency and clarity, a quality noticed by AMPAS when it awarded the film the Academy Award for Best Sound at the 65th Academy Awards. The soundscape brings to the fore the noise of activity, the running and swooping and slicing and shooting that are the fundamental skillsets of frontier life. There's exhilaration in witnessing the offensive and counter-offensive moves of the fighters here, combat styles that are no doubt the product of Mann's intensive pre-production research into handling edged weaponry. In this regard, the fighting scenes in *Mohicans* contrast strongly with other related films of the period such as Bruce Beresford's equally excellent but tonally different *Black Robe* (1991), a film in which frontier combat is rendered as something intensely ugly and reprehensible rather than supremely skilful and exhilarating. Although both these aspects – combat as something ugly and combat as something skilful – can be inherent to violence of this sort, the notion of professionalism can only really emerge from the latter, from *Mohicans*' style of representation which asks the audience to watch and be thrilled by the process.

Hawkeye, Uncas and Chingachgook save Cora, Alice and Heyward by skilfully slaying Magua's soldiers with a combination of blows that Mann captures using shot/reverse shot edits. Magua moves to shoot Cora with his long rifle but, using slow-motion photography, Mann shows Hawkeye to be the faster and more professional of the two combatants. In the time it takes Magua to take aim, Hawkeye has taken his rifle down from his shoulder, raised it up to the target and fired. Magua's rapid exit from the scene is like that of a phantasm or spectre, a ghostly presence who slips away and is now free to haunt Hawkeye once more. This is very much like the character of Waingro in Mann's next film, *Heat*, who evades McCauley (Robert De Niro) at the start by seeming just to disappear into the jungle of Los Angeles before going on to torment him until the end.

Hawkeye prevents the ignorant Heyward from shooting Chingachgook, since he has mistaken him for one of Magua's warriors, before Mann cuts to a beautiful shot of Chingachgook unfurling his massive tomahawk. It slices through the air and the shot's depth of field in a manner that's bordering on showy – as the audience, however, we allow it, allow the moment its slight contrivance, because this trio's skill and professionalism is the corrective that Mann wishes us to acknowledge.

Hawkeye, Uncas and Chingachgook now accompany Heyward, Cora and Alice to Fort William Henry in relative safety. They move against the flow of waterfalls, a sequence with some particularly fine editing, the best of which is when Mann exits the scene by cutting back to the rapids and the white noise of the river before fading out the sound completely. (This is something he would do again in *The Insider* to intimate the change in Wigand's relationship with Bergman while the two talk at length by the Colgate clock near the Ohio River in Louisville. Mann marks the change by not only having Bergman move from the back seat to the front passenger seat of Wigand's car but by also cutting to a shot of a river barge glimpsed through a rain-soaked windscreen and then gradually fading out the sound.) The party pass through the murder scene at the Cameron homestead and along the fringes of a tribal burial ground at dusk, before finally arriving at Fort William Henry later that same night.

As Hawkeye and the group gain access to the fort via the sally port, the French forces pound its walls with mortar rounds and cannon fire while hundreds of French soldiers move forward along shadowy ridges, glimpsed only by the momentary illumination of the explosions. This is undoubtedly Mann's centrepiece, a grand evocation of history wrought from both his own labour and the film's production designer Wolf Kroeger. While the French attack on the fort perhaps lacks the percussive digital augmentation that would be found in similar sequences in years to come – the assault on Jerusalem in Ridley Scott's *Kingdom of Heaven* (2005) comes to mind – it more than makes up for it with its production design that includes the working fort (complete with interior decoration and basement levels), operational cannons and trenches. For the construction of the fort itself Mann and Kroeger revisited the original design elements and recreated something along the following lines:

> Fort William Henry was an irregular square fortification with bastions on the corners, in a design that was intended to repel Indian attacks, but not necessarily withstand attack from an enemy armed with artillery. Its walls were 30 feet (9.1 m) thick, with log facings around an earthen filling. Inside the fort were wooden barracks two stories high, built around the parade ground.[17]

Mann usually rebuts accusations of this being nothing more than slavish adherence to actuality by insisting that there is no better alternative than the real thing and, on this occasion, he is likely correct. The fort, particularly in its interior spaces, has a used quality to it, an air of workmanship and a patina of wear, that help it sidestep the pitfalls of seeming like a set (in a way that the interior spaces of the Overlook Hotel in Kubrick's *The Shining* (1980) do not). Mann's 3-D recreation of the fort has real heft and ballast, something that in this instance can only come from a working building with both visible exterior and interior dimensions. Though the talented product of no doubt hundreds of joiners and builders, the decision to actually construct the fort in the first place – rather than rely on scale models or rear projection – must lie squarely with Mann and his overall vision for this film. This wish to recreate reality on its own terms, meaning Mann's preference for travelling to a real location rather than using a set decorator or for constructing a real building rather than a model or for shooting in camera rather than with digital effects or for casting real prisoners and police officers rather than actors, is, as our assessment of his films will make clear, merely an extension of the ethos of professionalism and proficiency that he equates with success. As *Thief* and *Manhunter* evidenced, often this reality-based project comes up against a deliberate design or stylisation that creates an interesting and ambiguous tension like that found in Scorsese's *Mean Streets* or *Taxi Driver*. While such design or style is normally a balanced projection of the environment of the film, *The Keep* presented a stark anomaly en route to *Mohicans* by priding its aesthetic far above and beyond considerations such as narrative coherence or interior meaning.

Hawkeye's time in the fort serves to bolster his credibility as an emblem of professionalism and competence. Mann shows him in heated dialogue with Munro, tending to his munitions and, in his most explicit display of skill, laying down increasingly more difficult covering fire for an escaping member of the colonial militia. Hawkeye is subsequently thrown in a basement cell for aiding the escape of the militiaman but manages to avoid execution when the French breach the walls of the fort and force Munro's surrender. The official surrender of Munro's English army to Montcalm and their exchange of terms is one of two scenes that harken back to the opening moments of *Manhunter* and the Renaissance perspective of Graham's beach house in Captiva, Florida.

Prior to Mann's take up of the newly emergent hi-def digital video technology for 2001's *Ali*, his films, particularly his 1990s films, were marked by an interest in the compositions and strictures of Western Renaissance painting, particularly in what filmmaker Mark Cousins terms the Z axis, but also the symmetry of things such as binary opposites. In *Manhunter* it's there when Molly talks with Crawford early on in the film about the dangers of asking Graham back to work; Mann's camera captures the discussion from within the sanctum of the dining room, its table delineating the *trompe l'oeil* of depth (the Z axis) and therefore loneliness and isolation. In the shot's design – figures blocked at the far end, table lines suggesting a deep perspective, parallel bars of the sliding windows – we are reminded of Renaissance paintings such as *St Jerome in his Study* (1460–75) by Antonello Da Messina, a work that operates on a series of planes and lines that lead the viewer's eye past St Jerome at the back of the room and on towards a distant and yet imaginary vertex. The first example of this viewpoint in *Mohicans* can be found at 58m 51s as Munro and Montcalm greet each other on the battlefield and discuss the terms of the British surrender. Mann shoots the scene with the French Army to screen left and the English to screen right. In front of those men are the three respective standard bearers for each side and in the centre of the frame, Montcalm, Munro and the two deputies of each. Like the lines of the dining table in *Manhunter*, the lines of the soldiers here guide the eye along the Z axis towards those Native Americans aligned with Montcalm at the extreme rear of the shot. Such perspective, when combined with the shattered remnants of trees and shrubbery on the ground between the armies, points to something like Paolo Uccello's *The Battle of San Romano* (1430s), a Florentine painting enthralled by the suggestion of perspective through broken lances and warriors on either side of the frame.

The sequence that follows on from this surrender to the French by the English forces is the second key distillation of Mann's love of symmetry and static forms in *Mohicans*. It is also a great scene for further exemplifying the reflexive notions of professionalism and precision that the film parades throughout its running time. The English, having left Fort William Henry and en route back to Webb, pass through a clearing in the forest with a road down the centre and trees to the left and right. As the party wanders through the pass, civilians and Redcoats together, the image becomes highly pictorial, painterly even in its composition and colour. The long shots are very static and symmetrical, with the party moving along the Z axis from front to back and an even distribution of grass and trees on either side of them balancing things beautifully. A reverse shot and the army is now coming towards us, moving along the Z axis from back to front. This second shot, however, is not a flagrant disregard for the 180-degree rule as it is shot from a different height and uses a cooler colour temperature so as to distinguish it from the previous establishing shot. Calm, measured, balanced. Some close-ups of individual faces we know – Cora, Hawkeye – and then Mann disrupts the equilibrium with a cut to the dark interior of the forest to the side of the pass. Like John Ford's repeated use of what several writers have termed "womb shots" in *The Searchers* (1956) – those pregnant images looking out from within a dark space, the most famous of which is obviously at the end of the film when Ethan is viewed in the doorway of the house, light outside but dark within – this image in *Mohicans* is fraught with a similar tension. It feels both safe and sinister in the darkness of these woods.

A Huron skirmisher speeds out of the darkness, in a shot that's perpendicular to the Z axis of moments before, and moves towards the English party, killing one of the soldiers in seconds. Now the disruption begins as Mann breaks down the static forms of the scene and instead offers battle violence and chaos, albeit chaos still marked by precision. As Hawkeye, Uncas and Chingachgook acknowledge what is happening, more Huron skirmishers emerge and attack along the flanks of the staid and restricted English Army. Mann is again foregrounding the professional dynamism of Native American tactics versus the outmoded fighting style of the imperialists here, a notion reinforced by the way in which the attackers disrupt the compositional harmony of this scene.

Through a series of choice editing decisions and that Oscar-winning sound design, the fighting that emerges is thrilling and clearly delineated, a counterpoint to the intentionally jarring camerawork and messy choreography of Mel Gibson's *Braveheart* (1995) – a debt Gibson owes to Akira Kurosawa – or the brooding and repugnant intensity of the aforementioned *Black Robe*. Mann's corrective to the disservice offered by Cooper's characterisation of the Native American tribes hinges largely on this, on his ability to present them as a professional and formidable force, both in their combat tactics – as ably evidenced here – and in their political organisation and economics. Both Hawkeye and Magua display a consummate skill in this battle scene. The two men carve out a path amid the melee of edged weaponry and death and each manifests a single act of violence that cements their reputations for the remainder of the film: Hawkeye saves Cora from going under the knife of a Huron warrior and Magua cuts out the still-beating heart of Munro. Mann singles out both events with tight framing that sidelines the background violence and renders each character an ambassador for this way of thinking in a war that was as global as any in the twentieth century.

The group flee to the now famous waterfall scene, Magua's group close behind them. Hawkeye explains that he cannot guarantee the safety of Heyward, Cora and Alice if they all remain together as a group. Hawkeye therefore jumps into the falls and escapes with Uncas and Chingachgook, allowing Cora, Alice and Heyward to be caught so that he can later rescue them with the advantage of surprise. Running and the sense of relentless motion re-enters the film as Mann recaptures that feeling of physicality that he remembered so fondly from the Randolph Scott version. Hawkeye and his brothers speed on to the rescue of Cora, Alice and Heyward from what they know will be either slavery or death.

The remainder of *Mohicans* seems now, by and large, to be a literal run uphill as Hawkeye moves from the lowlands of the forest floor to the rocky precipice of the Smoky Mountains climax. Mann fixates on the running bodies of our three heroes as they track Cora. Shot after shot of their athleticism is stitched together into a compendium of images that remind us of *The Jericho Mile*'s running sequences, an activity of transcendence and heroism. Halfway up the mountain Magua leads his captives to the village of the Great Sachem, the political and spiritual leader of this area. Magua attempts to parlay his prisoners into a greater wager for the Sachem's favour. Magua proclaims how great a warrior and leader he is, how he has vanquished many English soldiers and is now deserving of recognition. The Sachem seems to go along with this until Hawkeye walks into the camp, unarmed and willing to sacrifice himself in order to save Cora and the rest of the group. Mann's direction of Daniel Day Lewis here is particularly fine. Lewis as Hawkeye boasts a powerful authenticity in his delivery of a monologue that lays bare Magua's intentions for Huron supremacy in the region. The Sachem listens, framed and illuminated in an almost beatific light and soft focus, such a representation a stark contrast to the film's treatment of the English and French leaders. The Sachem is persuaded by Hawkeye. Magua leaves in disgust, headed for the Huron of the Great Lakes, while Heyward deliberately mistranslates Hawkeye's words to the Sachem, thereby saving Hawkeye and Cora but sacrificing himself in the process. The Sachem takes Heyward to burn in the tribal fire as an awful form of war reparation and Cora is released with Hawkeye.

The climax of *The Last of the Mohicans* thrills with crisply edited sequences of edged weapon combat and some epic *mise en scène*, compositions that dwarf the characters against enormous rock faces as in Roland Joffe's *The Mission* (1986). Uncas charges ahead to rescue Alice. He ambushes Magua's soldiers on a high ledge and works his way towards the warlord, the stunning Foley work punctuating his movements. Despite being powered on by his new love for Alice and fighting with true conviction Uncas is quickly felled by Magua, who is clearly the more seasoned combatant here. Mann's camera, in its angles and framing choices, treats those characters now left as titans, giants in a giant landscape. As Magua delivers the *coup de grace* to Uncas the camera is

The Films of Michael Mann

Figure 10. The Last of the Mohicans

low and tracks along the side of the pedestal of rock they stand on. The film is building operatically towards one of its final images, the elemental positioning of Magua and Chingachgook. Uncas is killed and thrown off the cliff, his body falling like a feather. Alice, acknowledging the hopelessness of her situation, chooses to throw herself into the void too in an attempt to reunite herself with her lost love. Magua is dumbfounded by the girl's choice of action, as is her sister Cora, who initially does not register shock or upset but rather confusion at the seeming insanity of Alice's suicide. Chingachgook, enraged by Magua's murder of his son, races on along the ridge as Hawkeye provides covering fire. Hawkeye is once again a visible emblem of professionalism as he reloads his long gun with powder and shot while running at speed towards Magua, something that the film's producers thought could not realistically be done until Lewis's trainer demonstrated it. Using their ammunition first, Hawkeye and Chingachgook shoot their way up to Magua, sometimes, as in Hawkeye's case, firing two rifles at once. Again, the editing rhythms here sustain the sense of professionalism that these two men exude, Dov Hoenig and Arthur Schmidt cutting with shot/reverse shots to capture both the superior aim of Hawkeye and Chingachgook and the felling of all the Huron leading to Magua.

When the final showdown does arrive the fate of Magua quickly becomes clear, Wes Studi's character being this film's incarnation of the doomed psychotic figure that we have seen before in *The Jericho Mile*, *Thief*, *The Keep* and *Manhunter*. Magua readies his tomahawk and knife, anticipating a waist-height frontal attack by Chingachgook. Instead Chingachgook rolls under Magua's lunge with the tomahawk and strikes Magua from behind. Then there's a deflection of Magua's counterattack, which rips open his right elbow joint, and another blow to his lower back,

The Last of the Mohicans and Professionalism

in effect winding him severely. A penultimate thrust down on Magua's left shoulder tears open the musculature there and renders both his arms useless. A reaction shot of Chingachgook reveals a look of disgust and also pity when confronted by this now pathetic adversary. Mann then reunites the foes in a wide-angle two shot that's held just long enough to become an intrinsic metaphor for the clash of civilisations and ideologies, an elemental rendering of conflict and the triumph of professionalism over greed. The *coup de grace* is a powerful blow to Magua's abdomen by Chingachgook's much larger tomahawk, in which the point actually pierces through and out Magua's back. Chingachgook then pushes Magua off his tomahawk, as you would prise a piece of glass from the sole of your shoe, and he falls to the ground dead. There's no denying the satisfaction when Mann's psychotic characters meet their demise in his cinema – the death of Jose Yero (John Ortiz) in *Miami Vice* (2006) comes to mind, blasted against a warehouse wall by Tubbs (Jamie Foxx) during the climactic shootout[18] – and Magua's falls into this tradition. He's framed falling to the ground, blood running from his mouth, much as Mann would later frame Dillinger's demise in *Public Enemies* (2009). From such heady heights, both these characters end up as diminished figures, broken and laid out on the ground.

The closing image of *The Last of the Mohicans* returns us to the heights of the film's opening, when Mann's camera peers across the vast landscape of the Blue Ridge Mountain range. The ascetic professionalism exemplified by Hawkeye and Chingachgook has made them the ultimate victors in this story, a film that makes no attempt to hide its wish to be a corrective to James Fenimore Cooper's skewed representations. As well as offering the best avatar of professionalism to date in Mann's canon, *Mohicans* also holds a light to Mann's own multidisciplinary, research-based methodology and his professional commitment to creating rigorously crafted dramas. The film is Mann's strongest testimonial yet that he is a director who wants to be regarded as worthy, a cinematic artist who can also be viewed as a professional in other disciplines, and as someone who invests heavily in what could be termed the totality of the milieu. With this film – and the others that bookend it – Mann spent months acquiring all the details and context and language of its unique environment in order to generate what he believes is a near-subliminal and yet integral component – visual credibility. Mann strives so fervently for credibility or authenticity because he considers it key to an audience accepting the events he's presenting onscreen. For Mann, the months Daniel Day Lewis spent training to he Hawkeye, to wield edged weapons properly, to hunt and survive in the wilderness, to reload his long gun while on the run, are key to creating a positive audience reaction. Audiences notice these aspects in the actor's performance and, at least according to Mann's assessment of the process, generate a value judgement in their mind that seems to say, "This feels real to me." This method or curriculum, this programme for the acquisition of skill and professionalism, is then applied to his own working style. Mann will learn the vocabulary of a given period, study its politics and the mindset of its people, and research the key events of the day in order to arrive at a point where he feels validated enough to then tell a story about that time.

In this way, *The Last of the Mohicans* is, after *Manhunter*, the most strongly emblematic example of Mann's auteurism we have so far encountered. The film satisfies a desire to see something technically competent – the construction of the fort, the period lighting – with both a directorial signature – professionalism – and an interior meaning to it – a cinematic redemption of the Native American tribes of the frontier.

Ideas about professionalism would continue into Mann's next film of the 1990s, *Heat*, but they would subsumed by something else, an environment of stark contrast to the woods of upstate New York and a determinant of much more significant import, the city of Los Angeles.

> **Key scene suggestion for professionalism – the opening deer hunt that introduces the twin ideas of movement and skill.**

Notes

1   Steven Rybin, *The Cinema of Michael Mann*, Lexington Books, 2007, 99.
2   Mann's film was the latest in a series of adaptations of Cooper's original novel that includes ten films and two television series.
3   Video interview with Mann found at http://michael-mann.blogspot.co.uk/search/label/Last%20of%20the%20Mohicans (accessed 26 December 2022).
4   Ibid.

5 http://www.mohicanpress.com/mo06053.html (accessed 26 October 2022).
6 John Harkness, "White Noise", *Sight & Sound* 2, no. 7 (November 1992): 15.
7 Interview between Mann and Gavin Smith, *Sight & Sound* 11, no. 7 (November 1992): 12.
8 Tim Robey, "Kubrick's Neglected Masterpiece", *Daily Telegraph*, 31 January 2009, 16–17.
9 Look again at the difference in approach of Sam Mendes's *Road to Perdition* (2002) and Mann's *Public Enemies* (2009) as an example of how artifice can swamp or complement the story.
10 See the director's commentary on the Blu-ray of *The Last of the Mohicans*.
11 The other notable example is Stanley Kubrick.
12 Excerpt taken from production featurette on the Blu-ray of *The Last of the Mohicans*.
13 *Mann Made: From L.A Takedown to Heat* documentary interview TV special, BBC; first broadcast 23 February 1997. Available on YouTube in two parts.
14 http://michael-mann.blogspot.co.uk/search/label/Last%20of%20the%20Mohicans (accessed 26 December 2022).
15 Mann has a cameo in his friend Peter Berg's film *Hancock* (2008).
16 Rybin, *The Cinema of Michael Mann*, 102.
17 David Starbuck, *Massacre at Fort William Henry*, University Press of New England, 2002, 7.
18 Some reviews at the time of *Vice*'s release seemed uncomfortable about the level of glee with which Mann appeared to imbue Yero's death scene. Nick James, writing in *Sight & Sound*, notes "But the spectacular blowing away of the chief villain elicits an uncomfortable bloodlust from audiences." Nick James, "*Miami Vice* review", *Sight & Sound* 16, no. 10 (October 2006): 68.

CHAPTER EIGHT

Heat and Los Angeles

I was not yet my best in those years – the late 90s – and it, the City of Angels, was way past its.

Mark Cousins

Does *Heat*, Chicago slang for the police and Mann's sixth film, prove Mark Cousins's observation wrong? Is this film the exception to a vast lineage of cinema set in Los Angeles that has, little by little and over the years, established a template for the city that somehow says *faded* or *worn* or *retrograde* or, perhaps worst of all, *parodic*? It's arguable that, prior to *Heat*'s release in 1995, the popular cinematic conception of Los Angeles was probably one characterised by a "familiar, anaemic yellow hue ... Vaseline soft focus and beach culture inflection" or a "nostalgic period sensibility" or a "shimmery, hallucinogenic insanity ... where Los Angeles played the role of a tropical hell hole indicative of Laos or Vietnam".[1] What these conceptions often reveal is that while Los Angeles was many things prior to the years leading up to the millennium, it was rarely viewed – at least within the confines of movies – as being relevant and modern (for Mann the postmodernity of Los Angeles would not emerge until *Collateral*). While films such as *Point Break* (1991), *Encino Man* (1992) and *White Men Can't Jump* (1992) revised and repeated the tired archetype of Los Angeles as a beach culture location for surfing, skateboarding and basketball respectively, and others such as *Chinatown* (1974), *Devil in a Blue Dress* (1995), *Mulholland Falls* (1996) and *L.A. Confidential* (1997) spent time looking reverently back in search of a period nostalgia, some films – *Lethal Weapon* (1987), *Falling Down* (1993) and *Predator 2* (1990) – sought to present Los Angeles as another place entirely, as an analogue of South East Asia that could re-examine the folly and insanity of the Vietnam War. In these modes Los Angeles was a city caught between the lure of the beach life, the regurgitation of old forms and the parodying of past conflicts. Such a summary of styles is hardly definitive and no doubt omits many other examples and styles that Los

Angeles has come to be known by over the years. It does, however, bring into stark view the notion that, while the city is protean in its cinematic nature, part of that mosaic has rarely been a piece that says "Here I am, a city that is alive and contemporary, a prize fighter on the global stage." Even in the bulk of its contemporary-set movie chronicles, from those earliest Los Angeles stories to those of the late 1980s, Los Angeles rarely felt modern or new. This chapter will argue that Mann changed all that in 1995. In generating for himself an indispensible determinant of his auteurism – Los Angeles – Mann also crafted a fresh vision for the City of Angels, something irrefutably modern in its look and post-millennial in its reach, a new style that would still be influencing filmmakers decades later.

Mann had lived in Los Angeles for some time before he chose to update his NBC TV movie *LA Takedown* (1989). During that time the city saw much of its business centre move away from the downtown core and out to the suburban areas. This decentralisation was due in no small part to the earlier emergence of the city's "horizontal, automobile culture", a mass shift in transportation habits towards car ownership, necessitated by the ever-growing expansion of the city.[2] Formerly well-to-do areas such as Bunker Hill started to fall to bits, many of its Victorian mansions now flophouses for transient workers and ex-cons – amid its myriad other concerns, *Heat* deals with this struggling social class through characters such as Breedan (Dennis Haysbert) and Waingro (Kevin Gage), small-time criminals who never achieve the financial independence of McCauley, Shiherlis or Cheritto. Downtown Los Angeles, rather than the locus of modern ideas and wealth that it now signifies in films, had become ghostly in its pedestrian emptiness. The complete lack of foot traffic led most streetside businesses to close up and move out. If a person was on foot in downtown it had to look odd and out of place and they were probably only there to run an errand and then leave. As pedestrians disappeared so did many of the centre's historic buildings, razed to the ground to make way for parking lots.

While downtown gutted itself in this manner, the other styles of Los Angeles remained at least partially true. The beach culture and sun-bleached haze of Malibu, Venice Beach and Santa Monica, typified in the likes of *Point Break*, persisted in these earlier years. So too did the melancholic nostalgia of *Chinatown*, a film which refused to let go of the period sensibility of buildings such as the Eastern Columbia on 849 S. Broadway, a wonderful Art Deco tower designed by Claude Beelman that evinced images of cigarette holders, evening gloves and dark wood interiors. Where the third style appears, those films that sought to draw parallels between LA's palm trees, sub-tropical climate and mental instability and these aspects of Vietnam (*Falling Down* being the best of these), you have one possible understanding of Los Angeles as a protean and shifting metropolis akin to what writer Mike Davis pinpointed in his late eighties book *City of Quartz*. By and large this was the Los Angeles where Mann lived during the years he made *Manhunter* and *The Last of the Mohicans*. It was a city with many cinematic facades but, notably, the idea of it being modern was not among them (even *Blade Runner* (1982), for all its pursuit of the futurism of Antonio Sant'Elia, is a film defined more by what David Edgerton calls the shock of the old, the idea that "the old will survive alongside the new and sometimes outlast it".[3] One need only look at Deckard's apartment in the film – a space based on the Mayan influences of Frank Lloyd Wright's Ennis House in Los Angeles – to see this in effect.) Mann himself recalled an older Los Angeles along such lines in a promotional interview given around the time of *Heat*'s release in 1995: "There were old factories, warehouses from the 1930s, wonderful Deco places ... just falling into abandon."[4] Like the burgeoning new ideas and crumbling old forms of *Blade Runner*'s Los Angeles, the city Mann saw around him in the 1970s and early 1980s was one caught in a similar flux.

That all began to change in the late 1980s when Bunker Hill, that downtown area of degenerating flophouses, was viewed with fresh eyes and an awareness that the new millennium was coming fast. Over the next ten years extensive redevelopment of the Bunker Hill area would be undertaken as city authorities sought to curb the mass exodus from the downtown area and restart its core. A new skyscraper was built nearly every year during this period, something that coincided with huge ground excavation efforts and the clearing of slum areas that had blighted the area for so long. The towers of finance, industry and tourism that now erupted from this hill, not so long ago the utilitarian living space of impoverished pensioners, would soon prove a crucial symbol of the modernist revitalisation of downtown Los Angeles, a revitalisation that *Heat* would arguably be one of the first to cinematically acknowledge. The emergent high-rise towers of downtown – the Wells Fargo Centre, the California Plaza buildings, the mighty US Bank Tower – became the tent poles of LA's new conspicuous modernity, their steel and glass replacing brick and mortar. Where this imagery fused with Mann's recognition of LA's ever-growing mass transportation systems (freeways, cloverleaf interchanges, air traffic bound for LAX and MTA lines), its economic polarisation and its markers of industry (the refineries of Wilmington, the hardware yards, the harbours and Port cartage) and we have *Heat*'s cutting-edge conception of the city, a Los Angeles that was now:

The locus for strange or new technologies (precious metals depositories, sulphur mines, cell phone communication towers, signal interception capabilities and bank alarm bypass systems), architecture, both corporate (Van Zant's office space, the downtown towers, Far East National Bank) and modernist (Hanna's "dead-tech" cubist 2 up/2 down, Neil's strictly minimalist Malibu beach abode, Trejo's perilous house on stilts) and a very specific look that went a long way towards exemplifying our 21st century expectations of what the city should look like.[5]

Heat begins with a brand new addition to the real-life modernist expansion of Los Angeles, the Firestone section of the MTA's Blue Line, a part of LA's rail network that was so new at the time of shooting that it wasn't even open yet to the general public. A train bound for Los Angeles comes through plumes of steam towards the camera as the distant headlights of cars move along a hillside freeway. A reverse shot has the train stop at the Firestone station. De Niro's character Neil McCauley gets off and heads for the escalator down to street level. Both in their cool evocation of colour – Blue Line, the blue canopy roof of the station, dark blue hue of the night sky – and their conception of the city as a place of perpetual transit where people and information are always moving, these opening images of *Heat* sketch out quickly and effectively the film's modernist thesis of Los Angeles. A low-angle shot captures De Niro as he steps on to the sidewalk outside the St Mary Medical Centre in Long Beach. He is dressed as a paramedic although his furtive glances at the people around him suggests he's a crook. The kerbside outside the hospital is pristine and free of the signs of wear that normally mark street concrete. There's no rubbish blowing around either. The Santa Ana winds are absent from this cool and calm conception of the city. Weather as a whole is very restrained in *Heat*; scenes seem to oscillate between clear days and airy nights and the only instance of anything different is when De Niro and his crew are escorting Waingro out of the diner after the opening robbery and it's raining. It's a rain that's barely visible though, because of the covered parking lot outside the diner building. That's the automobile culture of Los Angeles at work again, this time disrupting weather systems with its insistence on protecting cars from water. We only see the rain after Waingro has fled the murderous intentions of McCauley and escaped into the city at large, the adverse weather a harbinger of McCauley's later line to Eady (Amy Brenneman), "When it rains, you get wet."

Aside from cinematographer Dante Spinotti's cool colour palette and its relevance in presenting Los Angeles as an inherently modern locale,

HEAT AND LOS ANGELES

the other early signifier of *Heat*'s wish to view the city through a new lens is its lighting choices. Despite the fact that the film opens at night, there is a concerted use of shadow here that's less about the evocation of a noir sensibility – although this does come later in the film – and more about stressing the three-dimensional nature of the city. Traditionally Los Angeles is presented in films as a hazy, flat plane disappearing into the distance, an aspect that, when viewed through a camera lens, tends result in the loss of a feeling of depth. 3-D becomes 2-D as the notion of the city as a dimensional construct is swallowed up by the scale of the horizon, or the Y axis (the aerial shots in Michelangelo Antonioni's *Zabriskie Point* (1970) provide just such an example). Thom Andersen notes this traditional view in the video essay *Los Angeles Plays Itself*: "In New York everything is sharp and in focus as if seen through a wide-angle lens; in smoggy cities like Los Angeles everything dissolves into the distance and even stuff that's close up seems far off."[6] The interplay of high-key spot lighting and deep shadow in the opening scenes stresses that Los Angeles is now a city that can be moved through in multiple directions, not just from front to back. Lines are sharp and in focus like New York. The petroleum jelly soft focus and the NO_2 haze are instantly forgotten, ostensibly because Mann quite deliberately chose to shoot *Heat* during the early part of the year when there is no smoggy marine layer hanging over Los Angeles. More than this, however, it's Mann's lighting, his love of a strong, directional exposure, which brings objects into high relief and lends mass, heft and depth to the city and its forms.

McCauley moves ghost-like through the emergency room of the hospital, past banks of vital signs monitors and medicines and gunshot victims, and exits by the back door where he steals an ambulance. A cut and we're on a construction materials yard where Chris Shiherlis (Val Kilmer) is buying demolition charges. There's more high-key lighting here and it helps to stave off the smothering and flattening morning sun as Shiherlis equips himself with the technology of his trade. In this regard the technology and industry at the heart of McCauley's crime spree across Los Angeles is one key to understanding the modernist nuances of Mann's vision for the city. As well as foregrounding the mechanics and technology of the crew - as Mann did in *Thief* – *Heat* also seeks to reveal the new age technologies and industrial thrust of Los Angeles itself, something associate producer Gusmano Cesaretti was instructed to find during the long months of pre-production on the film. Cesaretti himself refers to this look as the "corrosive architecture of Los Angeles", those elements of the city made from metal and imbued with an industrial function.[7]

As the film ambivalently demonstrates, this industrial function need not always be legal or in the interests of the city's power base or the LAPD. Indeed, lying in between *Heat*'s tour of its legitimate industry and infrastructure – the refineries of Wilmington, the Port of Los Angeles, the 110 freeway – are the mechanics of the city's crime as they appeared in Los Angeles at the dawn of the new millennium. The result of six months' worth of "ride-alongs" with the LAPD every Friday and Saturday night, the criminal environs of Los Angeles that Mann offers us are also characterised by a sense of the modern, the notion of an industrial or technological activity that is just as relevant as those legitimate areas noted above. From the high-end chop shop owned by Albert Torena (Ricky Harris), where stolen cars are reconfigured for resale, to the hilltop house of Kelso (Tom Noonan), the bearded mastermind who organises robbery packages by intercepting financial air traffic communication with a bevy of antennas, repeaters and satellite dishes, to McCauley's own interests in metallurgy and *Stress Fractures in Titanium*, crime in *Heat* is bound to its larger evocation of Los Angeles as a modern metropolis of industry.[8]

Pacino's Vincent Hanna, the gifted detective in LA's Robbery Homicide Division, is another character who is defined by, and therefore defines in return, the city around him. Hanna lives in the house of his current wife Justine (played by Justine Venora), a cubist/minimalist dwelling that uses metal sheeting and cubes of glass to carve up its interior spaces and thus fragment the bonds between those who live there. Mann shoots Hanna with a tight framing as he and Justine make love and, from here on, rarely permits him much more space whenever he is in this domestic environment. He is shown in the shower next and it's another tightly framed shot. Mann cuts to Justine smoking in bed, her smoke a tenuous connection to Hanna's shower steam. Lauren, Justine's daughter from a previous marriage, arrives upstairs looking for something. As he would later do in *The Insider* during the scene where the Wigand family have dinner together, Mann directs this familial exchange in *Heat* as something based on evasion and disconnection. Characters pose questions that are left answered or are responded to with unrelated questions directed towards another character entirely. This is the family unit as a heterogeneous group, all pursuing different agendas and essentially talking different languages. The exchange in *Heat* proceeds as follows:

Justine to Hanna: "Hey, taking me to breakfast?"
Hanna to Justine: "I can't, I'm meeting Bosko."
Lauren to Justine: "Hey Vincent ... Mom, where are my barrettes?"
Hanna to Lauren: "Hey sweetie."

Justine to Lauren: "I said on the kitchen table."
Lauren to Justine: "They're not there, I already checked."
Justine to Hanna: "Want me to make coffee?"
Hanna to Lauren: "No school today?"
Lauren to Hanna: "My Dad's picking me up. He's taking me to the new building and then to lunch."
Justine to Lauren: "Try under the cushions on the sofa."
Justine to Hanna: "He's already a half an hour late."
Hanna to Justine: "Is he gonna show or is that sonofabitch gonna stand her up like last time?"
Justine to Hanna: "I'll make coffee."
Hanna to Justine: "Another time baby."

Lauren goes back downstairs to continue her hunt for her hairclips, unaided by her mother or stepfather. Hanna collects his gun from the side table in the bedroom and leaves for work. Justine, alone and sitting on the side of her bed, reaches for a bottle of pills. To date Mann has yet to portray a conventional and well-adjusted family.

Despite this family fragmentation, these disconnections between a husband and wife and their troubled teenage daughter – caused, as the film seems to suggest here, by environment – *Heat* is not a film that presents Los Angeles as a postmodern city where chaos and irrationality rule. As will become clear, the Los Angeles Mann crafts here is one generally shot along quite rational lines (in many ways the opposite of the Los Angeles of *Collateral*). While there might be some variation on popular conceptions of the postmodern Los Angeles – Ed Soja's "horizontal, automobile culture"; hints at economic fragmentation (poor Waingro and Breedan on the one hand versus rich McCauley and Cheritto on the other); the conspicuous hallmarks of industry and how they separate the city into domains as Jane Jacobs discussed in *The Death and Life of Great American Cities* – the Los Angeles of *Heat* assiduously avoids those other key indicators of what, according to Soja again, constitutes the ultimate in postmodern living.[9] These include the racial enclaves of Los Angeles, those compartmentalised neighbourhoods that are almost "self-sufficient and inward turning", or what Soja terms the "citadel" of Los Angeles, those obvious power structures of the city itself that include iconography such as City Hall, the Stanley Mosk Courthouse and the Hall of Records.

The idea of fragmentation is key to the notion of postmodernism, and while *Heat* trades in a certain degree of splintered individuals and fragmented locales, its central characters rarely appear lost in their environment. McCauley and his crew or Hanna and his team appear consistently secure wherever they go and dispel the idea that they are mere tourists in this place; *Heat*'s characters know where to go, where to hide safely and where to dine out. The security that they feel in their environment is played out in the next scene, where McCauley and his crew mount an audacious robbery of an armoured car carrying the bearer bonds of businessman turned criminal Roger Van Zant (William Fichtner).

Waingro (Kevin Gage) exits the bathroom of a taco stand and demands a refill of coffee from the guy behind the counter – one of the film's many views of the disenfranchised service worker. Mann foregrounds the mural on the side of the building – a Latino woman and a man playing the accordion standing amid cacti and flowers – and you get the feeling that in this newly adopted city of his, this post-millennial successor to Chicago, he is attempting to show that which went before alongside that which is to come. Waingro spots the truck he's hitching a ride with and speeds off towards it without his coffee. The driver is Michael Cheritto (Tom Sizemore), one of McCauley's crew members, and he is in no mood to chat. Already, Waingro is someone who Mann is very carefully characterising as despicable and – worst of all in this cinematic conception of the world – unprofessional.

As the two drive to what will become the film's first robbery, there's a replication of that sense of composure and structure we saw in the shot choices and framing of *The Last of the Mohicans*. There is an obvious "mind" behind the direction of *Heat* in these opening scenes, a directorial thought process that is not only eliciting new visions of Los Angeles but also recalling previous forms of expression from past films. The Renaissance sensibility of *Mohicans* is back as Cheritto backs the truck into its temporary hiding place between the vertical columns of a freeway overpass. Look again at how Mann has the shadow of the column on the right fall on the truck until it covers, in a uniform way, the front grille and window and you cannot help but acknowledge the presence of the Renaissance ethos of symmetry and composition. There's a singular intent here, a deliberate voice and internal meaning that wants to be recognised. Before the film's end we will have witnessed the relevance of *The Jericho Mile*'s prison culture, the criminality of *Thief*, the future-looking modernism of *Manhunter* and the rigid professionalism of *The Last of the Mohicans* to *Heat*'s individuals, both good and bad. In short, *Heat* offers both the post-millennial exegesis of Los Angeles and the first crucial way point en route to Mann's hard-earned auteur status.

The robbery of the armoured car by McCauley's crew is perfectly executed with regard to the principal players. Mann stages the robbery at the junction of the 110 Harbor and Santa Monica Freeways, just south of downtown Los Angeles. In the text of the film, this location for an armed robbery is justified by the cop Hanna when he explains to his deputies that the fleeing criminals would have needed a good escape route (even though we never actually see McCauley's crew using the freeway to get away). However, this location's relevance to *Heat*'s modernist treatment of Los Angeles is far more crucial and revealing. Throughout *Heat*, and beginning with the opening scene, Mann is constantly leading us on a tour of the imagery of the mass transit systems of Los Angeles. With this robbery it's specifically the freeways, but there are also, as we have seen, the tracks of the MTA and, later, the taxiways and runways of LAX. By 1995 Mann was no doubt aware of the way in which the freeway and other, related mass transit operations had become a byword for modernism, systems synonymous with the rapid exchange of people and ideas from the past to the future. In *Heat* he capitalises on these concepts, rendering Los Angeles as a city to be moved *through* and where such movement is an indicator of capability, intent and productivity. In the film the characters are never encumbered by the crippling traffic jams and suffocating smog normally associated with LA's automobile culture. The film presents a somewhat idealised version of transportation in the city, something akin to Reyner Banham's "autopia" or the Disneyland attraction called *Tomorrowland*, where patrons can visit the freeway of the future and experience "driving" free of collisions or jams.[10]

The armoured car robbery proceeds perfectly to plan up until the point where the highly unpredictable and amateurish Waingro feels his masculinity is being threatened by one of the guards. The guard, deaf from having his eardrums blown out by the shock wave of the charge the crew used to gain access to the vehicle, cannot hear Waingro's demands for him to "move back". Waingro, taking this as a refusal to cooperate, kills the guard before the crew then flee to their cars. The chaos of Waingro's psychopathology temporarily disrupts any sense of control or rationality represented by McCauley or Los Angeles up to this point. As Waingro prepares to shoot the guard Mann frames him in front of a multistorey parking lot, its dark and vacant spaces mirroring the black holes of Waingro's hockey mask – we know that he's the archetypal psycho of *Heat* because he is made up like this, like a bogeyman with a mask that's not too dissimilar to Michael Myers's in *Halloween* (1978). Elliot Goldenthal's score completes the idea of emptiness with its echoing, almost hollow drumbeats disappearing into the distance of the city.

The crew escape and McCauley is next seen exchanging paperwork with Nate, his handler of sorts. They have met in another multistorey car park – transportation again – that's clearly in the downtown core of the city. The towers of glass and steel loom up in the background although you can sense Mann's frustration with exposing them properly on celluloid as they appear quite black and formless here. Nevertheless, the fact that McCauley and Nate choose to conduct their criminal business in the downtown area bespeaks volumes about the Los Angeles of *Heat*. In this film, crime is not something that's relegated to the seedy recesses or outward bounds of the city. The Los Angeles of *Heat* is a city of industry and opportunity throughout, where transportation allows the free movement of people, information and, most importantly, criminal activity.

A tour of the domestic spaces of McCauley, Shiherlis (Val Kilmer) and Hanna now follows and each is fraught with loneliness or marital angst. Architecturally these spaces are very linear with lots of bisecting lines and parallel shapes and each is encased in glass in one way or another. McCauley goes off to a bookshop where he has an encounter with Eady, a clerk at the bookshop and someone looking for a meaningful connection with a man. They end up back at her house above Sunset Plaza, a hillside spot so high above the city that it has, in the words of Thom Andersen, "jetliner views".[11] From Eady's balcony Mann shoots the night-time sprawl of Los Angeles with a very wide-angle lens. The sheer size of the city – 1302 square kilometres – is made clear in what is probably Mann's first real treatment of the Los Angeles horizon. The magnitude of the scale in these shots is matched only by the extent of light pollution that Mann shows emanating from the city's sodium vapour street lighting, something that reminds us of the three-dimensional nature of cityscapes at night. As Mann shows here, rather than a vast settlement that lies on a flat plane, the Los Angeles of *Heat* exists in all three dimensions, the X, Y and Z axes. The light pollution reflects up and off the bottom of the cloud layer and produces what Mann refers to in the commentary for *Collateral* as the feeling of a "dark afternoon", a weirdly luminous or crepuscular aura that suggests a city in 24hr operation, where there is no optical demarcation between day and night.

By this point in the film we can see what Los Angeles has become for Mann, a more updated, more contemporaneous and more evocative variant of Chicago. Mann notes:

> As interesting as I found Los Angeles before I shot the film Heat, I find it even more exciting now. Because of the way it's laid out, lots of people move through self-imposed cultural ghettos that track through different parts of the city's topography… It's a culturally complex, commercial-industrial conurbation.[12]

HEAT AND LOS ANGELES

Figure 11. Heat

Mann's comments are revealing about Los Angeles and how it arose as a city. Rather than emerging from a core district of houses and factories clustered around, say, a river or port, Los Angeles coalesced from a series of independent villages and small towns, similar to the way in which water pools when encouraged, or simply forced. More often than not it was only the freeways that became the boundaries or separations between these previously unincorporated "ghettos" and yet, despite the fact that Mann acknowledges this aspect of the city as something fascinating for him, it is not an element of Los Angeles that *Heat* seeks to portray. It would not be until 2004's *Collateral* that Mann would explore the ethnic fragmentation of the city, where the notion of a decentralised space would prove central to the story's themes of existential isolation and abandonment. In *Heat*, Los Angeles is many things, but heterogeneous is not one of them.

Even in scenes such as the one following McCauley's tryst with Eady, where Hanna visits his informant Albert Torena to berate him for not meeting up when they had agreed, the location – a very old varrio called Dogtown – still feels part of Mann's total vision for the city. At the time of shooting Dogtown (which takes its name from the dog pound located in the area) remained a totally unincorporated part of the Los Angeles area and one not patrolled by the LAPD in any way. The dog-fighting pit and the car chop shop, both of which Torena runs in the film, were real, working locations and were situated next to an unlicensed abattoir. And yet, despite of all this seemingly alien *mise en scène*, Mann brings Dogtown firmly into the fold of his vision for the Los Angeles of *Heat*. The scene establishes Dogtown as part of the city's larger technological and industrial base via a fleeting but revealing shot of a sulphur refinery behind Drucker – Hanna's deputy – as he gets out of the car. The huge pile of yellow sulphur and the various pieces of heavy plant machinery

125

help to render the potentially lawless Dogtown as a location equally as valid as the precious metals repository or the Far East National Bank. They are all loci of industry and activity that support the post-millennial reading of Los Angeles in the film.[13]

In the ongoing tour of the domestic and crime dramas of its principal characters, *Heat* continues to chart the geography of a Los Angeles that is looking headlong into the future, even while lamenting the past. Scenes such as the ghostly shootout between McCauley's crew and Roger Van Zant's hired guns at the abandoned drive-in movie theatre on Centinela Avenue offer the audience a meeting point for the old and the new, where defunct movie nostalgia fuses with end of the millennium criminal pursuits. Where *Heat* seems to offer other, older architectural forms or ideas (the diner where Breedan reports for work after his release from jail) or cultural ideas (the after-hours club where Hanna meets Torena), it is actually drawing upon progressively modern aspects of Los Angeles as they existed in 1995. To take the diner, the exterior shot that Mann gives us reveals that it is actually the famous Bob's Big Boy restaurant on Riverside Drive, a building designed by Wayne McAllister, an architect noted for his adherence to the Googie style and streamline moderne, movements both intensely concerned with space age ideas, the incorporation of transportation elements such as fins and chrome and sloping, curvy lines. These influences, coupled with the undeniably Hopper-esque quality of the diner – the angle from which Mann captures the building accentuates the sloping, curvy lines just as Hopper does with the diner in *Nighthawks* (1942) – mean that, however antithetical it seems to the towers of glass and steel downtown, Bob's Big Boy is in truth just as modern as they are, just as much a manifestation of LA's post-millennial reach as the US Bank Tower.

Other moments in *Heat* support its future-looking aspect, not so much by virtue of the architecture to be found there but by the ideas. When Hanna goes to meet Torena and his brother at an after-hours club in Koreatown, there's a shot of Hanna standing in the club office where he is on the phone to his deputies organising the wire tap and transponder surveillance of McCauley's crew. On the wall behind him are portraits of Malcolm X and Miles Davis, both ultra-cool progressives in their respective fields and men who looked to the future for as yet unheeded ideas and ways of being. Although, as Mann notes in the commentary for *Heat*, Malcolm X would have excluded after-hours clubs like this from the awareness he tried to generate, his presence on the wall of the office nevertheless fits with *Heat*'s overall view of Los Angeles as a site of the future, both for architecture, industry and, here, ideas about racial

Heat and Los Angeles

Figure 12. *Heat*

equilibrium (something that Mann would explore more intricately in 2001's *Ali*). Equally, the image of Davis playing the trumpet – alongside the way his image bolsters Mann's view of Los Angeles – invokes both the time the musician spent in California (he lived in a house on the Malibu beachfront) and his presence in other works in Mann's career, such as when he played the role of Ivory Jones in a 1985 episode of *Miami Vice* or the way in which he heavily influences the jazz club scene and overall ethos in *Collateral*.

When *Heat* does occasionally diverge from its ultra-modern, future-looking aspect, it is to draw upon those outdated remnants of an older or trashier Los Angeles, something theorist Thom Andersen refers to as "the pastness of the present".[14] These are the environments in *Heat* where a kind of aesthetic arrested development is used to comment on the moral degeneracy of certain characters. After fleeing from McCauley's crew following the armoured car robbery, Waingro is next seen in a grubby motel room with a young prostitute. The scene is highly critical of Waingro and rightly so. He is the true psychopath of *Heat*, a detestable white supremacist with a swastika tattoo, beneath which it says "White Power". He remains a petty criminal throughout the film, a small-time player who murders the girl before him with total indifference. The choice of location and the décor of the room – all drab colours and awful wallpaper – show that Waingro can never occupy those modernist environments of Los Angeles traversed by the professionals of *Heat*. He is corralled or relegated to the dingy and more rundown parts of the city and is blocked in these environments by Mann in such a way as to highlight both his capacity for violence and his insignificance. In the motel scene he looms in towards the camera as he grabs at the prostitute's head, consuming the screen space with his attempt at profundity – "the grim reaper's visiting with you", he intones to the girl. But the framing of the shot, like the décor of the room, conversely cuts Waingro down to a marginal figure, rendering him pathetic even in his moments of extreme violence.

One of the finest editorial decisions Mann then makes in *Heat* is to immediately follow the shot of Waingro grabbing the girl's head with an abrupt cut to a close-up of a bartender snapping off the cap on a bottle of beer. The rapid cut to this image offers a metonym for Waingro's horrible treatment of the girl, while also providing a through line to this next scene, one that further diminishes Waingro's stature via its *mise en scène* and dialogue. The beer is for Waingro who now sits in a grubby little bar. He is advertising his supposed criminal credentials to the bartender who, it becomes evident, also moonlights as a middleman between the corrupt businessman Van Zant and petty criminals like Waingro looking for work. Waingro extols his prison history – SHU Pelican Bay and New Folsom, B Wing, both tough, end-of-the-line prison environments in the greater Los Angeles area – before Mann cuts to a long shot of the bar, at the end of which, perched on a stool and thoroughly alone, sits Waingro, imbued with a false sense of pride and purpose. The tacky neon sign reading "Cocktails" above his head is perhaps a sly attack on Waingro's self-inflated sense of masculinity. At the very least it forges a link back to the shady motel where only moments ago he murdered the girl.

Heat's modernising of the city of Los Angeles extends also to its view of the LAPD. When we look at the character of Hanna we see a detective who, while riddled with personal and familial failings, is absolutely driven to avenge crime and serve the moral order. There's an addiction to police professionalism here, both because it provides Hanna with an adrenaline high and because the film is seeking to represent anew what a city police force should be like. In the 1940s and 1950s the LAPD was a potently corrupt institution that, in effect, ran Los Angeles. With Mann, those shameful days are gone and what stands in their place is *Heat*'s representation of the police as a homogeneous family, career cops who extol the virtues of work and professionalism as much as McCauley's crew do. There's no police corruption in *Heat* and the film's only instance of police ineptitude – during the scene where Hanna has staked out the precious metals depository, hoping to catch McCauley's crew in the act, one of the officers stumbles back and bangs the side of the trailer, alerting McCauley to their presence – actually serves to benefit Hanna's deductive abilities, allowing him to intuit the eventual location of McCauley before the airport shootout.

Heat's modernising of the LAPD also extends to the environment in which they station themselves. Most likely filmed at the Parker Centre, the real HQ of the LAPD between 1954 and 2009, the police station scenes in *Heat* are notable for how much they avoid including any reference to those hallmarks of Los Angeles that were perhaps once associated with police corruption or what could now be considered old-fashioned forms of representation. City Hall, which features prominently on the LAPD badge, is ignored in *Heat*, both in general shots of the cityscape and also when Hanna and his deputies are very specifically shown at police headquarters. In the first instance, this avoidance of City Hall, a building that Ed Soja considers indicative of the "citadel" of Los Angeles, is possibly down to its association with seminal but now period police dramas such as *Dragnet*, a TV show that reinforces Soja's notion of City Hall as a dominating and perhaps even manipulative force in a city full of what Mike Davis termed "fools, degenerates and psychopaths".[15]

Heat sidesteps this, avoiding all notion of Los Angeles as a city run from the top down by dismissive Sergeant Friday types. There are no obvious power structures here, no indication that the power of Los Angeles comes from a civic core of mayoral or police privilege. Instead, *Heat* shows Los Angeles to be a place of relative moral equilibrium, where both crime and justice have equal weighting and where one is as competent as the other. Secondly, via an architectural understanding of the Los Angeles of *Heat* – something that's inseparable from its general narrative – the police station locale that Mann chooses to use once again complements the film's wish to reconstruct Los Angeles as something coolly evocative of modernism. The MCU control room where Hanna and his team piece together the movements of McCauley's crew is all smoothly poured concrete, symmetrical patterns of small windows and a linear overhead lighting system that reinforces spatial depth. There's no sense of hierarchy here, of the clichéd scenario of a mayor pressuring the police captain, who in turn takes to berating his underlings. Still less is there any reference to those popular and outdated images of embattled detectives chain-smoking their way to an early retirement or the taupe wallpaper and cheap wooden desks of the *Dragnet*-era situation rooms.[16]

Hanna now closes in on McCauley. He's in a police helicopter, navigating the spaces between the vertiginous towers of downtown Los Angeles. In a film of standout visual moments, this sequence is Mann's nocturnal masterstroke, a series of lustrous images so obviously in love with the X, Y and Z axis linearity of the Los Angeles sprawl at the end of the twentieth century. It's a moment that reconfigures and outdoes the heavy-handed futurism of the LA flying sequences that open Ridley Scott's *Blade Runner*. Minus the hellish columns of fire and the portentous electro scoring by Vangelis that made the city so specific in that film, the Los Angeles of *Heat* carries with it an epic but relativistic openness, the option to inscribe upon its limitlessness whatever you will, be that good or bad. This fits well with the film's modernist ambitions because, if *Heat* is about anything, it's about the ability of a person or indeed a city to determine something new for itself, to remake old ideas and dismiss hackneyed forms of representation. The open expanse of the Los Angeles skyline here distils these ideas and writes them large across its breathtaking horizon, conjuring something akin to *Blade Runner*'s science fiction but without the didacticism of that film's production design (a sensibility Mann would return to again and again with *The Insider* and then *Collateral* and *Miami Vice*).

As *Heat* moves through its vast narrative tapestry, through the pivotal meeting of Hanna and McCauley at Kate Mantilini's on Wilshire Blvd, through the odd silence and noise of the bank robbery and its noirish fallout, where many of the principal characters are killed, through Hanna's deterioration as McCauley seemingly escapes and then his regeneration after his stepdaughter's tragic suicide attempt, Mann continues to tease out the futuristic potential of Los Angeles. It's there in the Jungian undertones of Hanna and McCauley's discussion of dreams and regret, in the passing acknowledgement of Michael Heizer's modernist sculpture *North, East, South, West* at 444 South Flower during the bank robbery, at the famous house on stilts at 1219 Dodds Circle (a building that defies the hillsides of East Los Angeles and upholds the X axis) and in the sci-fi treatment of familiar locations such as the Wilmington refineries, glimpsed as spaceships when McCauley is driving past the area after having killed Trejo. When the climax of *Heat* does arrive, it seems perfectly apt that it should happen against the backdrop of the Los Angeles airport, LAX, a major hub for the movement of people, commerce and information. By 1995, the year of the film's release, LAX was handling over 53 million passengers, 732,000 aircraft and more than 1 million tons of freight a year. The choice by Mann to locate the epic climax of *Heat* here, amid the complex taxiways and terminal buildings, is a perfect final statement about the modernist regeneration of Los Angeles that the film seeks to evoke.

Having caught sight of McCauley exiting the Hotel Marquee after he has killed Waingro for his earlier betrayal, Hanna gives chase and pursues McCauley on to the runways of the night-time airport. Here the two men are allegories, metaphorical titans who have navigated the future landscape of Los Angeles and ended up here at a paragon of modernity.

If there's one shape that defines the airport shootout and complements its summation of *Heat*'s concerns, it's the cube, that most modern of shapes. The climax of *Heat* is a cubist dream of airline cartage containers, luggage crates and chequered junction boxes, around which Hanna and McCauley skirt and weave in pursuit of domination over the other. The odd interstitial silence of the bank robbery returns to this deadly meeting of cop and robber, the only sounds being the occasional reverse engine blast of landing planes, the barely audible whisper of crickets in the grass and a customary piece of electronic scoring that is so well integrated into the visuals that it's hard to acknowledge.

As the two men move through this cubist space their shadows appear disconnected from their bodies, so tangential is Mann's lighting of the scene. As with the similarly cataclysmic moments in *Manhunter* and *Thief*, this collision of minds at the end of *Heat* is fraught with notions of divided psyches and bodily fragmentation. Consider the shots at 2:33:02 into the film, when McCauley takes aim at Hanna from behind a freight container; Hanna appears to be in two places at once as McCauley shoots at him. We are never sure which "Hanna" is the shadow and which is the real man. McCauley then crosses the path of a taxiing aircraft and heads off into the barren scrub behind the runway blast walls. With Hanna's shotgun now empty, he's reduced to using his handgun, its ivory-style handle reminiscent of the affectation of some Old West sheriff. The editing rhythms now begin to reflect the internal state of each man. McCauley is treated with some rapid and oblique cuts, some point-of-view shots and some objective glimpses of him as he looks for a redoubt amid the cubes. Hanna, by turn, is graced with much longer shots and shot/reverse shot editing. He is calm and composed, closing in on his quarry with care. As McCauley's shadow betrays him and he is shot and killed by Hanna, the landing aircraft overhead reminds us that, while these men are crafting the epic endings to their respective stories, Los Angeles remains a functioning modern metropolis where information and people converge. As Mann notes:

> And you see the amount of air traffic and it's almost as if the air traffic in my mind is almost a metaphor for this whole layer of data. You'll see eighteen planes, the lights of eighteen planes all lined up on the approach to LAX, on two runways, one and a half minutes apart, helicopters all over the city. And you see this three-dimensional layer, you see the microwave dishes, the data being transmitted … this is Los Angeles.[17]

Heat is perhaps the quintessential expression of Michael Mann's status as an auteur up to this point in his career. The film's rendering of Los Angeles as *the* modern city reclaims it from those more prevalent conceptions that declared it moribund and adrenalises it with a sensibility still being imitated today with films such as *Nightcrawler* (2014) and TV shows such as *Southland*. *Heat* takes what was patinated and flat about Los Angeles and crafts something dimensional and modern, a post-millennial hub of crime and punishment that, twenty years later, has aged remarkably well. In its moral relativism and architecture, its psychology and representations, *Heat* summarises Mann's work from the films before it and points out the path that would lead the director to his next film, 1999's *The Insider*.

> **Key scene suggestion for Los Angeles –** Hanna's night-time helicopter flight over downtown L.A as he chases McCauley to their coffee shop meeting.

Notes

1 Deryck Swan, "*Heat*: An Appraisal", *Media Education Journal* 50 (2011): 22.
2 *Los Angeles – City of the Future?*, documentary, BBC Open University Productions, 1992. Available in four parts on YouTube.
3 Leader article, "The Shock of the Old", *The Guardian*, 25 August 2007, https://www.theguardian.com/commentisfree/2007/aug/25/comment.comment2 (accessed 22 February 2023).
4 *Mann Made: From L.A Takedown to Heat* documentary interview TV special, BBC; first broadcast 23 February 1997. Available on YouTube in two parts.
5 Swan, "*Heat*: An Appraisal", 22.
6 Thom Andersen, *Los Angeles Plays Itself*, 2003, video essay, edited by Seung-Hyun Yoo, narrated by Encke King. Available on YouTube.
7 *Heat – Return to the Scene of the Crime* documentary featurette on Blu Ray edition of the film.
8 The exception here – and quite deliberately so – are the heinous crimes of Waingro (Kevin Gage), the archetypal Mann psychopath who, in *Heat*, remains distinct from McCauley's crew because of his behaviour, his look and where he frequents in the city.

9 *Los Angeles – City of the Future?*
10 The concept of *autopia* as found in Banham's book *Los Angeles: The Architecture of Four Ecologies*, University of California Press, 1971.
11 Andersen, *Los Angeles Plays Itself.*
12 R. Barton Palmer and Sanders Steven (eds), *Michael Mann: Cinema and Television Interviews, 1980–2012*, Edinburgh University Press, 2014, 55.
13 As does the name of the bank in *Heat* – Far East National – which helps invoke the futuristic influence of the Far East on American West Coast culture as in *Blade Runner* or *Die Hard*.
14 Andersen, *Los Angeles Plays Itself.*
15 Mike Davis, *City of Quartz: Excavating the Future in Los Angeles*, Verso, 2006, 251.
16 This is something Mann reinforces on page 332 of his novel, *Heat 2*: "Downtown at Parker Centre, Hanna sweeps into RHD. The fluorescent lights give off a magnetic hum. The concrete-and-glass offices of the Major Crimes Unit spread across the floor, open plan, industrial minimalism." Michael Mann and Meg Gardiner, *Heat 2*, HarperCollins, 2022.
17 *Mann Made: From L.A. Takedown to Heat*, Part 2.

CHAPTER NINE

The Insider and Cinematic Space

> Who would guess that a story like this – set mostly in courtrooms, hotel rooms, newsrooms and cars – could be turned into a suspenseful, heart-pounding thriller?
>
> Margaret A. McGurk

McGurk's quote about the seeming incongruity between the spaces and locations used in *The Insider*, Mann's last film of the 1990s, and its success as a thriller is instructive for what will follow in this chapter. The film, the story of tobacco whistleblower Jeffrey Wigand (Russell Crowe) and his tense relationship with CBS producer Lowell Bergman (Al Pacino), marks the beginning and end of several important stages in our search for Mann's auteur status, not just in terms of space but also story material and the medium of film itself, celluloid. *The Insider* is to date Mann's last fully fledged use of celluloid in the making of a motion picture. It also marks the end of his formal experimentation with the symmetry and balance of the Renaissance aesthetic, something of profound importance to films such as *Heat* and *Thief*. Lastly, it is the first of his films to deal with a complete and expansive true story, albeit with a degree of dramatic licence based upon reported but unproven claims by the Wigand family. As the chapter proceeds, these factors will be dealt with in more detail. They will, however, remain subsidiary to the assessment of *The Insider*'s greatest quality, its bold experimentation with cinematic space and its role as a key determinant of Mann's future work.

From the film's very first moments, spatial construction and its ability to comment upon point of view and experience is something that is foregrounded, literally. The opening image of *The Insider* is a point-of-view shot of a blindfolded man, later revealed as Bergman. The depth of field can only be a centimetre or so but the weave and pattern of the fabric of the blindfold is clear and in focus. This is a bold, destabilising way of beginning a film, one that uses space – or its complete reduction – as a way of aligning audience with a particular character and creating

135

a sensory, tactile experience. A reverse shot from just outside a moving vehicle makes it clear that the blindfolded man in being escorted in a 4x4 by soldiers of some kind. This image of the blindfolded man coupled with the exterior *mise en scène* of desert shrubbery, dust and posters of Grand Ayatollahs, immediately brings to mind the common themes of Middle Eastern kidnap and government rendition that would characterise much of American cinema from 2002 onwards.

However, this was the late 1990s and Mann quickly allays our fears, again through the use of space. A cut and this time the space within the vehicle has been opened up some more. We have been permitted an exterior close-up of the blindfolded man, a move that thereby humanises the point of view from moments ago. We see that the man is "looking" around, clearly inquisitive about his surroundings. The mixture of Pacino's gestures and the spatial proximity to his face means that we instinctively feel that this man is not in danger, despite the connotations of his situation. The convoy passes through a military checkpoint at speed and Mann's camera, now on the side of the road, uses a crash zoom – that aspect of cinematographic vernacular so common to the 1970s conspiracy thriller that *The Insider* builds upon – to close the space between us, the convoy and a young Lebanese soldier smoking (the only instance of actual smoking in the entire film). The moment has a wonderful sense of accidental verisimilitude to it that helps bolster the film's real-life credentials.

The convoy now reaches the town of Baalbek and winds its way at speed through the close quarters and tight corners. The blindfolded man turns his head to follow the sounds of music being projected from outdoor speakers. Other diegetic sounds of the street intoxicate him and capture his attention before the convoy arrives at a building and he is hurriedly escorted inside. The blindfolded man is seated in a room on a single chair. In a separate shot, the Shia cleric Sheikh Fadlallah is introduced. Spatially, this scene is all about establishing an oppositional tone that is sometimes classicist in its proportions and balance, like some great piece of Palladian architecture, and sometimes jagged and disruptive, as when one character or another goes on the offensive. A blend of over-the-shoulder shots and classical perpendicular two shots lends the exchange a sense of convivial formality while cleverly avoiding the commonplace atmospherics of paranoia and incipient violence that we have come to associate with the whole "Westerners in the Middle East" scenario. When Mann wants to punctuate a moment, such as when Bergman refuses to allow the Sheikh access to CBS's interview questions ahead of time, he then spatially disrupts the formality by surging across the 180-degree line and completely reversing the shot composition.

THE INSIDER AND CINEMATIC SPACE

At the end of the scene a clever, near over-the-shoulder shot of Bergman sees the Sheikh sneaking out of the meeting after a date and time for the pivotal CBS interview is agreed. Bergman then removes his blindfold and moves to the window to phone Mike Wallace, the famed CBS journalist and broadcaster. Before speaking Bergman whips aside the curtain that had obscured the room from the wider world. What is revealed is a beautiful panorama of this Lebanese town, an image of space that forms a strong counterpoint to the tight organisation and orientation of the meeting room. This use by Mann of a larger vista as glimpsed through the framing of an internal space, such as a window, is used throughout *The Insider*, most often as it is here, with a character on the phone or engaged in some other work activity. In this respect the image evokes Edward Hopper's 1953 painting *Office in a Small City*, with its office worker figure looking out on a much larger cityscape from the confines of a small space. In the work of Hopper and Mann, space is often used to suggest the perception of an exterior world that is, at times, wholly distinct from the interior environment of the character. While Bergman in *The Insider* is not trapped by the interior spaces he inhabits – unlike the vast majority of Hopper's protagonists – he and, to a degree, Wigand are nevertheless frequently presented as viewers of the outside world from an interior space. Wigand's introduction in the next scene is equally revealing in this respect, in the way that the spatial dimensions of his environment are manipulated by Mann in order to arrive at quite an affecting statement about this character's mental condition.

Jeffrey Wigand is first seen leaving his ghostly monochromatic office at the Brown & Williamson tobacco company in Louisville, Kentucky. Via framing and some shallow depth of field Mann marginalises him, excluding him – quite literally, as it happens – from the party his scientist colleagues are having on the other side of the glass. Wigand then leaves his office for the last time via an odd, almost waist-height camera shot that recalls something the great Japanese director Yasujiro Ozu would do. The office door closes behind him, swiping across the screen from right to left, a camera move that will also characterise Bergman's exit from the CBS building at the end of the film. We then cut abruptly to an aggressively close tracking shot of Wigand as he descends in the lift and makes his way across the Brown & Williamson lobby for the last time as an employee. Mann keeps the camera extremely close to Wigand's right ear and moves with him at this point-blank range until he approaches a security guard. The space between the lens and Wigand's head is about as reduced as it could be before the image lost meaning or became abstract, and the effect is quite startling. The shot generates something that a conventional

Figure 13. Insider

point-of-view shot would not, namely the sense that Wigand's mental state is chaotic and his movements are unsynchronised. As Mann notes in *Directors Close Up*: "Wigand was an obsessive-compulsive, very dystonic, very arrhythmic, and I wanted to bring you into his perceptions. So there's a lot of use of negative space…"[1] This extreme close-up tracking shot employed by Mann allows us to understand Wigand from the outset, just as the interior blindfold shot did with Pacino's character at the start of the film. Recourse to a conventional point-of-view shot here would have denied the audience this dissonant view of Wigand as an unstable force who erupts out of the Brown & Williamson building intent on doing something radical.

Mann's use of negative space in *The Insider* extends across several characters and a series of different scenes, often for subtly different but interconnected reasons. And although such framing and camera placement also appeared in *Heat* and *Thief* – normally related to those moments of inner loneliness experienced by McCauley and Frank respectively – such devices reach their apotheosis in *The Insider*. In the next scene Wigand is viewed via yet more hand-held, aggressive close-ups as he enters his mansion home earlier than usual. As Wigand pours himself a drink, one of his daughters sits on a couch watching cartoons. Look again at the perfect alignment of the pattern on the cushion with the surrounding sofa and we can see how Mann uses space and, here, *mise en scène* to reflect Wigand's obsessive-compulsive viewpoint. This linear reflection of an interior condition was also present in McCauley's Pacific beach house in *Heat*, but in that film its use is more obtuse and less well integrated into the narrative (*Sight & Sound* editor Nick James suggests that, in a film with a less established director, the scene in *Heat* where McCauley stands by his balcony window and looks out to sea would have been cut – it serves no concrete narrative purpose).² With *The Insider*, however, Mann offers a new degree of refinement of such a technique.

The frequency of aggressive close-ups and hand-held tracking shots continues in a manner that's related to both the evocation of character and the pseudo 1970s conspiracy thriller genre that *The Insider* seeks to revise and modernise. The CBS interview with Sheikh Fadlallah takes place, with Mike Wallace (Christopher Plummer), in his customary style, destabilising his guest with a difficult first question – "Sheikh Fadlallah, thanks so much for seeing us. Are you a terrorist?" The Sheikh replies "Mr Wallace, I am a servant of God." "A servant of God", Wallace responds, "really? … Americans believe that you as an Islamic fundamentalist are a leader who contributed to the bombing of the US embassy…" This last line, perhaps in reference to the 1998 bombings of US embassies in several East African capitals, diverges into a hazy close-up shot of a box being delivered to Bergman's house in Kentucky. The intention here is clear; the use of space and editing to imply a connection between the dangers of Middle Eastern affairs and the threat posed by the story that is literally being delivered to Bergman's door.

By this point in *The Insider* (and indeed Mann's canon as a whole) space, narrative and, as we shall soon see, music have become indivisible components of his project. In how these aspects are deployed by Mann, *The Insider* takes things further still, rendering them wholly integrated into the world of the film. This triumvirate shows but is not showy, is stylish without stylisation, something that Steven Rybin highlights in the introduction to his book *The Cinema of Michael Mann*:

> Expressive mise-en-scène … exhibits what Martin [critic Adrian Martin] calls a "textual economy" … pitched more at the level of a broad fit between elements of style and elements of subject … general strategies of colour coding, camera viewpoint, sound design and so on enhance or reinforce the general "feel" or meaning of the subject matter.³

For Martin, this expressive approach to *mise en scène*, which the majority of Mann's films exhibit, sits between two other types that, taken together, form a kind of cinematic litmus test for understanding film style. At the left end of this spectrum is the "classical" style, an approach mostly – although not exclusively – associated with the golden age of Hollywood (roughly speaking the 1920s to the early 1960s) where notions of style are subtle and transparent, subsumed into the narrative and only revealing themselves when the story really demands it. *The Jericho Mile* is perhaps

Mann's strongest example of this approach. At the opposing end of this scale is the "mannerist" style, the approach that is most easy to deride because, as Martin points out, it "performs out of its own trajectories, no longer working unobtrusively at the behest of the fiction and its demands of meaningfulness".[4] With *The Keep*, however, Mann demonstrated (at least in a partially successful sense) that where style overrides the demands of narrative, a more fantastical or, as Mann put it, *relativistic* world can emerge, one where effects do not always proceed from causes. *The Insider* sits squarely in the centre of this spectrum, an expressive work that reaches new levels of subtlety in its integration of *mise en scène* and narrative but that can also draw upon moments of obvious "style" – the CGI morphing of Wigand's hotel room mural into a diorama of his old home life springs to mind – when called for by that narrative.

The package delivered to Bergman's house turns out to contain the results of a study into the prevalence of people burning to death from falling asleep while smoking. The source of the package is anonymous, but Bergman is put in touch with Wigand by an associate – a nervous associate who is shot very aggressively by Mann with tight framing and huge tracts of negative space to the left of him – at the Food and Drug Administration. The link between these two men has thus been made, although in a tangential manner, and the scene where Bergman calls Wigand for the first time is a typical example of the film's economical handling of *mise en scène* and, specifically, negative space. Using a kind of geographical dialectic that will be deployed throughout the film, Mann films Bergman making that first phone call to Wigand from a payphone in busy downtown Louisville. While Bergman speaks first with Wigand's daughter and then his wife, he is seen wearing rose-tinted sunglasses and simultaneously gesturing to a co-worker in an adjacent coffee shop to bring his drink outside to him. The shot is overexposed by Mann, Bergman's face appearing almost bleached out from the white light, a deliberate ploy that helps to establish the contrast with Wigand's locale. A cut and Mann's camera is now hiding behind the Wigands' sofa and peeking through a doorway into another room where Wigand's wife and daughter are glimpsed in a timid and marginalised way. A cut again and Bergman takes his coffee from Bob, his co-worker, and places the other coffee on top of the phone stand. He explains who he is to Wigand's wife. Mann now shoots Wigand's wife (played by the wonderful Diane Venora from *Heat*) frontally, a very slow zoom-in revealing their familial opulence and all they stand to lose. When Bergman calls again moments later, Mann finally permits a shot of Wigand at work in the office of his home, this time the answer-machine picking up Bergman's request for a

THE INSIDER AND CINEMATIC SPACE

meeting between the two. The way that technology both permits interaction and divides people is a staple of *The Insider* and much of the film's key dialogue exchanges are conducted by phone, fax and pager. The way in which Mann frames these interactions – contrasting locations behind the speakers being one strategy – is the key to infusing the otherwise potentially banal exchanges with zest and pathos.

Wigand's office is wonderfully organised by Mann and production designer Brian Morris. It's a space of evident work and accomplishment but very much along the lines of Wigand's burgeoning OCD. Everything is aligned perfectly and in the choice of porcelain bowls and vases that line the table against the far wall, there's more than a passing reference to the orderly Japanese culture that the real Wigand so strictly adhered to. Mann notes:

> The real Jeffrey Wigand knew Japanese. And his appreciation for Japanese culture is because this is a man who is avidly, very aggressively, ordering the present, because he perceives schizophrenia right over there on the horizon kind of coming his way, so it's a desperate kind of maintenance.[5]

Like the perfectly aligned pattern on the sofa and cushion earlier on, Wigand's office is an external expression of an internal conflict. Within this space, one that Wigand no doubt fiercely protects from outside influence, including his own family, Wigand is in a state of relative peace. Mann's camera, both in its soft angle and subtle movement, is conducive to this understanding of the character at this point in the film, as is the lighting, which is warm and free from harsh shadow. There is lots of space to the left of Wigand but it's not negative and is instead filled with the carefully chosen *mise en scène* of a man who wants to control things.

Counterposed with this sensibility is Bergman in his office as he initiates his first contact with Wigand. Somehow in the spirit of the New Left political movement of which the real Bergman was an important proponent, a movement predicated on dissent, activism and agitation, the scenes of Bergman in his office space are, more than anything, characterised by a relentless and roving camera style that's hand-held and whose movements are dictated by those of Bergman himself. There are abrupt cuts here too as Mann tracks the active process of Bergman's investigative abilities. The lighting is overexposed as it was in the earlier scene of Bergman at the payphone – something somehow suggestive of Bergman's pragmatism and realism – and, most rewarding of all, we have the posters and other images of the New Left philosophy that adorn Bergman's walls.

Whether the famous painting of Cesar Chavez, *Portrait of La Causa*, by Octavio Ocampo, a stylised version of an 1887 photo of the Bedonkohe Apache Geronimo in which he kneels with a rifle in his hands, or the great dissident of the period, Allen Ginsberg, Bergman's office space is all about invoking the revolutionary spirit and political activism of the 1960s. In comparison to Wigand's, it's a messy office too, the desk space littered with papers and the overriding sense of deliberate disarray that accompanied the New Left movement.

As these two men collide, the cinematic space of *The Insider* continues to be used in interesting and often radical ways. As well as a means of commenting on the divergent philosophies of Wigand and Bergman, space remains something that Mann uses as a way of investigating and modifying those traits common to the 1970s' American conspiracy thriller. Paranoia, lack of personal agency, mental instability, themes all clearly apparent in the likes of Alan J. Pakula's unofficial paranoia trilogy – *Klute* (1971), *The Parallax View* (1974) and *All the President's Men* (1976) – or *Marathon Man* (1976) or *Three Days of the Condor* (1976) or *The China Syndrome* (1979). Of the above films, three stand out in particular for how they could be said to presage the corporate/political nature of the conspiracy that lies at the heart of *The Insider*: *The Parallax View*, *All the President's Men* and *The China Syndrome*. Each of these three films, the first two directed by Pakula and the third by James Bridges, prominently features journalists battling against clandestine corporate or government bodies in an attempt to expose a certain truth. It is in this idea of the investigative battle between often very limited individuals and massive, faceless, corporate/political entities that lies the template for *The Insider*'s leftist fight against big tobacco and the US corporate media. In the character of Lowell Bergman we find an amalgam of the revolutionary spirit of Warren Beatty's reporter in *The Parallax View*, Hoffman and Redford's Bernstein and Woodward in *All the President's Men* and Jane Fonda's Kimberley Wells in *The China Syndrome*, all characters who cling to liberal notions of truth and integrity regardless of the cost.

Each of these films, *The Insider* included, also uses the reverse conceit of the unreliable narrator at times as a means of casting doubt on the credibility of the events we witness as audience members. This goes with the territory in the sub-genre of the paranoid conspiracy thriller and is indeed often the source of much of the enjoyment of watching the likes of *The Parallax View* or *All the President's Men*. Is the threat real or just in the headspace of the protagonist? Much of the visual treatment of, say, Wigand in *The Insider* – very tight close-ups, off-centre framing, tracts of negative space – means that we're forced into his character's way of thinking about, and seeing, the world around him, a viewpoint that may not always be trustworthy. Nick James writes in reference to *The Insider*, "It takes place mostly inside Wigand's head."[6] As Russell Crowe plays him, Wigand is a fascinating incarnation but one whose staccato rhythms often threaten to undermine what we might otherwise take as objective reality in the film.[7] Of the many great instances of this in *The Insider* the night-time driving range sequence is perhaps the most subtle and most perfect example.

The scene begins with a return to the kind of beautiful visual abstraction of *Thief* or *Manhunter*, or, indeed, the opening moments of *The Insider* itself. Dots of white litter a dark and featureless landscape. Are we looking at the night sky through Wigand's eyes? Is he seeing stars after his disastrous and dizzying meeting with Brown & Williamson CEO Thomas Sandefur? Lights move into the frame from the right, sitting atop some kind of vehicle. A cut back from this telephoto image reveals the vehicle to be a motorised collector for golf balls. It trundles along in relative silence like one of those rovers on the moon. Another cut and we're shunted back into extreme close proximity to Wigand's face. Mentally, he's becoming unhinged by the fallout of his firing from Brown & Williamson, and cinematographer Dante Spinotti renders this in a chilly palette by giving Wigand a pallor that recalls the almost leached appearance of De Niro or Pacino in *Heat*, bloodless ghouls in the city of the dead. Wigand is clearly in the throes of rage here. He stomps about, thumping his driver on the ground and throwing golf balls. He's also far from hitting his best distances. A long shot now reveals that another golfer is at the range, far away down at the other end of the platform. He wears a suit and has perfect form. Wigand does not notice him at first and neither do we. Wigand's staccato rhythms keep things disjointed and off kilter. He's trying to focus on his drive but, mentally, he is terrorised by the betrayal he has suffered at the hands of his employer. Mann manages to convey all this through some hand-held camera work and some assiduous editorial decisions that evoke the twin feelings of edginess and neurosis in Wigand and his situation.

As the man at the other end of the platform becomes more than just another golfer, the soundtrack is subtly modified to include some abstract electronic notes and clever diegetic noises of what seems to be a plane circling close overhead and a train in the distance. As in the previous scene, where the diegetic blast from the horn of a passing truck signals Wigand's misplaced rage as he phones Bergman, sound effects are once again used to imply a deteriorating mental state and an increasing level of paranoia. The space between Wigand and this other golfer is now figuratively reduced as Mann cuts in closer to him and his perfect golf swing. Wigand tries to dismiss his misgivings but he is now convinced that the presence of this man has suspicious connections to the Brown & Williamson tobacco company. What follows is a beautiful dilation of cinematic time and the suggestion that this mysterious man is both feared and envied by Wigand, whose own golf swing remains mediocre at best. Mann now cuts in close to the other golfer as he makes his solid drive for the last time. An eerie and lonesome soprano voice rises on the soundtrack – Lisa Gerrard most likely – and we then cut back to Wigand's face as he realises who this apparition might be.

Crowe's silent, facial communication of an inner annihilation here is masterful. There's none of the usual cinematic bravado that typically accompanies a threat to our hero's pride and status. This is as much about the real world as Mann can muster and that world includes characters who react to threat in a customary way, typically with a mix of adrenaline and fear. Wigand, like all Mann protagonists, is good at what he does, but psychological warfare is not part of his skillset. Mann cuts back again to the threatening golfer and we watch as he assumes a pose of steely determination, a corporate hitman who uses looks instead of lethal weapons. The scene moves on and the golf ball that was struck three shots ago is still in the air! Mann cuts back again to Wigand's face before the sequence's most beautiful and most abstract shot appears, an image of that same golf ball hitting the safety net at the back of the driving range, something easily in excess of 250 yards. It's a superficially puzzling shot in that it breaks with the point-of-view template established by the rest of the sequence and takes the viewer way out beyond the reach or gaze of Wigand. What the shot does do, conversely, is continue this sequence's reflection of Wigand's fluctuating *mental* state. This shot disassociates both him and us from actual events and projects us into Wigand's fantasy, a dream where Wigand is visualising where the man's golf ball will land (at a distance far greater than what Wigand can achieve). In short, both time and, more importantly, space are manipulated in this scene in order to show Wigand's diminished mental health and this other man's formidable skill, both in golf and as an agent of Brown & Williamson's assault on whistleblowers. Wigand is simultaneously threatened by this man and in awe of his clearly superior golf swing, so much so that the possibility remains that this man is nothing more than a manifestation of Wigand's paranoia and obsessive behaviour.[8]

The floodlights at the range go dark, via another percussive diegetic sound effect, and the mysterious man is now shrouded in blackness like a demon. Out in the parking lot Wigand and the other man return to their cars. The man stares at Wigand as the soundtrack reaches some high, sustained notes typical of a tense horror moment. Wigand then exits his car with his golf club in hand, ready for a physical confrontation. The man, however, drives off as Wigand insists, "You stay away from me." Wigand is then left alone in the parking lot. Mann shoots him from an oddly angled and elevated position. Wigand and his car cast enormous shadows that run from left to right and, standing as he is between the parking bays on either side, it looks as though he is caught in the teeth of some giant urban monster. A slight zoom out and Mann captures perfectly the significantly denuded agency of this man, someone who is nearly at his lowest ebb.

Since *The Jericho Mile*, Mann has evinced a clear interest in cinematic space and the opportunities afforded to him by its exploration and manipulation. In *The Jericho Mile* space was often flattened during the running sequences by the use of telephoto lenses, in order to make a statement about Murphy's entrapment and the physical struggle to liberate himself. With *Thief* the opposite was usually true. Wide-angle shots stressed that the city belonged to Frank, that it was an environment seen from his expansive perspective and it was his to move through and exploit and nobody was going to take it from him. In *The Keep* Mann used vertical pans, reverse zooms and overhead shots to conjure a space fraught with insanity and multi-dimensional dread. With its bars and windows, through which space was viewed, sometimes longingly, sometimes with trepidation, *Manhunter* moved things closer to the kind of Renaissance perspective that would later characterise *Heat*. And with *The Last of the Mohicans*, space was something to be moved through and traversed at great speed by both its characters and Mann's cameras.

Of these various experiments in space, *The Insider* lies somewhere near *Thief*, an obvious bedfellow when we consider how the spatial environment of both films is rigorously determined by the mental state of the central characters. This approach by Mann is less about a tricksy take on the point-of-view film – Brian de Palma's *Snake Eyes* (1998) or Gaspar Noé's *Into the Void* (2009) come to mind – and much more to do with his ongoing desire to provide audiences with what he terms an "internalised experience", as opposed to some traditional and very linear docudrama or character piece. So *Thief* and *The Insider* are not at all obviously point-of-view films in the sense that *Into the Void* is, with its relentless p.o.v. shots, obtuse, singular perspective and savvy marketing; rather, these are films that seek to offer an *approximation* of a life, sketched in often close proximity to their characters and with editing, *mise en scène* and sound designs that try to ape their mental conditions.

Neither is *The Insider* a didactic piece of filmmaking on the dangers of smoking. In 1999, around the time of the film's release, there was no doubt that smoking was bad for you. Hundreds of thousands of people in the US alone were dying each year from illnesses related to tobacco. Despite this, the tobacco industry at this time was a formidable force that expended vast sums of money on litigation and the enforcement of confidentiality agreements. People were buying cigarettes and companies such as Brown & Williamson and Phillip Morris were posting huge revenue streams. And it is here that *The Insider* diverges from those more traditional conspiracy thrillers mentioned above. Unlike *The Parallax View* or *All the President's Men* or *The China Syndrome*, where neither audience nor characters know the truth and seek to find it, by the time the real-life events dramatised in *The Insider* were taking place, everyone knew how damaging smoking could be to the human body. The conspiratorial issue at the heart of *The Insider* then is not that cigarettes are bad for you – "no shit", as Christopher Plummer's Mike Wallace says in the film – but that companies such as Brown & Williamson were making those cigarettes *worse* for you. What Wigand discovered was that Brown & Williamson were adding compounds such as coumarin to their cigarettes, a chemical that increased the nicotine content of cigarette smoke and made it significantly more harmful.

But even this major crime is not really what forms the backbone of Mann's film. It is instead the stimulus for an exploration of the professional response to an existential crisis, a determinant that has cropped up in every Mann film that we have examined so far, bar *The Keep*. There are conspiracy and paranoia, dark shadows and empty spaces in *The Insider*, but ultimately these aspects are part of the main characters' responses to crisis rather than evidence of any actual threat being made against them. Not one gun is fired in the film and the next closest thing, the "bullet in the mailbox" scene, may actually have been entirely fabricated by Wigand, deliberately or as a result of his questionable mental state during this time in his life.[9]

The Japanese restaurant scene, which occurs nearly an hour into *The Insider*, is the first formalised meeting between Bergman and Wigand in the film. It is worth exploring, in a chapter dedicated to cinematic space, for the way in which it replicates and builds upon the strategy of the opening scene of the film, where Bergman met with the Sheikh in Lebanon (it is also another instance of Mann's interest in detailing the influences of the Far East on Western culture that we saw in *Heat* and will see in *Collateral* and *Miami Vice*). The scene begins with the two men, blocked to the left of screen, sitting at a low table in the restaurant. Wigand, speaking in Japanese, places their order with the waitress and then asks Bergman about his early history at the University of Wisconsin

THE INSIDER AND CINEMATIC SPACE

and his mentor, Herbert Marcuse. Mann films this initial exchange in a series of two shots that are emblematic of the burgeoning friendship here. The two shot moves in a little closer as the men reveal truths about the impact of their fathers – another common trait in Mann's work – on their respective outlooks. Bergman then cuts short this discussion and moves things quickly on to the *60 Minutes* interview about big tobacco. Bergman informs Wigand that he needs to know everything murky about his past before Brown & Williamson try to use it in a smear campaign. "I drink ... couple of occasions more than I should have", offers Wigand. Mann directs Pacino's Bergman to take a drink of sake at the delivery of this line from Wigand, perhaps an attempt to suggest that there was a degree of manipulation of him on Bergman's part, a concern that Wigand verbalises later in the film.

Mann continues to move the camera in closer to the two men. The two shot has now become an over-the-shoulder shot of each man as they exchange more barbed remarks about people being nothing more than media commodities to the large TV networks. Traditionally, at this point, where the camera is in close to the characters, the scene would either end or revert to the previous establishing shot that opened the scene. Mann, however, does not do this. He instead cuts to a very destabilising two shot that's perpendicular to the original 180-degree line, where Wigand is now seated on the left and Bergman on the right. The shot has the same wonderful zero-point perspective that Stanley Kubrick loved to use – most notably in *The Shining* (1980) – and this effect is aided by the two stripes of detail on the carpet that run parallel to each other from the foreground to the background. It's as if the world is caught in the flux of some perpetual slippage.

As Wigand questions the integrity and purpose of Bergman's adherence to the *60 Minutes* format (*infotainment*, as Bergman refers to it), this perpendicular two shot is now brutally reversed so that Bergman is on the left and Wigand on the right. The notion that these two men are now heading into stark opposition is thus implied in a dramatic visual and spatial way, but one that avoids the didacticism of the kind of shoddy expositional dialogue that Mann and screenwriter Eric Roth wished to avoid. "It [the shot/reverse shot] would give" instead, as Mann notes, "a punctuation that would signal the conflict"[10] – cinematic space used as an exclamation mark. It's also a bit of technical legerdemain. When considered analytically, this oppositional two shot/reverse two shot technique would require two separate takes of the same dialogue exchange, both of which would then have to be matched perfectly at a

147

key point in the interaction, therefore giving the impression of a seamless transition from one end of the new 180-degree line to the other.

In a further move to avoid the conventional, Mann then cuts back to the tight, over-the-shoulder shots as the men's discussion reaches its most fraught point. "Maybe for the audience", Wigand states. "it's just voyeurism, something to do on a Sunday night. And maybe it won't change a fuckin' thing. And people like myself and my family are left hung out to dry, used up, broke, alone." Bergman's reply is both a formidable defence of the CBS method and a further hint at Wigand's mental deterioration and the dissociative personality that Mann alluded to when he spoke of Wigand's schizophrenia being very nearby: "Are you talkin' to me or did somebody else just walk in the room? ... No, don't evade a choice you gotta make by questioning my reputation or *60 Minutes* with this cheap scepticism." Wigand avoids committing to the interview at this point by diverting attention to his need to phone his daughters before they go to bed. Bergman is left alone at the table and the scene ends with a focus pull that blurs his image and brings into relief the trees and lights outside the restaurant window. The larger framework of the world, its horizons and skylines, is, after all, what Mann truly loves to look at in his work.

When the time comes for Wigand's pivotal decision about whether to testify in the Mississippi court, this notion of the horizon as a framing device attains its fullest realisation. The actual location where Wigand made his choice is Pascagoula, Mississippi, specifically a lawn right on the banks of the Gulf of Mexico where vertiginous trees bisect the strongly linear horizon. For this moment in the film Mann chose to restage the scene in exactly the same location as where the real event happened, not, as he would say, out of some slavish adherence to actuality but because there could not be a better location for the realisation of this decision on film. What's startling is how aligned the real location is with Mann's artistic sensibilities, with his wish to stage the existential dramas of men and women against the endless horizons and vistas of nature. Drawn from the aspect ratio that Mann chose to use for *The Insider* – 2.35:1 – we find images like the one at 1:22:46 into the film, the view of two men reduced to bit parts in the far larger panorama of the Mississippi coastline.[11] The 2.35:1 ratio is used by Mann here to capture the sheer scale of what lies before these men while, at the same time, avoiding the common cylindrical perspective distortion that can occur in this format.[12] The result is a horizon line that is beautiful in its relative flatness, a perfect liminal zone that divides the expansive sky above from the human drama below. That drama is something that unites the two men of the image, Bergman and Wigand, although here they are shown to be responding to it in

THE INSIDER AND CINEMATIC SPACE

Figure 14. Insider

their own distinctive ways. From the different directions of their glances to their carriage and attitude, these men stand before the same existential dilemma but are reacting to it in hugely divergent ways. In this way the moment recalls the painting *Two Men by the Sea* by the German Romantic landscape painter Caspar David Friedrich, an artist whose style at times seems eerily reminiscent of Mann's. As Vincent Boele describes it:

> Friedrich's paintings characteristically set a human presence in diminished perspective amid expansive landscapes, reducing the figures to a scale that, according to the art historian Christopher John Murray, directs "the viewer's gaze towards their metaphysical dimension".[13]

Friedrich's *Two Men by the Sea* foreshadows this image from *The Insider* in the way that it places human figures engaged in deep introspection before this "metaphysical dimension" of nature. At least from *Manhunter* onwards, there is a moment like this in every Mann film, where a character or characters consider the impact of their actions against the enormous backdrop of the natural or urban environment (Mann's 2015 film *Blackhat* features a wonderful instance of this as hacker Hathaway looks to the horizon from a runway and contemplates his future). However, it is in *The Insider* that we find the dimensions of this recurring composition at their most extreme. Here Wigand and Bergman are Mann characters who appear at their most marginalised, dwarfed by the lawn, the water, the trees and the distant horizon. In his continual attempts to thwart the "pan and scanners" – those TV networks and home media companies that crop the filmmaker's image to best fit the dimensions of domestic TVs – these horizons and vistas have become integral components of Mann's work and are perhaps his best weapon in preserving the integrity of his images. The recurrence of these images also reinforces the distinction that Mann seems to perceive between the anomalous and indifferent exterior world of nature and the interior chaos of human experience. He is constantly setting the two in opposition to each other, even in a film like *The Last of the Mohicans*, where the relationship between the two worlds is at its closest and most reciprocal. Look again at the closing shot of *Mohicans* – for all its seeming harmony and calm, this image still holds within it a sense that the distant horizon of the Blue Ridge Mountains is completely indifferent to the dark and uncertain future that the Mohicans now face. These characters are looking for solace in nature but are, in the end, hugely diminished by it. At the close of this sequence in *The Insider*, the distant horizon also proves to be a motivational force for Wigand, a means of making the kind of yes/no decision that Mann favoured so much in *Thief* and *Heat*. Wigand goes to court and makes his crucial deposition.

The immense fallout from this brave deposition results in Wigand's wife leaving him and Bergman being banished from CBS on a forced vacation. Wigand ends up staying in the hotel where he first met Bergman at the start of the film. It's Sunday night and Wigand stops his marking (he's now teaching Japanese and chemistry at a high school) to watch the crucial *60 Minutes* show about his whistleblowing. A vast mural of a man galloping on a horse through a woodland landscape on the wall behind Wigand gives the hotel room an almost endless spatial dimension, a trick of the eye like the best *trompe l'oeil* of Renaissance art.[14] Mann starts with this wide shot and replicates it as he cuts to all the other interested parties who have a hand in Wigand's crusade: first to Bergman and his wife in their holiday beach hut, then to Don Hewitt, and finally to Mike Wallace. When we return to Wigand it is through a tightly framed close-up of his face to the right of frame and the rider on horseback (from the mural) to the left. Mann holds this devastating close-up as Wallace can be heard narrating the *60 Minutes* episode on TV. Crowe communicates the inner annihilation of Wigand as the show reveals that his full interview won't be aired at this time and that Wigand's face and voice have been hidden from the viewing public. The space around Wigand is reduced further still to bold shots of his right temple or left eye. The framing of these images obscures the rest of Wigand's body as the extent of CBS's failure to remain true to its original agreement with him become clear. Wigand is now as vulnerable and physically marginalised as he will be in the film. An earlier vertical pan shot, rising up behind Wigand as he sits alone in his hotel room staring out of the window at the Brown & Williamson building's 10th floor Legal Department, communicates an unsettling sense that

Wigand wants to kill himself now. Like the rear shot of McCauley's head as he exits the train at the start of *Heat*, this rising shot in *The Insider* forces the audience to project themselves into Wigand's state of mind. Only here, rather than a master criminal at the height of his powers, we imagine a broken, former tobacco executive getting up from his chair, running to the window and throwing himself into oblivion.

The final part of the hotel room sequence returns to the bold stylistic departure that we saw earlier at the driving range, where Wigand imagined seeing his tormentor's golf ball hitting the safety net at the very back of the range. Bergman is desperately trying to get in touch with Wigand from his beach hut in the Caribbean. True to the form of the film, Mann is again bringing two people together on the phone who are in very different spatial environments. At first, Bergman has to go through the hotel manager, who is having great difficulty gaining the attention of Wigand from the door of his room. Bergman's mobile reception is ropey, further heightening the tension that's already being communicated by the use of Lisa Gerrard and Pieter Bourke's "Meltdown" on the soundtrack. The track's wonderfully unreal quality and very dreamy rhythm allows what happens next to seem, somehow, perfectly natural within the subjective context that the film has established from the beginning. A profile shot from the left side of Wigand shows him sitting side-on to the mural of the horse and rider. As "Meltdown" continues in its ethereal slumber the mural slowly begins to morph into Wigand's back garden. We see the lawn appear, the flower beds and his daughters' swing set. Wigand is seen silently talking to himself as he turns to look at this diorama of his former life that has replaced the wall mural. His daughters acknowledge his presence and even wave at him. Like Frank's postcard collage of his dream life in *Thief* or McCauley's fantasy about fleeing to Fiji in *Heat*, Wigand's vision of what really matters to him sees Mann once again exploring the surreality that lies at the heart of realism. As the hotel manager barks at Wigand to "get on the fuckin' phone" (at the behest of Bergman), Wigand rises from his reverie, snatches the phone from the manager and slams the door. The "Meltdown" track stops dead and Wigand rebukes Bergman for manipulating him into this position. Now Mann almost reverses the nature of the space around these characters – Wigand is strictly back to reality and filmed with some shaky hand-held camera work, while Bergman is now in the dream world, standing knee-deep in the blue waters of the ocean. The lighting also demarcates these divergent spatial environments. Wigand's room is a pool of darkness punctuated with strong uplighting, reminiscent of those secretive meetings between spies, whereas Bergman's space is saturated in the colour blue, with the incoming waves appearing like ripples in some silky fabric stretched out to the horizon.

Despite his faltering belief in the primacy and sanctity of his career path and the legitimacy of the *60 Minutes* show, Bergman pushes this to one side and successfully manages to talk Wigand down from his state of panic and desolation with appeals to the heroic nature of his whistle-blowing. In the next scene, Bergman recalibrates his motivations in the hugely contrasting, wintry locale of Lincoln, Montana. He has been tipped off about the major FBI manhunt for Ted Kaczynski, otherwise known as the Unabomber, and finds two agents posing as geologists in a local coffee shop. Even as he seriously questions what CBS is doing with regard to the Wigand interview, Bergman is still involved in these side hustles, here threatening to expose the FBI's investigation unless he gets advance notice for his news programme. There's great satisfaction in watching Pacino play Bergman, the intellectual worker, at these moments in *The Insider*. The character is adroit at these social and professional manoeuvres in a way that Wigand is not. Their collision as characters was one of the primary interests Mann had in the material when he first became aware of the story via Marie Bremner's 1996 *Vanity Fair* article, "The Man Who Knew Too Much".

From the Montana sequence, *The Insider* then tracks Bergman's dangerous gambit of leaking to the *New York Times* the fact that CBS Corporate pressured CBS News to pull the inflammatory interview with Wigand from broadcast over fears that the network could face a multi-billion-dollar lawsuit for tortious interference. Spatially, the film collapses more and more into itself as this and the other hallmarks of the paranoid conspiracy thriller signpost the fallout from Bergman's rebellion from CBS. There are some wonderfully bellicose verbal fireworks between Bergman and his boss Don Hewitt (played by the wonderful Philip Baker Hall), while Wigand is shown excelling in his new role as a high school chemistry teacher. At great cost to himself, Bergman finally convinces CBS to air the original interview with Wigand after highlighting that big tobacco's attempts to destroy Wigand's character and reputation in the *Wall Street Journal* were a sham. Ten minutes before the end of the film, Wigand finally receives the credit and vindication for his courageous actions, serving his daughters noodles for their evening meal (another reference to the Far East) as he watches the show. Bergman is in an airport bar waiting for his flight home. Other passengers bear witness to his and Wigand's achievements in exposing the corrupt practices of Brown & Williamson. The truth is out.

The Insider is without doubt a film that bolsters Mann's status as an auteur. It has become as integral to his directorial persona as *Heat* or

Manhunter and continues some of the key determinants found therein. In its fusion of a grand 2.35:1 aspect ratio with some extreme experiments in tight framing and negative space, *The Insider* takes the relationship between character and environment explored in *Thief* and *Manhunter* and shows that such a device is also perfectly applicable to real stories and real people. Where the reality of *The Insider* – some of the scenes of domestic or professional drama, the courtroom and school sequences – gives way to expressing the chaotic interior world of Jeffrey Wigand or the political philosophy of Lowell Bergman, this departure still feels part of the same genetic material of the film. The film's surrealism is never jarring when understood from the subjective viewpoint of either of the main characters, and it is, indeed, a testament to the powers of Michael Mann that he can marshal this spatial interiority without ever resorting to more obtuse or gimmicky point-of-view material. Its use of space aside, *The Insider* continues many other aspects of Mann's growing canon, such as the idea of the binary opposite that was seen in *The Last of the Mohicans* and *Heat* and the obsessive detailing of the practices of work found in *Thief* and *Manhunter*. Lastly, it is a film that accurately perceives the destruction of investigative journalism by news networks beholden to the corporate state.

> **Key scene suggestion for cinematic space – the pivotal scene that takes place on the lawn in Mississippi when Wigand is wrestling with the decision to go to court or not.**

Notes

1 Jeffrey Kagan, *Directors Close Up*, Scarecrow Press, 2006, 174.
2 Nick James, *Heat*, BFI Publishing, 2002, 34.
3 Steven Rybin, *The Cinema of Michael Mann*, Lexington Books, 2007, 11.
4 Ibid.
5 Kagan, *Directors Close Up*, 154.
6 Nick James, "No Smoking Gun", *Sight & Sound* 10, no. 3 (March 2000): 15.

7   Indeed the results of an FBI search warrant that were released just prior to *The Insider*'s release seem to indicate that Wigand may have fabricated many of the supposed threats that were made against him and his family by Brown & Williamson.
8   Stimulating as it is to propose that the driving range sequence is, within the text of the film, a fabrication of Wigand's deteriorating mental state, in actuality it never took place. The real Wigand did indeed observe several figures staring at him in different places over the course of his whistle-blowing ordeal but never at a driving range. Of this decision Mann notes in the Taschen book *Michael Mann*: "Eric Roth and I both felt an obligation to be very authentic and very truthful about what happened. So when we made three characters into one, or when we made an eight-part event into a two-part event, we used a process that collapsed events but kept them authentic." Duncan Feeney, *Michael Mann*, Taschen, 2006, 127.
9   Lucretia Nimocks, Wigand's wife at this time, believes that Wigand planted the bullet in his own mailbox. See D.M. Osborne, "Real to Reel", Brill's Content (July/August 1999), 75–80.
10 Interview with Mann in Kagan, *Directors Close Up*, 176.
11 Interestingly, all Bollywood films released since 1972 have been filmed in this aspect ratio.
12 This distortion takes place when there are horizontal lines in the image that lie above or below the lens axis level. It results in such lines appearing curved. For Mann this is probably something he would wish to avoid, yet Wes Anderson, for example, seeks it out at every opportunity for his zany tracking shots and tableaux.
13 Christopher John Murray, *Encyclopedia of the Romantic Era, 1760–1850*, Taylor & Francis, 2004, 338.
14 The mural was specially commissioned for the film by Mann. The primary artist was John Stewart.

CHAPTER TEN

Ali and Recreating History

> Production designer John Myhre relates the way they rebuilt The Tiger Lounge in Chicago where Ali danced with his first wife Sonji. The former club had become a furniture shop, but "they pushed away the furniture, put up a couple of walls and shot the scenes on the site where Ali's first romance had blossomed".
>
> Claire Denis

If *The Insider* sought to recreate an event, the real-life whistleblower Jeffrey Wigand's battle with big tobacco, then Michael Mann's first film of the twenty-first century would seek to go one better, the recreation of an era. With a production budget of $107 million, his second biggest to date, 2001's *Ali* would chart a key ten years in the career of the eponymous boxer, from the early bout with Sonny Liston to the almost superhuman athletics of the Rumble in the Jungle with George Foreman. After the exploration of Nazism and the macabre in *The Keep*, Native American Indigenous culture in *The Last of the Mohicans* and the battleground of corporate America in *The Insider*, *Ali* represents Mann's fourth foray into what could be termed real history. As theorist Vincent M. Gaine sees it, these historical films border on a kind of movie activism, where their grand narratives take the form of a social conscience and their protagonists "actively seek to improve the world in which they live".[1]

Muhammad Ali is a historical figure who certainly embodies this notion of activism and social engagement, a man who formulated an intelligent counteroffensive against the gargantuan racist structures in place in America in the 1950s and 1960s. He was a dedicated and professional sportsman who used boxing as a means to combat what Mann terms the "de facto apartheid" that existed throughout these times, and he did so with verve, grace, integrity and good humour. That Ali also had numerous wives and girlfriends during this time, could be very antagonistic towards other fighters (notably Joe Frazier), and would take such principled stands against things he didn't believe in that it often damaged his career potential were surely things that Mann must have been aware of when he decided to market the film with the tagline "Forget What You Think You Know". What this chapter aims to do is account for the way in which Mann recreates the reality of Ali and his times and filters it through the prism of the same creative sensibility that gave us *The Keep* or *The Last of the Mohicans* or *The Insider*, those works that show us Mann as the visual historian.

Via this exploration of the film's successes in evoking the streets of Louisville, the ascendant militancy of figures such as Malcolm X, Ali's conscientious objection to the war in Vietnam and his *raison d'être* bout with Foreman in Kinshasa in 1974, the chapter will evaluate the visual and aural strategies Mann put in place to realise his desire to bring the audience into an internalised understanding of Ali and avoid a "Xerox" copy of the man himself, as he terms it. The overall relevance of all of this to the aim of this book lies in making clear how important the pursuit of realism and verisimilitude (whatever those terms amount to in cinema) is to Mann. As was detailed in the chapter on *The Last of the Mohicans*, extensive background research and tailored training programmes for the key roles are always indivisible components of any Michael Mann film. As he has explained previously, whatever the central activity of a character is, the actor playing that role should be able to perform that activity just as well. In seeking to understand a historical period or event, Mann applies this dictum to himself as well, often spending years learning about, say, John Dillinger's life philosophy and its relationship to the Great Depression of the 1930s or models of the post-millennial drug trade in Miami in order to feed this learning into the worlds of *Public Enemies* and *Miami Vice* respectively.

Just as was the case with *The Insider* or *Thief*, the world of *Ali* is presented to us very much through the conduit of the central character. And, like *The Insider* or *Thief*, *Ali* uses a visual strategy that manipulates onscreen space to imply this individual agency, rather than resorting to obtuse point-of-view devices. One thing in *Ali* that Mann adds to his toolkit for tying our perceptions to those of the central character is the subtle use of an interior monologue that permits the audience to witness Ali's decision-making process, his determination to succeed and his occasional fears. As written by Mann, Eric Roth, who worked with Mann on *The Insider*, Stephen J. Rivele and Christopher Wilkinson, these interior monologues have a lyrical quality to them very much akin to those of Terrence Malick in *The Thin Red Line* (1998) or *Tree of Life* (2011). This device, coupled with more of Mann's aggressive close-ups, this time of Ali's face, makes for an experience of 1960s America and Africa that is both authentic in its construction and myopic in its gaze. This tunnel vision is most certainly an intentional aspect of *Ali*'s intent as a film. As he would show to wonderful effect in *Public Enemies*, such a singular gaze helps Mann to avoid making trite and passive historical statements in favour of a boots-on-the-ground sensibility that demands active participation from the audience. As a small but paramount example of this approach, one need only look at how Mann uses his expensive and highly accurate exterior recreation of the Biograph Theatre on Lincoln Avenue in Chicago in *Public Enemies*. In the hands of most other directors the theatre would be treated with lots of widescreen largesse and obvious screen time that went above and beyond the demands of the script. What Mann does is take this important historical element of Dillinger's demise and pass it through the prism of the film's subjective viewpoint so that it's just *there*, present when it's needed to establish location and the gathering of Melvin Purvis and his lawmen and then gone like any other building on the street. As will become clear, *Ali* makes use of this strategy, so that famous sites important to Ali's story – the 5th Street Gym in Miami where Ali honed his skills, the Audubon Ballroom in North Harlem where Malcolm X was assassinated, the Rumble in the Jungle's Stade du 20 Mai in Kinshasa, Zaire – become less about being obtrusive picture postcard icons and more integrated backdrops that support the film's impressionistic stance.

The film begins on 24 February 1964 in Chicago. Ali (a totally committed Will Smith) is out running at night in preparation for what will be a crucial bout against Sonny Liston for the world heavyweight championship. With his hood up and his leather shoes ill suited for running, Ali appears in these opening minutes as a lovable social delinquent and someone totally underestimated by the pugilistic cognoscenti. These opening minutes are captured not on film but a very early stage high-definition video camera – the Sony Cine Alta camera – that, in 2001, formed an important marker in the evolution of Mann's visual style. A low-angle tracking shot captures the saturated whiteness of Ali's hooded top, the whiteness of the walls by the pavement, the cloud cover and the moon overhead. It's evident that these moments are not shot on celluloid. The night sky looks far too clear and detailed, nothing like the usual mass of amorphous black that we have been accustomed to seeing on film. There's a jitteriness at work in the images here, an off-the-cuff kind of visual grammar that would, in retrospect, prove to be the inauguration of a new film-making style from Mann, one that would see him turn his back on the Renaissance formalism of *Heat* and dominate all his new work as far as 2015's *Blackhat* and beyond.

A police car slows to a crawl next to Ali and the officer enquires, "What you runnin' from son?", a sly turn of phrase, the literal answer to which you can imagine being "segregation, racism and slavery". Ali ignores the police and continues running as they drive off to a call. Ali runs past a large white arrow on the tarmac that's pointing in the direction opposite to his – just as McCauley does at the start of *Heat* after he's alighted from the train – and Sam Cooke, whose glorious voice we have heard since the opening seconds singing "Feel It", appears again onscreen. He's singing to a live audience in what could be the famous Harlem Square Club recording of 1963.

From Ali making his pivotal preparatory run in early 1964 to Sam Cooke laying down his historic recording in 1963, the opening montage then takes us to the famous 5th Street Gym in Miami where Ali is seen training, perhaps for the Liston fight or perhaps not, such is the patchwork chronology of these opening scenes. Mann uses a point-of-view shot of Ali pounding the speed bag to both summarise Ali's skill – his trainer Angelo Dundee noted that Ali would open and close the 5th Street Gym – and permit us access to his thoughts as he anticipates the upcoming bout with Liston and remembers his life as a child. The analepsis that now takes us back to Ali as a boy in 1950s Kentucky homes in on his father's adherence to the dominant WASP culture of the time, an adherence encapsulated here by his father's painting of, in the words of the film, a "blonde haired, blue eyed Jesus". The young Ali looks on in confusion; the artwork is beautiful but has no bearing on his world. Ali, even at this age, regards the painting as suspect, another manifestation of what he sees as his father's servility and his "double consciousness", in the words of W.E.B. Du Bois.[2]

More shots of Ali on the speed bag precede another flashback, this time to a young Ali getting on to a segregated bus with his father. As he walks past several white people luxuriating in the front, the credit "Directed by Michael Mann" appears on the back of the young Ali, an authorial stamp on another great Mann protagonist. A point-of-view shot shows Ali looking up at the "Coloreds Only" sign and then noticing the newspaper headline, "Nation Shocked at Lynching of Chicago Youth", a story referencing the real-life murder of 14-year-old Emmett Till in Mississippi in 1955 after he was reportedly caught flirting with a white woman. The man reading the paper then thrusts it forward at the young Ali's face as if to admonish him for letting such a heinous thing happen.

A break in Sam Cooke's ongoing medley then takes us to another principal character of the age, Malcolm X, as he addresses a congregation in his customarily militant manner. As played by Mario Van Peebles, Mann's Malcolm X is an honourable and dignified character but one who is frequently viewed behind things, behind podiums and kitchen tables, encumbrances that restrain his potential and foreshadow his untimely demise. We hear Malcolm's fiery rhetoric as Mann cuts back to Ali training in the gym. Drew Bundini Brown (Jamie Foxx), Ali's corner man and poetry writer, is seen walking into the gym eating an orange but does not receive an official introduction until the next and final component of this audacious montage. Half of the screen is blue, the other fuzzy. A focus pull and into the shot walks Bundini. He's addressing someone just to the right of the shot but it could just as easily be us, the audience:

> I'm called Bundini. Rhymes with Houdini. He was a Jew too. Some people call me Fast Black. Some call me Daddy Mac. Gave Sugar Ray Robinson my power for seven years. My voodoo. My magic. Now Shorty done sent me here to work for you. Call him Shorty 'cause he likes 'em circumcised. Original people. Like Moses. And I was a babe in a basket too. Born on a doorstep with a note across my chest that read … "You do the best you can for him, world." I wanna be your inspiration. Your motivator in your corner. Can I be in your corner, young man?

Foxx's delivery of these lines is off-centre and impressionistic. Framed against the blue of Ali's house wall, addressing an Ali we rarely see, there's the air of a soliloquy here, of performance art and of a character almost breaking the fourth wall (surely something Mann would never actually entertain). This is the lyricism that Bundini was famous for, the poet laureate to Ali's pugilist.

Taken together as a whole, this extraordinary opening montage is one of the most accomplished things Mann has ever shot, a perfect condensation of the complex history and salient events of Ali's times. It's also one of his least characteristic, when viewed as part of his larger canon. In the way the images and sounds float in and out of alignment, in the way any sense of chronology is warped, in its playful manipulation of cinematic convention, the opening sequence is perhaps closest to that other weirdly phantasmagorical entry in Mann's canon, *The Keep*. Like that film, *Ali*'s opening sequence is a dreamy coagulation of textures and contours, specifically an impression of the Civil Rights struggle as seen from Ali's viewpoint, a rumination on racism, boxing, music and religion that is not constrained by time or location. In this regard it is also very closely connected to Aaron Douglas's highly impressionistic series of paintings *Aspects of Negro Life* (1934), a quartet of panels that presents key aspects of the African American experience. The second of these panels, entitled

From Slavery to Reconstruction, is closest in its intent to what Mann wanted to achieve with the opening montage of *Ali*. Like the opening of Mann's film, Douglas presents key portions of the history of the African American experience as a collective memory, a mass thought process that is at once fluid and fragmented. The panel is read from left to right in three sections: the first details the progression from the dark days of slavery to Lincoln's Emancipation Proclamation; the second charts the importance of black leaders in the Civil Rights struggle; the last depicts the ascent of white supremacy as a virulent reaction to black empowerment. With this in mind, when we look again at Mann's opening sequence we find something very similar going on. As part of his reverie we witness the de facto apartheid of Ali's youth (the slavery section of Douglas's panel), followed by the importance of figures such as Sam Cooke and Malcolm X (the black leaders on the panel) and finally the institutionalised racism characterised by the police officers asking Ali what he's running from (the rise of white supremacy as embodied by the Ku Klux Klan on Douglas's panel) and the "blonde-haired, blue-eyed Jesus".

Both in their content and visual design, Douglas's painting and Mann's opening sequence have much in common. Understanding the opening montage of *Ali* as a form of hazy and subjective memory is the key to understanding Mann's approach to recreating the reality of Ali's times. The way that those times are closely tethered to the perception of the main character is indeed a similar strategy to that used in *The Insider* and *Thief*, but that is where the similarities end. As stated above, *Ali*'s closest stylistic bedfellow in Mann's canon, at least if we take the opening sequence as being representative of the whole, is *The Keep*, a film that, as we saw in Chapter 4, remains the great anomaly in Mann's film roster. In terms of how playful the film is with time, structure, memory and objective reality, *Ali* is perhaps closer to Mann's Nazis 'n' Zombies epic than it is to, say, *The Last of the Mohicans*. The majority of Mann's films, *Mohicans* included, operate on what could be termed a "here and now" basis, meaning that their narratives are both linear and completely contemporary relative to their time period. The films start and end in the "now" and do not use devices such as flashbacks, dissolves (an instance in 2006's *Miami Vice* and 2015's *Blackhat* being the exceptions to the rule), dream states or freeze frames to tell their stories. That element of Mann's style that demands realism, verisimilitude and veracity means that his narratives are, generally speaking, as unobtrusive as possible and often totally free of things such as unnecessary exposition, either visual or through dialogue. While *Ali* continues this trend of an exposition-free narrative, particularly in its fight scenes, it also brings into the fold those other, perhaps more flashy, devices that had previously been relegated to *The Keep*. This makes the recreation of history in *Ali* both highly credible and highly impressionistic.

This tension between realism and stylistic impressionism that lies at the heart of *Ali* is not new. As we have seen, it's there in other Mann films such as *Thief* and *Manhunter*, as well as the films of other directors such as Martin Scorsese, most notably *Mean Streets*, *Taxi Driver* and *Raging Bull*. Beyond the fact that it's also about a famous boxer, the last of these three Scorsese movies, 1980's *Raging Bull*, shares another interesting connection with *Ali* that is useful when trying to understand its balance of realism and impressionism. On its release *Raging Bull* was lauded for the brilliant realism of its fight sequences and scenes of domestic turmoil, but only one of these observations is really accurate. The domestic scenes in the film are indeed shot through with a flat and stark realism that makes the brutality of Jake La Motta all the more pronounced and horrifying. But to state that the fight sequences of *Raging Bull* are also realistic is to entirely miss the point of the film's intentions during these moments. What people have misconstrued as realism – the percussive violence, the animalistic sound effects, the sweaty *mise en scène* – are actually part of La Motta's persona and the film's stylistic manifestation of his rage. By and large, the fight sequences in *Raging Bull* are *anti-realist*, cacophonous instances of mortal combat that have more to do with the comic book battles between Superman and Batman than with capturing a boxing match as it actually appears to the fighters and the audience alike. Of course, this was entirely the point, Scorsese's wish (via the genius of DOP Michael Chapman) to present an outward expression of La Motta's inner, sadomasochistic mania.

This teetering balance between making certain things look real and other things look fanciful is something seized upon by *Ali*, albeit in an inverted way. History here is something that is realistic in the ring and often fanciful outside it. As we have seen, the opening prologue of *Ali* establishes a fanciful and impressionistic view of events, the world of apartheid America from within the fragmented space of a collective consciousness akin to Aaron Douglas's panels. Its dreamy sensibility of hazy memory and partial perception bleeds into the film's subsequent portrayals of the dual assassinations of Malcolm X and Martin Luther King, as well as those tender moments between Ali and Sonji Roi (Jada Pinkett Smith) and, most notable of all, the extended sequence of Ali running through the slums of Kinshasa, Zaire, to the track "Tomorrow" by Salif Keita. Between the prologue and these moments, however, we have the first fight of the film, the initially inauspicious bout between

Figure 15. Ali

Ali and Sonny Liston where Mann moves us in the opposite direction to Scorsese, away from fancy and into realism.

The camera starts low, peeking into the ring from underneath the bottom rope. Ali's dancing feet come into view and Mann's camera, wielded by DOP Emmanuel Lubezki, tracks them with a shaky indeterminacy.[3] A cut to Jon Voight's Howard Cosell captures one of the forgotten relics of 1960s live radio broadcasting, advertisements for products such as hair cream delivered by the commentator himself between his remarks on the fight. Here we get a sense of just how effective Voight's uptake of Cosell's mannerisms and speech patterns is; he looks little like Cosell himself but the cadence and timing of Voight's delivery is spotless and reminds the audience of the erudition of the key journalists of the time, figures who would include Walter Cronkite and, from Mann's *The Insider*, Mike Wallace. Mann presents all these initial moments as a series of glimpses, caught from between the boxers' feet, the ropes of the ring and the flurry of fists as the fighters get in some last-minute warm-ups. As the fight nears its start, Mann brings the camera in tight on Ali's face (he is still, at this point, referred to as Cassius Clay, Clay being the slave name forced on his ancestors by white landowners) just as he did with Wigand in 1999's *The Insider*. Historical perspective as personal introspection.

The fight begins and Mann simultaneously moves the camera forward towards Liston while zooming in on his face. The effect is a massive compression of screen space and the depth of field of the ring, as if the weight of events has collapsed into this pivotal moment and the two fighters have been thrust together less by gravity than by history. In conceiving the key fights of Ali's early career, such as this one between him and Liston, Mann has talked of the way he came to recreate their reality through a mixture of the famous blows and images of the time

– such as Neil Leifer's photo of Ali standing over the fallen Liston after the much-debated "phantom punch" – and improvisational boxing generated by the actors on set. This methodology coupled with actually having Will Smith land punches and be hit himself by his opponents (some of whom were actual fighters, such as Michael Bentt) and innovations in miniature camera technology – the Elmocam, a wireless, lipstick-sized device that permitted Mann and DOP Emmanuel Lubezki to interrogate those highly dynamic interior spaces between the boxer's flying fists – helps to generate both fight scenes and a film that has the odd quality of being subjectively immediate while also paying detailed deference to historical record. This is a duality that fully defines both *Ali* and Mann's later historical work, *Public Enemies*, both period films about real figures that pay strict adherence to actual recorded events while, at the same time, viewing them through the filtered subjectivity of a highly mobile brand of cinematography.

Ali manages to overcome the tactics of Liston, including the liniment oil that he reputedly applied to his gloves towards the end of the fight so that Ali would have trouble seeing, and beats him into psychological submission by the start of the seventh round. The moment of Liston's defeat is beautifully captured by Mann. Liston has taken to the stool in his corner and spits out his mouthguard. It roves and flips about on the canvas before coming to what seems like its final position, teetering vertically for a beat and then falling flat just as "Set Me Free" by Dungeon East & Wild Peach drums itself back on to the soundtrack. Contrary to the expectations of much of the boxing community and the press at the time, Ali wins the fight and becomes the world heavyweight champion. He unleashes his famous "eat your words" grimace to the world and acknowledges the presence of his parents and Malcolm X in the crowd as, all the while, Elijah Muhammad watches these events with interest on television.

By the end of this first fight it has become clear that the template Mann is using for his evocation of history is one dependent on this interplay between veracity and impressionism, between factual recreation and subjective speculation akin to something like that found in Aaron Douglas's panels. Like *The Insider* before it and 2009's *Public Enemies*, *Ali* is historical record framed by the limitations and speculations of a character's (or characters') perspective, rendered with an emergent brand of cinematography that now includes digital technology. Furthermore, within the purview of the boxing film genre itself, *Ali* sits closest to Martin Scorsese's *Raging Bull* in the way that it sets in opposition (albeit in an inverted way) the fights and the social/domestic arenas of the period, the former being viewed with some strict adherence to the actual events while the latter are presented as dreamy conflations of time, memory and perspective. The remainder of this chapter will serve to further this reading of Mann's historical storytelling in *Ali* by looking at three additional salient moments in the film: the assassination of Malcolm X, the assassination of Martin Luther King and Ali's jog through the slums of Kinshasa, Zaire.

By the time we reach the scene of his assassination on 21 February 1965 at the Audubon Ballroom in New York City, Malcolm X has moved from the black militancy of his earlier years to the somewhat more restrained, though no less dedicated, pursuit of African American civil rights. As has become customary with *Ali* up to this point, the Audubon assassination sequence refutes the heightened realism of the boxing ring in favour of a more dreamlike and somnambulistic approach, like the slow-motion destruction of Jake La Motta in his fight with Sugar Ray Robinson in *Raging Bull*. The scene begins with Malcolm walking down a corridor to the stage with two associates to his right and left – he's about to give a speech to the Organisation of Afro-American Unity. Martin Tillman's "Ceremony" comes in on the soundtrack, its chamber cello strings providing a seemingly Eastern inflection to Western events, the reasons for which will soon become clear. As Malcolm enters backstage, Mann's camera tracks behind him, still shooting in slight slow motion. We see a graphic on the wall to Malcolm's right of a Japanese woodland scene and then, in the background, the small figure of a woman appears, standing at the entrance to the stage. She is Yuri Kochiyama, the tireless Japanese civil rights worker who fell prey to the anti-Japanese sentiment that flooded the US after Pearl Harbor before going on to live in Harlem and work for Malcolm X and other causes. Here she smiles in admiration as Malcolm takes the stage to rousing applause.

A wide shot from the audience shows that the backdrop to the stage is the reverse of the Japanese woodland scene from moments ago. Mann then cuts back in close to Malcolm's right ear, just as he did with Wigand as he exited Brown & Williamson for the last time as an employee in *The Insider*. The associates who walked Malcolm in now circle the audience as his security team. "Assalamu alaikum", says Malcolm as he quiets the crowd and readies himself to speak. The combination of the dreamy slow-motion photography and the Japanese inflection produces another moment in the events of *Ali* that reminds us not only of this film's approach to the recreation of its history but also the larger interest Mann's recent films have had in the culture of the Far East and its interconnection with American stories. Like the Far East National Bank in

Heat or the Japanese restaurant in *The Insider*, this moment in *Ali* excels in rendering what might be considered a quintessentially American event into something exotic and otherworldly, as if in an attempt to relay the complete absurdity of what happened next.

A disturbance arises in the audience. "Get your hand outta my pocket!", one man bellows to another to create a diversion. Meanwhile a third man gets out of his seat with a sawn-off shotgun and shoots a puzzled Malcolm X in the chest. He is blasted back through a line of chairs before falling hard on to the stage. Mann captures this from above, looking straight down on the fallen figure. The man with the shotgun fires again, quickly followed by five further shots from other men with handguns, while Tillman's "Ceremony" still plays on the soundtrack. As the crowds flee in terror, Mann closes in on Malcolm's face as his pupils dilate and Kochiyama cradles his head as people try to attend to his horrific wounds. As we are shown Ali's reaction to the shooting from his car in Chicago, Al Green's version of "A Change Is Gonna Come" replaces Tillman's "Ceremony" and the scene reverts to a perhaps more typical aural expression of this tragic moment in modern American history. A tear falls from Ali's eye before he pounds his steering wheel in a private expression of rage and regret. It is, however, Mann's subtle genius here in choosing to craft the majority of Malcolm's death scene in a Japanese and not American aesthetic that makes this part of the film so interesting, creatively bold and useful in our discussion of how history is dealt with in the film. This is a history that is, of course, dutiful in its adherence to fact and recorded events – something that Mann takes more than a little relish in pointing out in the director's commentary – but is also singular in its expression of those events.

The assassination of Malcolm X is presented from a disassociated perspective, less his own and more from the position of Kochiyama, the silent witness of all that he represented for the 99%. Tillman's scoring and the woodland backdrop on the stage remind us of Mann's wish to positively destabilise our collective memory of history by rendering this moment in otherworldly textures and sounds.[4] By contrast, the assassination of Martin Luther King in *Ali* is both the same and different. As a restaging of real-world events, the sequence of King's shooting at the Lorraine Motel in Memphis on 4 April 1968 is just as oblique and alien as the scene just discussed. It destabilises our expectations of what we *should* see and instead manages to arrive at a highly idiosyncratic interpretation, one tied closely – like Malcolm X's killing – to an unanticipated perspective. Where King's assassination in *Ali* diverges from this template, it is in the simple fact that, unlike before, here we are denied an actual view of King's shooting. We see the before and after, but Mann withholds the moment when King is hit, standing on his balcony on that fateful Thursday. As we shall see, there are several reasons why he might have done this.

In 1968 Ali was still enduring his exile from boxing, having only served one year of the three-year ban handed down to him for refusing the Vietnam draft of 1967. As Mann noted at the time of the film's release, we never saw the best of Ali in these years, a span of time when he would have reached his physical and strategic peak, had he still been competing. Running up to the film's treatment of King's assassination, Mann conveys Ali's monumental frustrations by relegating him to the tight confines of a petrol station office that people in general and Ali in particular would frequent when seeking shelter from the weather or conversation with others. From this office Ali is shown on the phone speaking to Chauncey Eskridge (Joe Morton), a friend and counsellor to Ali and King in the fight for civil rights. Eskridge is on a public phone next to the Lorraine Motel, tightly framed by Mann's camera, while King and his entourage are one floor up on his balcony. Ali and Eskridge talk about the possible legal grounds for Ali's appeal against the boxing ban while the cover of "All Along the Watchtower" by The Watchtower Four plays on the soundtrack.[5] The two men finish their conversation, and Ali then returns to watching TV while Eskridge makes another call.

While the building Eskridge is standing next to is undoubtedly a motel of sorts, Mann denies us the comfort of an establishing shot or the kind of slow track to the stage that presaged Malcolm X's death scene earlier in the film. What we get instead is an aural signifier of what has occurred, a shot ringing out, to paraphrase Walter Cronkite's coverage of the assassination of John F. Kennedy in 1963. This, once again, is the presentation of history as a fragmentary memory, a disassociated interpretation hewn from a different perspective than the one most of us are used to seeing. As Eskridge dials the number of his second call the crack of the gunshot rouses us from the feelings of camaraderie and brotherhood that had been established moments earlier between Eskridge and Ali. He instinctively ducks for cover and then sprints upstairs, having obviously intuited the intended target of the assassin's bullet. Mann's camera comes to rest on one of the steps, instead of following Eskridge up into the melee, before that image dissolves into the famous shot of King lying dying on the balcony floor while members of his group point off to the left of frame towards the shooter's position. Laid over these two last images, the Watchtower track reaches its zenith. This interpretation of the Bob Dylan track – despite having no lyrics – shares qualities with Jimi Hendrix's

ALI AND RECREATING HISTORY

Figure 16. Ali

1968 cover of the song rather than Dylan's original. Like the Hendrix reworking, the track here is a much more muscular and plucky version that embodies the sense of protest and angry determination that erupted in the wake of King's murder.

Despite the film's revealing approach to delineating both the murders of Malcolm X and Martin Luther King, an approach based upon divergent and fragmentary perspectives, the way in which *Ali* treats the fallout from the killings appears quite different from each other. If Malcolm's death was all about signalling the fall of a titan, with the subsequent shots of people openly mourning in the streets, Ali crying in his car and the plaintive musical background of Tillman's "Ceremony", King's assassination is treated much more in the way of a call to arms. There's no outpouring of grief here, no hymn to the fallen. Mann doesn't permit us to see the killing of King as he did with Malcolm. We needed to witness the senseless murder of Malcolm X so that the film could properly inaugurate this dark era in American cultural and political life, an era that really began with the assassination of JFK and would not end until 6 June 1968 with the murder of Robert Kennedy. With King's death and how it is staged in *Ali*, with no actual scenes of violence, it's surely more about how Ali used the event to bring himself back to life, as it were, to reinvigorate himself from the physical slumber imposed by his boxing ban. The way Mann moves from King's killing to Ali training makes that link explicit. Where Malcolm's connection to Ali was physical, emotional and spiritual, King's is more tangential, a more distant figure who Ali uses a springboard for his comeback. Seen from what looks to be his own balcony, this next short scene that immediately follows King's death begins with a close-up of Ali shadowboxing outside at night, fires, rioting noise and smoke erupting in the streets behind him. Mann again intercuts this with more footage from his *17 Days Down the Line* documentary, further imagery of rioting and burning cars that takes on an acute contemporary resonance in the wake of the racist shootings in Ferguson, Missouri, in 2014 and the horrendous murder of George Floyd. If the murder of Malcolm X caught Ali off guard, King's murder served to imbue him with a renewed fighting spirit as he begins preparations for his return from exile and his first bouts with Oscar Bonavena and Joe Frazier.

Ali uses for its climax the famous Rumble in the Jungle, arguably the pinnacle of Ali's career and a fight that assumed huge cultural significance for a variety of reasons. For the film Mann moved his entire production to Kinshasa, Zaire (now the Democratic Republic of the Congo) and recreated the Stade du 20 Mai where the real fight took place. The specific scene in this part of the film's third act that is of most interest to this chapter's assessment of Mann's restaging of history is not the fight itself but the jogging sequence where Ali runs through the slums in preparation. As was made clear earlier, the fight scenes in *Ali*, while wonderfully realistic (in opposition to Scorsese's *Raging Bull*) are not always the most revealing if we are interested in how Mann recreated history here and, later, in *Public Enemies*. It is the jogging sequence and not the extended battle between Ali and Foreman that most clearly continues the template of a fragmentary, sometimes hazy but always singular view of historical events. The fragmentation begins with an overhead tracking shot that looks straight down into the iron-oxide dirt of urban Kinshasa. Ali then runs into the frame, after which the camera banks back down and levels off into a conventional tracking shot behind Ali and his coterie of runners. In many ways this subtle opening to an important sequence is about the way in which Ali's consciousness now *precedes* him. It may take him time to catch up to it, so to speak, but by the end of this extended jog, he will have caught his free-floating self and come to realise the extent to which this bout with Foreman is about more than his own comeback.

A series of advertising billboards and street banners line the road to Ali's left as more and more local people stream out from their homes and businesses to run with the champ. At the moment, Ali is just out for a run; his realisation of the social and political import of what he is about to do in Zaire has yet to dawn on him. Salif Keita's track "Sanni Kegniba" appears on the soundtrack to underscore this initial ignorance on the part of Ali, its upbeat vibrancy mixing with Mann's images of movement and colour. The presence of President Mobuto looms ever closer, though, with each step Ali takes.

Ali quickly veers off the beaten path, much to the annoyance of his trainer Angelo Dundee, who is seen desperately trying to find him from the back of an off-road vehicle. The boxer is now running down narrow alleys between the slum buildings. Mann's camera tracks in front of him and behind him, picking out street murals with tags like *Ali Bumaye* and featuring Ali standing triumphant over a fallen Foreman (by this point in Foreman's career he had aligned himself more with the centre right and what Ali considered the establishment, whereas Ali was much more populist and centre left). Tens of people now follow behind Ali as he runs past the domestic living conditions of urban Kinshasa. Mann gives us lots of cutaways to local cars, corrugated iron walls and women buying food before returning to a tracking shot from the right-hand side of Ali, only now in slow motion. Point-of-view shots from Ali's perspective show us more murals, only this time they seem more political, more about activism and ideology than simple idolisation. Our first shot of the all-important man with the green radio (as mentioned earlier in the book's discussion of *The Jericho Mile*) appears as Ali runs past him, demarcating Ali's crossover point from ignorance to enlightenment. The Salif Keita track fades out and is replaced by the opening notes of his much more sombre and melancholic "Tomorrow". Throngs of people now run with Ali, clutching at his arms and cheering "Ali Bumaye" or "Ali Kill Him", in ostensible reference to Foreman in the upcoming fight, but also perhaps an appeal for the destruction of the people's other foes, the tsetse fly and Mobutu's corrupt political dictatorship.

The man with the green radio is now to Ali's left. The scene is almost entirely non-diegetic. What we are witnessing is the true emergence of Ali's political consciousness, brought about by the grassroots movements of an impoverished people. A mural of Ali battling disease and poor healthcare appears. The green radio is prominent in these shots, held by the man who now stands directly in front of Ali as he surveys the rest of the same mural; Ali battling the tanks and aircraft and bombs of Mobutu's war machine. The radio will soon be Ali's saviour in the Foreman fight but here it acts as a visual signifier of his transition, an identifiable way of exploring the history of Ali's decision-making process. As Mann noted at the time of the film's release in his director's commentary:

> I wanted to try and find some way to represent the impact upon Ali of the realisation of what he meant to a lot of people all over the planet, to find a way to represent their expectations, what they were invested in … the idea occurred of a … people's art of muralisation … to try and represent the expectation of a kind of global consciousness.

The image that then closes the running sequence shows Ali with a determined look and a fixed gaze, moving ahead to the fight with Foreman and the liberation of the impoverished and underprivileged peoples of the world. He is now out of the tight confines of the back alleys and into a large housing project. Mann cuts to a tracking shot of the rows and rows of federalised housing and the balconies on which these poor people stand to get their only view of the Champ. As Mann notes in the same commentary, these people were too poor to attend the actual fight, so they recreated its significance in murals and street art. Like Bergman in *The Insider*, Ali has now become the left-wing, populist crusader for truth and justice. If Bergman's visual icons for this movement were Cesar Chavez, the Bedonkohe Apache Geronimo and Allen Ginsberg, then Ali's are arguably himself in these murals, a situation ideally suited to Ali's own brand of egocentrism.

This notion of a strong, centred ego is something that lies at the heart of Mann's approach to recreating history in *Ali* (and, to an extent, in his other historical works, *The Insider* and *Public Enemies*). It's the quality that gives *Ali* its sense of a singular perspective navigating an amorphous period of historical tumult. It's the organising principle for Mann's approach to the film's cinematography, its use of voiceover, the musical cues and the editing rhythms. It governs how time and history are marshalled together in the opening sequence of the film, how Ali's first fight with Sonny Liston is presented and, now, how Ali's run through the slums is used to arrive at a deconstruction of his move from celebrity to freedom fighter for the impoverished underclasses of the world. It is also, of course, the means through which we gain an understanding of the huge amount of fear Ali had going into the climactic fight with Foreman that closes the film.

As a marker of Mann's auteurism, this individualistic approach to the exploration of historical events is a common and identifiable element of his films based on real figures. *Ali*, like *The Insider* and, later, *Public Enemies*, stitches together a large backdrop of historical, social and political events, but the focus is always pulled back towards that lonely figure whose charge is to navigate the maelstrom. Like the saxophonist who stands at the centre of Aaron Douglas's highly detailed and dense panel *From Slavery Through Reconstruction*, pointing the way to the new freedoms of the African American citizen, Ali is the focal point in Mann's history of the African American experience in the middle of the twentieth century, the cartographer for our times. He is our conduit to a better understanding of this historical period and the method for grasping Mann's approach to recreating reality.

> Key scene suggestion for recreating reality – the virtuoso opening montage that manipulates time and memory as it introduces key characters.

Notes

1 Vincent M. Gaine, *Existentialism and Social Engagement in the Films of Michael Mann*, Palgrave Macmillan, 2011, 5.
2 W.E.B. Du Bois, *The Souls of Black Folk* (1903), Gramercy Books, 1994.
3 There's contemporary music here too, a pulsing synthesised hum that underlines the anticipation of things to come. For some commentators this choice of score undermines the film's striving for period realism. From selected tracks such as "Memory Gospel" by Moby to the remix of "Death Letter" by Johnny Farmer, it is true that *Ali* melds music that is relatively contemporary with 2001 with images expertly crafted to seem like the 1960s. But the dissonance that writers such as Steven Rybin feel this generates – according to Rybin the soundtrack to *Ali* gives the film a mannerist *mise en scène* – is, I feel, not nearly as pronounced as they make out. The majority of the tracks are updates of blues and soul classics particular to the period; a Baz Luhrmann-esque postmodern rehash this is not.
4 To a degree, Spike Lee also does this in *Malcolm X* (1992) but his approach veers more towards Black Dandyism, a style befitting of his wish to expose the European exploitation of Africa and the racist notion of the "luxury slave".
5 There's documentary footage here too, footage that Mann shot himself for a 37-minute travelogue he made in 1972 entitled *17 Days Down the Line*.

Key scene suggesting an escaping
reality – the virtuose opening montage
that manipulates time and memory
as it introduces key plot points.

CHAPTER ELEVEN

Collateral and Hi-Def Night

> I wanted to shoot the whole film at night, and right away I knew I'd never be able to get what I wanted by shooting 35mm. It just doesn't pick up all the little details and gradations of colour and tone that the naked eye picks up at night. And L.A. at night is this whole other character, and the only way to be able to see it the way I'd pictured it was to go digital video.
>
> Michael Mann

Collateral is about the failure of men to successfully navigate the postmodern world, in this case Los Angeles at night, which is perhaps the archetypal expression of this world. In this film, Mann's ninth, women (as they often are in Mann's work) are the key to men's liberation and occupy roles such as successful assistant district attorneys or former schoolteachers. The men, by contrast, are either criminal by-products of the former Cold War security apparatus, victims of crippling self-confidence issues that inhibit their potential careers or reasonably skilled police detectives who nevertheless end up way in over their heads, punished for their radical approach to detection. By night's end, Los Angeles will have borne witness to these men being either killed by other men or saved by better women. These failures of men – and the generalised idea of a flawed contemporary masculinity – sit very well within the confines of *Collateral*'s post-millennial and postmodern view of Los Angeles, a city that is portrayed as a physically fragmented and socially isolating place (by Mann and cinematographer Dion Beebe) with no single means of access or egress, like an Edward Hopper painting.

A flawed masculinity combined with the postmodernity of Los Angeles and the fact that *Collateral* is mostly set at night – a condition that further augments these ideas of fragmentation and isolation – and you have all the makings of what Mike Davis terms "post-noir" in his excellent book *City of Quartz*. Davis sees *post-noir* – or *neo-noir* as it is more commonly

173

The Films of Michael Mann

called in the new century – as "the popular and… 'populist' anti-myth of Los Angeles".[1] Davis cites films such as *Chinatown* and *Blade Runner* and writers such as Wambaugh and Ellroy as some of the key elements of this enduring movement, a movement that has sought, and still seeks, to undo the dominant myth of Los Angeles as a Hollywood confection (something also tangentially explored in Chapter 7).

Collateral, then, was 2004's addition to this corrective movement. The story of lonely LA cab driver Max driving hitman Vincent around the scuzzy refineries of Wilmington and the shadowy jazz bars of Leimert Park, the film presents a future-proofed, nocturnal evocation of the city and is something that Davis would undoubtedly have included in his list of key films and local chronicles. But alongside its place in that small but perfectly formed pantheon of LA neo-noir – something that will be evidenced further as we progress through this chapter – *Collateral* also marks something far more important in Mann's development as a filmmaker, his first near fully fledged embrace of a digital video aesthetic that would allow him to *see* the noirish night of Los Angeles for the first time. Digital video had been used in a number of film projects prior to *Collateral* – 1998's *The Last Broadcast* was a small-budget horror film that was shot and edited entirely on readily available digital equipment, while George Lucas's *Star Wars Episode I: The Phantom Menace* (1999) featured several extended sequences shot with digital cameras – but in both these cases (and most others during this time) the use of digital cameras was masked either by the nature of the story (*The Last Broadcast* was a found footage film and therefore it had to look like a home movie) or flashy effects work that effectively hid the use of digital cameras from the viewer. This is what Mann was talking about when he used the analogy of steel being hidden by bricks and mortar in architecture prior to Louis Sullivan's pioneering liberation in the 1890s; with *Collateral*, Mann was saying that the steel can be the scenery as well as the skeleton.

Daylight in *Collateral* is relegated to the two or three minutes that open the film and the precious few crepuscular seconds at the end when Max (Jamie Foxx) emerges from an MTA train with Annie (Jada Pinkett Smith). All that's in between is the virtuoso survey of a normally unseen cinematic topography of Los Angeles that would prove to be highly influential to a number of other filmmakers in the years to come.[2] Vincent the hitman's arrival at LAX is cool and steely and slightly slow-mo just like Hathaway the hacker's departure from an Indonesian airport would be eleven years later in Mann's divisive *Blackhat* (2015). Vincent controls his environment here in a way that Max cannot in the next scene. The cab depot is all chaotic cutaways to tools and engines and Thai newspapers and

COLLATERAL AND HI-DEF NIGHT

Figure 17. Collateral

sports footage on TV and cabbies arguing with one another. If Vincent's world demonstrates the single-minded intent of major narco-trafficking cartels then Max's world is emblematic of the energised multiculturalism of post-millennial Los Angeles. To distance himself from this positive chaos Max uses his taxi in *Collateral* like Hathaway uses his headphones when in jail in *Blackhat*, as tools for asserting their sense of control and removing the noise of the world. After wiping down the cab's interior surfaces and carefully placing a postcard image of a deserted island on his visor (an image as important to Max as Frank's collage is to him in *Thief*), Max begins his shift around 4 p.m., launching out of the depot dwarfed by a recreation of a mural from Estrada Courts, a housing project in East Los Angeles, featuring a headless vaquero on horseback chasing down a bull. Vincent, arguably the bull, is out there already, prowling around the new towers of old Bunker Hill waiting on the headless and guileless Max to track him down and rein him in.

With the two principal characters introduced, Mann gets his chance to demonstrate the technology of the Viper Filmstream and Sony F900 video cameras, something teased at in those early jogging sequences in *Ali*. Max has picked up Annie, an assistant US attorney, and is taking her from the airport to her downtown offices at 312 Spring St. (555 West Fifth St. in real life), via the 105 Freeway. Mann's opening evocation of the night of Los Angeles is introduced as these two move through the gorgeously depopulated landscape that bounds the freeway. Inside the cab, things appear gloomy and paradoxically lustrous, a kind of velvety darkness where any whites – Annie's teeth, headlights in the background – appear bright like phosphorous. Using flexible, low-luminosity light strips that were easily concealed behind the front seats or above the actors' heads in the roof of the cab, Mann lights the interior of the cab in such a way that the actors don't *look* lit. The light-sensitive hi-def video removes the visual artifice that audiences had become accustomed to via the use of 35mm film (because film needs lots of light to achieve at least a minimum exposure, a scene like this shot on film would look simulated due to the oddly bright light sources emanating from within the vehicle, not to mention the fact that, outside the cab, there would be little to look at but indistinct blobs) and replaces it with visuals that come very close to the actual experience of driving in a car at night. The Sony F900 also produces a wonderful colour palette in these scenes that would go on to dominate the look of the whole film: silvers, blues, tungsten oranges and flashes of red and purple, like some hellish bruise at night in the city.

Mann further uses the meeting of these two characters to establish the primary spatial orientation of the environment within the cab – Max to screen right with empty space to the left and vice versa for the passenger. Like the old cinematic convention of two people talking on a landline phone, and having one person to screen right with the phone cord trailing away to the left and vice versa, Mann uses space to establish a connection between driver and passenger, whether Max and his love interest Annie or Max and the hitman Vincent. The camera is also shaky here, a small detail but something that hints at the liberalisation of the cinematography in Mann's films, a modification that has occurred in tandem with his uptake of digital video technology and would find its fullest and most radical expression in 2015's *Blackhat*.

As the towers of LA's financial district creep into view, the virtues of digital video's ability to see the night become clear. From the appearance of a "rusty ceiling" created by the sodium vapour from thousands of street-lights bouncing off the bottom of the cloud layer to the almost ghostly, skeletal look of the skyscrapers of downtown, this is a noir Los Angeles updated and revised for the twenty-first century, less shadowy, smoke-filled backrooms and more post-industrial, science-fiction wasteland. Mann interjects long shots of the night-time skyline with cutaways of various corners and angles of Max's cab, as Scorsese does throughout *Taxi Driver*, and aerial shots that look straight down on to the complex grid system of the Los Angeles centre. If *Heat*'s view of Los Angeles was as being homogeneous, modern and technological, *Collateral*'s medley of fragmentary camera shots, its presentation of LA as a kind of dead zone and its night-time emptiness suggest a postmodern world where the modernist experimentation of *Heat* has gone wrong or, more so, worn itself out.

As night properly asserts itself, the noirish characters emerge from their daytime hiding places. Vincent's scarred hand keys in a code that opens the door to his night of murderous mayhem. He's in the same building that Annie works in, leaving and headed for a cab just as she arrives for her night's work on a deposition. On his way out he scans the front desk as McCauley does at the airport hotel in *Heat* while the camera tracks close to his face like any number of moments from *The Insider*. If in title only, *Collateral* shares its fascination with the darker side of night in the city with a number of other films, including Jim Jarmusch's *Night on Earth* (1991), Jules Dassin's *Night and the City* (1950), Joseph H. Lewis's *So Dark the Night* (1946) and Frank Tuttle's *This Gun for Hire* (1942).[3] Like *Collateral*, these films are enthralled with what night in the city feels and looks like, with how it changes characters and encourages certain behaviours. In his use of digital technology, Mann is extending this lineage to its logical conclusion so that the night now becomes an active participant in this process, something that can be moulded and directed as much as the hitman or the US attorney.

Now that night has descended, other key noir elements begin to enter the text of *Collateral*. Vincent's first hit goes wrong and the victim, having been shot, falls from his first-floor window on to the roof of Max's cab. The classic noir tropes of cynicism and irony feature in Vincent's response to Max's question, "You killed him?"; "No, I shot him ... the bullets and the fall killed him." Explained in the director's commentary as a debt to Billy Wilder, a director responsible for one of the best film noirs ever made, *Double Indemnity* (1944), this use of irony forms a larger part of the world-weary cynicism that is such an integral part of noir's view of crime and humanity, while, in the case of *Collateral*, helping to form a counterpoint to Max's unbridled humanism.

In the scenes that follow Max's discovery of who Vincent really is, Mann layers on to his painterly images of night-time Los Angeles a soundscape that serves a number of functions, the most important of which is to bring into focus Max's shock and deteriorating mental state after witnessing the murder of Vincent's first target. The whoosh of passing cars, horns, shouting, insults, dance music and screeching tyres all form part of the diegetic sound of Max's new situation. Max's humanism struggles to comprehend Vincent's actions and his subsequent attempt back in the cab to ameliorate the seriousness of killing someone by bringing up the spectre of the Rwandan massacre or the nuclear bombings of Nagasaki and Hiroshima. Given that Max didn't try to stop the slaughter in Rwanda, why, asks Vincent, should he care about the death of one Angelino he didn't know? In these early stages of *Collateral*, this cynical reasoning is somewhat persuasive and remains in place throughout other encounters in the film, including the jazz club scene and after the nightclub shootout, until such time as Max sees Vincent for who he truly is, towards the end.

An interesting divergence from the more familiar film noir tropes, however, and something that helps link it to the idea of a postmodern worldview, is *Collateral*'s seeming antipathy towards determinism. As they are typically understood, film noirs normally exhibit a deterministic view of human behaviour, the notion that the corrupt cops and crazed killers, barflies and femme fatales are all stuck in pre-determined patterns of behaviour of which they may be aware but which they cannot escape. The narrative of *Collateral*, in contrast to this, seems to refute such ideas in favour of a series of coincidences and unforeseen happenstances that permit the events of the film to unfold in a relativistic way. Gone is the heightened determinism of *Heat* or *Thief*, where the principal characters ride pre-determined tracks that give rise to the great sense of tragedy at the end of each film. From the way in which Vincent nearly gets into another cab outside Annie's building to Vincent's first victim accidentally falling on to Max's cab to the good timing of the more urgent call that comes through to the police who have pulled Max over for having a smashed windscreen, *Collateral*'s take on noir is founded on the indeterminacy of chance encounters rather than the fixed choices of automatons.

Part of the film's appeal as a postmodern take on the traditional "night and the city" narrative is the way in which such relativism – moral, social, cultural – reinforces *Collateral*'s view of Los Angeles as a barren metropolis where the gulf between people and places is not fixed but instead formed by arbitrary choice.[4] This model runs concurrently with Mann's revision of the traditional dramatic Hollywood narrative – something that normally dictates a simplistic, cause-and-effect structure, heavy on exposition and scene-setting where characters possess easily identifiable goals and motivations – the seeds of which are planted here in *Collateral* but would not be fully realised until *Miami Vice* (2006).

When the obligatory noir nightclub scene arrives in *Collateral*, it's once again tailored to the postmodern emptiness of the city, a quality that's already been highlighted by the desolate alleyways of 7565 Fountain Avenue and the seemingly abandoned petrol station in Koreatown. The jazz club scene is no different in that, while doing away with the characteristic low light levels, plumes of cigarette smoke and gangsters' molls, it still trades in the other, more vital thematic elements that tell us this film is part of the neo-noir lineage. Vincent and Max appear to be the only customers in the club and they sit and listen to a cover version of Miles Davis's "Spanish Key" from the *Bitches Brew* album. The lead trumpeter is the owner Daniel, the third victim on Vincent's hit list for the night.

Collateral and Hi-Def Night

Once Daniel finishes his set, Vincent buys him a drink and, along with Max, they talk about the dying popularity of jazz and the regret attendant on not acting spontaneously in life when chances present themselves (an issue also dealt with in the 2014 music film *Whiplash*).

Through these dialogue exchanges, the film doffs its cap to the classic themes of the noir genre – loss of agency, faded masculinity, ageing, obsolescence – while developing its own relativistic agenda predicated on improvisation, chaos and the impact of one's own choices on the world around you, all postmodern concepts. Furthermore, the ghost of Miles Davis in this scene, both as a topic of conversation and as a metaphor for improvisation and individual choice, forms another part of Mann's larger interest in the rise of social awareness and racial consciousness that he had been cultivating, in earnest, since *Heat*.[5] Easily missed on the first viewing, look again at Pacino's embrace of the murdered prostitute's mother or the tragedy of Breedan's fated choice in the restaurant or the fatherly presence of Malcolm X in a picture behind Pacino as he makes a call to his deputies from a nightclub office, and you will see both Michael Mann the director and the ethnographer at work.

Vincent kills Daniel after he fails to fully answer his question about where Miles Davis learned music. Max wanders off in a state of complete shock towards his cab. Vincent catches up with him after suffering his paroxysm of remorse over the body of Daniel. Max gets a radio call from dispatch informing him that his mother, who is in hospital long term, has been "callin' and callin'" and the film enters its second hour where more coincidences, chance encounters and torn edges bolster the claim that *Collateral* is a continuation and a development of Mann's revision of the traditional dramatic narrative. The detective, Fanning, who is trailing in the destructive wake of Vincent, now meets him in a hospital elevator without knowing it as the duo, Vincent and Max, ascend the floors to visit Max's sick mother Ida. In Ida's room, after some funny and touching exchanges between the three characters, Max finally decides to manifest some direct action and make his environment the product of his choices, something he has only witnessed Vincent do up until this point.

Max steals Vincent's briefcase and runs off in an attempt to thwart his ongoing murderous rampage across Los Angeles. Vincent gives chase and the two end up fighting on an elevated walkway that rises over the 5 Freeway as it runs through City Terrace. With the hi-def video technology, Mann gives us yet another glorious night-time view of one of the main arterial traffic routes through Los Angeles. As Max and Vincent fight above, thousands of vehicles move freely beneath them on another major freeway, serving to remind us that the LA of *Collateral* is a broken-up, porous place that is depopulated because it is dehumanised – lots of cars and no people.[6] There is such free and unbridled movement in this film's view of Los Angeles that there are rarely large congregations of people in any one place. Where there are groups – the upcoming sequence in Fever, a Korean nightclub, being about the only example – it is only so that people can flee *from* such a place and disperse again. This is, then, a Los Angeles that goes against the grain of some of the most popular, modern films set there, films that Mike Davis terms "carceral": *Escape from Los Angeles* (1996), *The Running Man* (1987), *Blade Runner* (1982) and *Die Hard* (1988), to name but a few.[7] In these films, Los Angeles was a place that entrapped people together in huge numbers, a dystopian hell to be escaped from, regardless of whether that hell was a game show, the Bradbury Building or a futuristic skyscraper in Century City. *Collateral*, by contrast, posits an LA that is fragmented and wide open to such a degree that there appears to be no one there at all – if, like those other films, it remains a prison, then the numerous doors and sally ports were flung open long ago.

For all that, however, the Los Angeles of *Collateral* is, above all else, beautifully atmospheric in its weird night-time geography. After their altercation on the pedestrian overpass, Max and Vincent head to a meet with the man calling the shots, cartel boss Felix played by Javier Bardem. Making their way there the cab passes through the oil refineries and industrial plants of Wilmington, a formerly unincorporated part of Los Angeles and home to the third largest oil field in the US. As Vincent toys with Max in revenge for Max destroying his PDA by throwing it on to the freeway in the earlier scene, the cab glides past refinery towers, giant exhaust vents and organised cartage containers that all sparkle with the floodlit intensity of night-time industry. These images, combined with the all-encompassing rusty hue emanating from the street lights, colour this section of Los Angeles as something akin to the opening shots of *Blade Runner*, a post-industrial netherworld that is both beautiful and totally devoid of organic life, aside from our principal observers. Having arrived at their destination (a club in Pico Rivera called El Rodeo), Max successfully pretends to be Vincent – his punishment for throwing Vincent's materials on to the freeway – in order to obtain from Felix a back-up pen drive of information on the remaining targets on Vincent's list. Federal agents, along with Detective Fanning, have been surveilling these events as part of an ongoing investigation and manage to work out the location of Vincent's penultimate hit of the night, the nightclub Fever in Koreatown. Felix, suspicious of "Vincent's" (Max's) behaviour when he was requesting the back-up information, dispatches his own gunmen to

COLLATERAL AND HI-DEF NIGHT

Figure 18. Collateral

the same club in order to kill this Vincent if need be. The convergence of these three "vectors" will result in a fallout from which few will survive, and those who do will be forever changed.

Before arriving at this moment of reckoning, however, Mann provides his principal characters with an interstitial pause, a moment that encourages reflection by forcing both Max and Vincent to think about themselves and their respective situations, perhaps *the* most essential element of the existential paradigm that Mann adheres to in all his work. The coyotes prowling and hunting across Olympic Boulevard reinforce the human lifelessness of this Los Angeles, a city that has been taken back by the desert wildlife. This wonderful moment in the appreciation of *Collateral*'s night-time tapestry has buried in its imagery a subtle thematic reminder of the fleeting shot in Terrence Malick's *The Thin Red Line* (1998) where a near-naked, native tribal elder of Guadalcanal walks past one of Staros's soldiers with complete and utter indifference. Like the coyotes that cross paths with Max and Vincent, the native in Malick's war movie is both unaware of and uninterested in the motivations for the soldiers' presence in his domain. The coyotes, like the elder, are the real landlords of this desert real estate; they were here before modern humans imported their urbanisation projects, their industry and their culture, and they will still be here when the city is finally evacuated for good.[8]

The increased light sensitivity of the hi-def camera renders this moment in a crepuscular twilight of greens and greys while disappearing colonnades of palm tree silhouettes provide added dimensions to the night in a way *Thief* could only have dreamed of. The trees seem to emanate from Vincent in one shot – arching away in ever-decreasing height into the nothingness of the night – and provide a forward link to the closing scenes when Vincent dies on the MTA and his soul escapes in the form of a tree. Audioslave's "Shadow on the Sun" brings the two men out of their pensive meditations on mortality and purpose (this moment of reflection is normally directed at the distant horizon but is here modified as a way of including both men) and bridges the rest of their journey to the reckoning at the nightclub in Koreatown.

The purge at the nightclub is significant. Among Vincent's victims is Detective Fanning (Mark Ruffalo), a character whose demise is unexpected and jarring in the way Marion's is in *Psycho*. The dispatch of this principal character – someone we had anticipated would have a hand in the resolution of events in the film – supports the notion of *Collateral* as a relativistic narrative set in a version of Los Angeles so porous that any fixed meaning or moral foundation leaked out long ago. Characters who would normally be the bedrock of the story are stripped away by the city of Los Angeles at a moment's notice and never replaced. The space they once occupied is quickly subsumed into that self-sustaining emptiness that was there in the alleyway or at the petrol station or on the freeway. This is a post-millennial view of Los Angeles where nature doesn't so much abhor a vacuum as feed off it.

The fallout from the nightclub is demarcated in perhaps the film's most powerful dialogue exchange, as Max and Vincent lay bare the respective understandings of one another that they have been forging since they first met. For the first two minutes of this scene Mann's camera follows, by and large, the template that was established in the opening minutes of the film, moving between Max in the front right of the cab and Vincent in the rear left. Max demands to know why Vincent had to kill Detective Fanning, to which Vincent replies, "Who the fuck is Fanning?", a response that, while perhaps suggesting his honest ignorance about the cops pursuing him, is more likely about Vincent wishing to antagonise Max with his seeming indifference as a form of punishment for being so vulnerable in the club. Max tries to help Vincent understand why killing Fanning should be considered morally heinous – "Why d'you have to kill 'im … he's probably got family, kids gonna grow up without 'im?" – but Vincent's pathology means he is incapable of intuiting any inherent significance to existence beyond living and dying – "That's the why, there's no reason, there's no good reason, no bad reason, you live or you die."

The point at which this sequence pivots into something else is when Vincent replies that he's "indifferent" to Max's query, "Then what are you?" As Vincent utters the word "indifferent" Mann cuts to a point-of-view shot (presumably Vincent's) of a speeding police cruiser passing the cab in the other direction, this time with no diegetic siren noise. This is imagery as punctuation mark, specifically a colon, after which comes the essence of Vincent's worldview, his "facile nihilism" in the words of Mann. For Vincent's delivery of these core lines, Mann cuts to a close-up of his face from a camera position directly in front, from where the passenger seat would normally be. It's more hand-held and shaky than the majority of previous setups in the cab, indicating the severity of the moment. This time, rather than a steadily shrinking colonnade of trees, it is a line of streetlights that seem to emerge from the back of Vincent's head as he expounds his bleak theory of Los Angeles and, thus, the universe – "Get with it. Millions of galaxies with hundreds of millions of stars and a speck on one, in a blink. That's us, lost in space. The cop, you, me ... who notices?" Vincent is truly alone in these images, both figuratively and physically, cut off from his driver in this vehicle and all the other lonely people moving through the equally empty spaces of the city. However much *Collateral* condemns this philosophy, it is ultimately one of the overriding themes of Mann's work, the notion that we are alone in this world and that our actions determine our nature. This essential element of existentialism in Mann's body of work is what gives rise to all the searching glances at the horizon by his protagonists, their focus on choosing a particular course of action, dealing with the consequences, and their possession of a personal moral and ethical code that they try to adhere to.

Max's struggle to articulate what he sees as the major failing of Vincent is very well realised by Jamie Foxx and Mann in the second half of this important sequence.

> What's with you man? ... As in, if somebody had a gun to your head and said "You gotta tell me what's goin' on with this person over here or I'm gonna kill you, what was drivin' him, what was he thinking", you know you couldn't do it, could you, cause, they would have to kill your ass 'cause you don't know what anyone else ... is thinking. I think you're low my brother, way low. Like, what were you, one of those institutionalised-raised guys? Anybody home? 'N'stand ... there ... there's standard parts that are supposed to be there in people and in you ... aren't.

The echoing instrumental noises on the soundtrack trail away into the night behind the cab, highlighting the devastating impact Max's words have on Vincent. Vincent readies his nasty retort but these two exchanges, Vincent's first and then Max's stumbling assessment of Vincent's soullessness, are the important ones here, the two principal characters framing the debate that's central to the film. Is Los Angeles a porous and meaningless city of empty public spaces or is there something integral that gives it life, a *standard part*, in the words of Max?

The hi-def night that surrounds this exchange in the cab is part of its success as a haunting deliberation on ideas and ideals. Without the kind of lunar transparency that Mann's new cameras provide, this battle between Max and Vincent would lose its sense of scope, its sense of the city beyond the windows of the cab. On motion-picture film this same sequence would be too closeted, too enclosed and encased in the underexposed blackness of the night to really achieve the necessary feeling of characters moving through an endless city plain that disappears beyond the horizon. The dual corollaries of this pivotal scene are that we now understand that, while Vincent sees life as meaningless, he nevertheless *lives* it by being improvisational and hedonistic. Max, on the other hand, imbues life with a clear purpose – family, steady work – but chooses not to live for himself. He is inhibited by his chronic failure to act ... until now.

Max crashing the cab into a set of roadworks on Figueroa Street is his dynamic cure for the inhibition that ails him and is the event that prompts the beginning of the end, a near 17-minute segue from the crash site downtown to the Marine MTA station on the Green Line. James Newton Howard's impressive scoring for this concluding sequence stitches together the various remaining city locations into one climactic chunk, the most interesting of which for this chapter is the rooftop sequence and office shootout.

After the crash Vincent flees the scene and heads off to kill his last target, Annie, the US attorney from the start of the film. Max deals with a clumsy cop who, moments earlier, arrived at the crash scene and then speeds off to Annie's aid when he sees her image on Vincent's PDA. En route to Annie's building, Max moves on foot through the deserted canyons of downtown Los Angeles (notably, Flower Street), deep, trough-like spaces that Christopher Nolan would use eight years later for parts of his Gotham City in *The Dark Knight Rises* (2012). Manifesting yet more improvisational behaviour, Max steals a man's phone at gunpoint and tries to alert Annie to the hitman coming her way. He's running through the underground car park of the Los Angeles Central Library and then up on to the roof to try and get phone reception. Here he stands amid the larger steel and glass towers of 777, 801 and 888 Figueroa Street, a rare human presence next to these skeletal structures where the dark office windows look like hollowed-out eye sockets. Once again, without the benefits of the higher sensitivity to light provided by the hi-def cameras, these dark window spaces would be indistinguishable from the darkness of the night sky or the building structures themselves.

Amazing close-up shots of Annie sitting at a desk from the point of view of Max on the library roof allow Mann to construct a tense sequence of shot/reverse shots without having to cut to the interior of Annie's space unless he wants to. Furthermore, when Vincent is sniffing around Annie's office Mann gives us an over-the-shoulder shot of a tiny Max outside the window, down on the library roof and on the phone pleading with Annie to get out of there.

These cameras allow Mann to maintain the film's view of Los Angeles as a place of yawning spaces and architectural canyons where the interactions between people are often conducted at extreme distances. This is the evidence for Mann's claim that, rather than being a hidden and alternative means of making a movie, hi-def photography can enter into the story itself and enhance the manner in which events are conceived and presented by the filmmaker. This sequence set in Annie's downtown building would have to be shot in an entirely different and far more conventional way if motion-picture film cameras were being used. To illustrate this point with the over-the-shoulder shot just mentioned, on film Mann would have to physically cut to Max on the rooftop rather than just pull focus from Vincent's face to Max in the distance in the same shot.

Vincent cuts the power to Annie's building and proceeds to try and kill her. The office she was working in is now in complete darkness, save for the illumination of the city – and key buildings such as the Staples Centre – outside her windows. This high contrast between the inside and the outside recalls the kind of inner sanctum of the Don's office in *The Godfather* (1972) or those dark spaces in Ford's *The Searchers* (1956), former havens that are now pregnant with threat and death except, of course, that in those films the outside was daytime and not the middle of the night. Vincent finds Annie hiding in the law library two floors above her office and is about to kill her when Max emerges from the shadows and, in response to Vincent's sly remark, "What are you gonna do about it?", shoots Vincent in the ear while aiming for his head. Max and Annie flee on to the MTA to Long Beach with a now-infuriated Vincent close behind.

Howard's tubular bells score reinforces the metallic milieu the three characters now find themselves in. Deserted concrete alleys and freeways have now given way to abandoned steel railway stations and train carriages. These closing minutes of the film bring home Vincent's apocryphal tale from his first meeting with Max at the start of the film, the one about someone dying on the Los Angeles MTA and their body then doing continuous laps around the city because no one is around to notice. Like Neil McCauley prefiguring his own death by walking past the pieta outside the hospital at the start of *Heat*, Vincent's homily about death and loneliness on a train to nowhere now becomes his own fate. Max and Annie are trapped in the end carriage of the train with Vincent fast approaching. With no other choice, Max fires chaotically at Vincent, who is standing on the other side of the carriage doors firing back at him. Max's break from his conventional and methodical approach to life's problems allows him to mortally wound Vincent while escaping injury himself. As Vincent turns to sit down, his face a picture of incredulity at the absurd outcome of this gunfight, we see an MTA advert with the words "Life's too short…" emblazoned over a bright orange background. This too recalls an earlier moment that Max and Vincent shared, when Vincent was telling Max to call Annie as "Life is short … soon, it's gone." Like the tragic sensibility of any great noir character, Vincent is the product of his own self-awareness. In expounding his philosophy to Max he is, in turn, perceiving his own demise. As he utters his refrain about dying on the MTA, a digitally composited Los Angeles appears outside the window at its most desolate and empty yet.[9] Vincent dies and his soul passes by the train in the form of a tree, a poetic reading of the moment alluded to in Mann's commentary for the film. Recalling the barren landscape beyond the runways at the end of *Heat*, this exterior environment of silhouette and silence offers a stark complement to Vincent's view of the world while also holding promise for a new Max, ready to start again with a clean slate.

If *Ali* was Mann's preview of the newly emergent high-definition technology, then *Collateral* represents his opening night. *Ali* was made in 2000/2001, but in its pared-down, third act narrative, its hi-def video-graphic look and its thoroughly liberated camera movements, it is *Collateral* that is truly the first film of Mann's new millennium. It marks the real beginning of his new aesthetic approach to film making, a kind of freeform visual and aural radicalism that seems to sit very comfortably with the new millennium's concerns of transnational crime, technological dependence and growing urban isolation. The film's deft update of the traditional noir norms and its consequent inversion of Los Angeles, from a place of incarceration to one of extrication, sit alongside those other Mann fundamentals that we have acknowledged over the previous chapters – factors such as professionalism, urban environments, the use of negative space, innovations in sound and an interest in modernism (here, modulated into postmodernism) – and allow a judgement to be made about *Collateral*'s value as an indicator of Mann's auteurism.

While it is a transitional film that saw Mann move from his twentieth-century proclivities – Renaissance symmetry, motion-picture film, more rigorously determined camera movements, more conventionally grand narrative ambitions – to the more unhinged characteristics that he exhibits in the likes of *Blackhat* (2015), *Collateral* blends these differing elements well and doesn't feel like a film of competing aesthetics. Consider again the scene where Vincent is prowling around in the law library hunting Annie and you will see the very early antecedent of the out-of-control camerawork of *Blackhat*'s foot-chase towards the Tsuen Wan drainage tunnel in Hong Kong sitting alongside a beautiful, Renaissance-framed, slow, downward panning shot of Vincent with his back to the ocean of downtown Los Angeles, like the coastal balcony scenes from *Thief* or *Heat*. This scene in particular, and *Collateral* as a whole, is about Mann bridging the gaps between motion-picture film and hi-def video, between the twentieth century and the twenty-first, between the formal framing of events and the feeling that we are witnessing something unscripted, unanticipated and unforeseen. Just as all Spielberg's films since *A.I.* (2001) remain unmistakably his, despite big changes to things like the colour temperature he uses and the way he lights exteriors from interior spaces – his exteriors are now very overexposed, in homage to Stanley Kubrick after their early collaboration on *A.I.* – *Collateral* is replete with the determinants that we have come to associate with Mann, in spite of the fact that it is also a hybrid work that spans the gap between the old worlds of *The Last of the Mohicans* and *The Insider* and the new millennial landscapes of *Blackhat*.[10]

> **Key scene suggestion for hi-def night – the rooftop sequence where Max desperately tries to warn Annie that Vincent is closing in on her location in the DA's building in downtown Los Angeles.**

Notes

1 See Mike Davis, *City of Quartz: Excavating the Future in Los Angeles*, Vintage, 1992, 21.
2 The most notable children of *Collateral* would be Nicolas Winding Refn's *Drive* (2011) and Dan Gilroy's *Nightcrawler* (2014), both films that are set

in Los Angeles, use digital video to explore the night and strive to undo the myth of the city as a Hollywood confection.

3   *Night on Earth*'s Los Angeles vignette is interestingly similar to Max and Annie's time together at the start of *Collateral*. In Jarmusch's film, a cab driver picks up an executive from LAX who is trying to conduct some business over the phone. Despite their different backgrounds, the driver and passenger develop a bond over the course of the journey downtown.

4   Of the film's postmodernism, critic Michael J. Anderson notes in his 2004 *Senses of Cinema* article: "Moreover, this focus on the city's design, though quite often exceeding the immediate exigencies of the narrative, echoes the film's moral universe. We see this in one moment when Vincent pulls Max up from the ground after a scuffle, revealing a striking vista of Downtown behind; or in the many moments when Mann utilises a technique of reverse shooting in the cab, wherein Max is presented in the right hand portion of the frame, frontally, with scores of lights out-of-focus to the left, while Vincent in the back right seat is presented on the left side with this same field of nocturnal light and colour to his right. Indeed, both the value system expressed by Vincent in particular as well as the architecture featured so prominently throughout the film represent instantiations of postmodernism. As such, the utilisation of the nocturnal urban landscape in *Collateral* is not simply a self-justifying preoccupation of its creator, though it is this, but is also an extension of the postmodern universe that defines the film's rhetoric." Michael J. Anderson, "Before Sunrise, or Los Angeles Plays itself in a Lonely Place", *Senses of Cinema*, October 2004, sensesofcinema.com/2004/feature-articles/collateral/ (accessed 23 February 2023).

5   Miles Davis is a character totem for Vincent in *Collateral* just as Cesar Chavez and Allen Ginsberg are for Bergman in *The Insider* or Okla is for Frank in *Thief*.

6   Thom Andersen exemplifies this idea further in *Los Angeles Plays Itself*. In Los Angeles "public space has largely been occupied by the quasi-private space of moving vehicles".

7   See Davis, *City of Quartz*, 223.

8   Indeed, Mann's script notes for this sequence feature the line: "Coyotes: we are immaterial to them." See Duncan Feeney, *Michael Mann*, Taschen, 2006, 174.

9   These final images of Los Angeles through the windows of the train were shot on green screen so that Mann could customise the visual experience. These are, in many ways, painted dreamscapes like those that Alfred Hitchcock had lovingly crafted for *Marnie* (1964).

10 Kubrick's *The Shining* (1980) is perhaps the best touchstone for the kind of harsh, overexposed exterior lighting that Spielberg began to employ in *A.I.* (2001) and then later in *Minority Report* (2002) and *Munich* (2005).

CHAPTER TWELVE

Miami Vice and Hi-Def Day[1]

> People who want Mann to go back to film are like those folkie drips who couldn't take it when Dylan went electric.
>
> Tristan Eldrich

Where *Collateral* was about the noirish darkness of Los Angeles as it appeared through the lens of a hi-def video camera, *Miami Vice*, Mann's 2006 movie reimagining of his and Anthony Yerkovich's important TV show, is chiefly concerned with the garish brightness of a very different set of environs. Set in a wide area ranging from South Florida to Cuba and all the way down to the tri-border area of Brazil, Paraguay and Argentina, *Miami Vice* was, as we shall see, both a logical next step for Mann after *Collateral* and anything but a simple, commercial rehash of a popular TV show from the 1980s. It is a film that takes those new incursions into narrative structure, framing and camera movement that were introduced in *Collateral* and melds them with an updated and greatly modulated interpretation of the criminal environment that the television show explored so well. One of those key modulations was to the sense of futility and foreboding that steadily crept into the TV series during its five-year run, a dramatic reality that sometimes grates against people's romanticised memories of the show as something jaunty and kitsch.

From the very opening of the film there is a sinister undercurrent at work that bespeaks the cynicism and poison that the show's co-executive producer Anthony Yerkovich perceived back in 1984:

> Even when I was on *Hill Street Blues* I was collecting information on Miami, I thought of it as a sort of a modern-day American Casablanca. It seemed to be an interesting socio-economic tide pool: the incredible number of refugees from Central America and Cuba, the already extensive Cuban-American community, and on top of all that the drug trade. There is a fascinating amount

of service industries that revolve around the drug trade – money laundering, bail bondsmen, attorneys who service drug smugglers. Miami has become a sort of Barbary Coast of free enterprise gone berserk.[2]

The film takes this understanding of Miami and the industries and ethnicities that were feeding into it at the time and runs with it, expanding the geopolitical scope far beyond the show's initial dramatic borders to places such as Ciudad del Este, the Paraguayan gateway city to Brazil and Argentina that is, in many respects, a lawless, ultra free-market paradise of international trade and crime. It also moves the show's interest in things such as the Art Deco architecture of Miami Beach into the dominant twenty-first-century movements such as neo-modern and neo-futurist that so now characterise Miami and the other major US cities.[3] Finally, and perhaps most important of all, the film offers a complete break from the traditional dramatic narrative structure that Mann has been slowly denuding from his cinematic work since the mid-1990s, a structure that was also, obviously, used in the TV series in a typical three-act form. Present all of these changes and modulations though the eyepiece of a Viper FilmStream hi-def video camera and you get *Miami Vice* the film, a largely misunderstood commentary on globalised crime patterns that is, as Manohla Dargis commented in her review of the movie, a "gorgeous, shimmering object…"[4]

The film opens with the camera emerging from the warm blue water off Miami Beach and into the maelstrom of an offshore powerboat race. Crockett and Tubbs are driving one such boat, a vehicle that remains a hallmark of the original series and is here deployed as part of the film's fascination with the innovative and new forms of transport being used in the world of narco-trafficking cartels. The presence of the Viper hi-def video camera is immediately apparent in the colours and tones of Mann's imagery here, the most startling of which must be the sheer whiteness of the frothy wake left behind by these boats and the luminous deep blue of the waters. In particular, this idea of whiteness, of an almost lurid, bleached-out but highly energising colouration, was the key motivator behind Mann's desire to use hi-def cameras once again. Of course there are night-time scenes in *Miami Vice*, wonderful evocations of the darkness of the city from the top of high-rise buildings that are only made possible with this high-definition technology, but it is in the opiated daytime exteriors of this tropical beach paradise that Mann's interests really lie.

In the daytime we see with clarity the attraction of this place, the stark addiction it generates in those who live and work there. The brightness

MIAMI VICE AND HI-DEF DAY

Figure 19. Miami Vice

of the whites goes with the streamlined formalism of this new Miami's architecture just as the TV show's pastel hues complemented its Art Deco buildings in the 1980s. This interlinking of technology and aesthetics reminds us that Mann openly uses digital technology to enhance the visual quality of his work rather than simply adopting it for the purposes of economy or efficiency. Crockett and Tubbs are undercover in this boat race in order to cut into a prostitution ring run by a pimp named Neptune. After the race they surveil another member of their team, Switek, arranging to meet Neptune at a club later that night as part of their sting operation. In its early focus on undercover work and pimps and prostitutes, this version of the opening of the film links more clearly to the idea of vice than the theatrical version does and, thus, to the interests of the original TV show, where most of the episodes explored either this topic or drug-running. At the nightclub called Mansion Crockett, Tubbs and the rest of the undercover team miss the chance to ensnare the pimp Neptune, but are then met with a frantic telephone call from a criminal informant (CI) whose world seems to be falling apart at the seams. It is at this point that the film quickly diverges from the parochial concerns of the TV show – pimps and local drug busts – and addresses something much more internationally pressing.

On the rooftop of the club the global scale of this new issue becomes clear as Crockett takes the call from his CI. The enormous depth-of-field generated by the Viper camera frames Crockett – who has his back to the world, confident in his supremacy – against the perpetual slippage of an infinite cityscape and Wagnerian night sky. As Tubbs joins him and the two try to divine some meaning from the CI Alonzo's scattershot delivery of info fragments and panicked exhortations, a plane can be seen behind them, high in the sky, climbing up into the air of the Miami night, its takeoff lights illuminating the stormy clouds ahead. Alonzo's deluge of info is mirrored by Mann's approach to shooting this scene and the one that follows soon after, where our duo meet with Fujima, an FBI man. As Graham Fuller pointed out in a *Sight & Sound* essay on *Miami Vice*:

> The urgency of this expository conversation … is emphasised by a kaleidoscopic flurry of dolly shots, low-angle shots, wobbling close-ups, reaction shots and a cutaway to a laptop screen showing the "go-fast boats" that Crockett wants to drive as part of his cover. This scene is an exemplary illustration of Mann's hectic formalism, which dispenses with the placid archaic grammar of scene-setting master shots and medium-length two-shots.[5]

While Fuller is absolutely correct in his detailed assessment of Mann's approach to covering even a seemingly simple dialogue exchange in *Miami Vice*, he makes it sound as if this has been Mann's methodology all along. Although things like master shots are rare in his canon, they are there in the opening imagery of, say, *The Last of the Mohicans* or *Heat* or *Ali*. Furthermore, the "wobbling close-ups" he mentions didn't really appear till 1995's *Heat*, and even then their use was slight compared to the 2000s. Finally, while they were never used in a perfunctory fashion to simply vary the view of, say, a dialogue scene, Mann did still use a series of highly idiosyncratic "medium-length two-shots" throughout his 1980s and, more importantly, his 1990s work in order to establish the binary opposition between characters and help develop his adherence to the symmetrical principles of Renaissance art. They are there in *Thief* when Frank meets with the fisherman on Lake Michigan, in *Manhunter* when Will sits on the log with Jack on the beach, in *The Last of the Mohicans* when Chingachgook and Hawkeye mourn the death of Uncas at the end of the film, in *Heat* when McCauley and Shiherlis sit together and drink coffee by the sea and, most brilliantly, in *The Insider* when Wigand and Bergman meet in the Japanese restaurant. No, what Fuller was recognising in *Miami Vice* was the fullest iteration yet of Mann's twenty-first-century creative impulses, of the new-millennial film-making grammar that began with *Ali* and arose more confidently in *Collateral*, a grammar indelibly tethered to his embrace of digital tech and his awareness of the globalised nature of crime and commerce. *Miami Vice* fearlessly distils Mann's many years' worth of R and D into the coverage of camera set-ups – the addition of the "wobbly close-ups" that only really began in earnest after 2001, the removal of any semblance of an establishing shot, the breakdown of the formal "medium-length two-shot", the insertion of cutaways – into a quintessentially post-millennial brew. This is the "kaleidoscopic flurry" of shots that Fuller spoke of, the camera shot collage that *only now* forms part of Mann's language for articulating the landscape of the twenty-first century.

Alongside the new language that Mann employs in *Miami Vice* sit his revisions to story structure, which are at their most radical yet. Although the opening montage of *Ali* is more ambitious in terms of the way in which it straddles multiple time periods and introduces different historical figures, the viewer is still guided by the fact that the film is a biopic and therefore, for example, the young boy looking at the painting of a blonde-haired, blue-eyed Jesus must be Ali as a child and so forth. The first 45 minutes of *Miami Vice*, by contrast, are a bold patchwork of tenuous connections involving fictional characters and, as yet, unknown relationships. The limiting contexts of the biopic are not available here to fall back on and Mann knows it. His guiding principle in the construction of this extended sequence was to render traditional dramatic forms obsolete and instead offer the viewer a cinematic experience based on the way events tend to unfold in the real world – messily, without discernible chronology and often lacking in full context.

As Crockett and Tubbs pace the nightclub rooftop trying to get in touch with Fujima to arrange a meet, the film cuts abruptly to the image of a family photo with Alonzo in it. The camera pans left and the image dissolves into a gold, damask curtain behind which we can see an out-of-focus figure standing in front of a refrigerator, all the while hearing Tubbs speaking on the phone back on the nightclub rooftop. Another cut and Mann's camera is now close behind this same figure at the fridge, only this time we can clearly see that he is a white supremacist covered in swastikas and other white power emblems. He's also wearing green rubber gloves, the left one of which is smeared with blood. Another cut and the camera is this time on the left side of the man where we can see past him to the same damask curtain from moments ago, this time across the room from us. The feet of a body are clearly visible at the bottom of the curtain. Another cut and Mann takes us back to the rooftop and Tubbs, who is still speaking on the phone. We then see Fujima in his office, followed by a further cut that takes us to yet another new location, a meeting of people by a dock somewhere near the Cobalt Blue Bridge at the Port of

Miami. We continue to hear Tubbs on the phone while witnessing these other locations.

Similar in strategy to what Oliver Stone does in key segments of *JFK* (1991), where he begins with a primary scene such as the *through the looking glass* sequence and then cuts in to the locations and events under discussion in that primary scene (which we remain privy to), this sequence in *Miami Vice* is about the deconstruction of traditional Hollywood storytelling. As Robert Kolker states of this process in *A Cinema of Loneliness*: "Stone sees time as perfectly malleable. More accurately, he sees time as entirely under the film-maker's control and as a tool for constructing and shifting points of view."[6] Some pages on he continues: "Stone breaks radically with conventional, linear narrative construction ... [he] insists that we pay attention not merely to stories, but to the images through which they are told..."[7] Like Stone's film, *Miami Vice* is enthralled by the investigative process. In its wish to present a hyper-real picture of Miami-Dade detective work that rebels against neat and tidy storytelling, the film takes up the latest in hi-def digital technology while dispensing with the narrative tropes of a conventional police procedural. The film replaces dramatic norms with the kind of deconstructed montage detailed above, an assemblage of overlapping dialogue, visual clues (the snipped cable ties around Alonzo's wrists) and interconnected locations that the viewer is expected to process and internalise.

Crockett and Tubbs track Alonzo down via the transponder they attached to his Bentley some months before. By the side of a freeway the detectives explain that Alonzo's partner has been killed by members of the same white supremacist prison gang that are meeting down near the Port of Miami. Acutely aware of what will now happen to him as a result, Alonzo walks out in front of an 18-wheeler and commits suicide in front of Crockett and Tubbs. His death sets in motion the rest of the film, which details Crockett and Tubbs's attempts to infiltrate the group responsible and follow the drug trail wherever it may lead. The opening assemblage of sound, noise and image is boldly perpetuated by Mann over the remaining 100 minutes as he refuses to regress into conventional story beats. As Jean-Baptiste Thoret wrote in his essay on the film for *Senses of Cinema*:

> The narrative develops then by jerks, flattens most of the peaks of action ... and multiplies the false starts ... then in a fraction of a second changes direction. Violence erupts in the shot, preceded by no ritual, blows up without forewarning and one enters into the film ... like a war reporter projected in the middle of a conflict in

progress. Without beginning or end, it is just 135 breathless minutes deducted from an uninterrupted flux of images and events.[8]

Along with the "kaleidoscopic flurry" of different shot choices that Mann perfects in *Miami Vice*, the narrative of flux with which he tells his story is the key to properly understanding the film and, in turn, his new-millennial project. Just as *JFK* was as much about Stone's investigation of the possibilities of editing and point of view as it was about the murder of a president, *Miami Vice* is an ultra-modern, hyper-realistic police film with the dual purpose of mimicking our media experiences of the twenty-first century. What were perceived as the film's failings upon its release – its narrative organisation, its hand-held freneticism, its repudiation of conventional dramatic cues – are actually the markers of Mann's perceptive new style, something that we might term *fragmentation cinema*. Like Steven Soderbergh's *hyperlink cinema*, where his film plots are organised laterally (radiating out in a democratised fashion from a central idea) rather than vertically (the traditional model of cause and effect with one or two privileged individuals), *Miami Vice* is shot and organised in a way meant to appropriate the "horizontal experience of human life, the spatial dimension of individual behaviour and social relations", things that the current generation is growing up completely accustomed to via the behemoth of social media and readily available film-making platforms.[9] The writers Edward Soja and Costis Hadjimichalis continues by saying, "It is scarcely any longer possible to tell a straight story sequentially unfolding in time … we are too aware of what is continually traversing the story line laterally."[10]

Crockett and Tubbs have successfully penetrated this new criminal group by posing as experienced drug traffickers. Their fabricated identities are sent to Ciudad del Este, the chaotic border town and gateway to the head of this new group, Montoya, played by Luis Tosar. In Mann's hi-def daytime, Ciudad del Este appears as a bright and colourful mess of street rubbish, knotted telephone wires, multi-ethnic populations and a laissez faire commerce protected by armed private security. The hot colour temperature of the Viper cameras and the vaguely sinister electronic music that is laid over these images cast this town – and most of the Central and South American locations in *Miami Vice* – as distinctly otherworldly and alien when compared to the film's view of Miami. As captured by Mann's cameras, both are beautiful in their own right, but it is Ciudad del Este that emerges as the new frontier of international, black market commerce, displacing Miami and the frontier role it enjoyed back in the 1980s.

As an Asian courier delivers the identities of Crockett and Tubbs on a USB to some middle-management players, there are strong overtones of the Hong Kong market scenes of 2015's *Blackhat*. Both environments are bustling but dangerous bazaars of product signage, shoppers, foreign-language menus and strewn cabling that act as metaphors for the twenty-first-century globalised experience. It was noted in the chapter on *Heat* that as early as 1995 Mann was beginning to show an awareness of the rising relevance of the Far East (specifically China, Japan and South Korea) and South America in global affairs. This awareness manifested itself in small ways in *Heat* – Pac Rim influences such as the Far East National Bank and Hanna's night-time rendezvous in Koreatown – and *The Insider* – the Japanese restaurant where Bergman and Wigand meet – before becoming more integral in *Ali* with the character of Yumi Kochiyama and the Audubon Ballroom sequence. By the time *Collateral* arrived Mann was visibly equating the new millennium with the rise of nation-states in Asia. In Vincent's back story his home is a province of Thailand while the fourth victim on his hitlist is a Korean gangster holed up in a Korean nightclub.

Miami Vice would expand on the narrative function of these kinds of locales and mine the new market economies of the likes of Haiti, Cuba and the tri-borders of Ciudad del Este for its street murals, clandestine meeting places, drug lords and shootout sites. But more than these visual details and character types, *Miami Vice* would develop Mann's interest in the twenty-first-century frontier by adopting the *sensibility* of these places as well as their look. This incarnation of Crockett and Tubbs is predicated on the notion of a diminished US hegemony, and the film is fraught with the feeling that new but dangerous things exist out there, across the sea, in exotic and undiscovered places.[11] Mann revels in the otherworldly big skies and deep oceans of the film's reconnoitres beyond the US border and uses his Viper cameras to capture the epic dimensions to be found there. As Crockett and Tubbs make their way to meet with Montoya's middleman, Yero, their flight through the towering cloudscapes above Haiti provides one such example. Mann's camera seems to float amid these clouds, the scale of which is immense. They could be replacements for the ones Jacob van Ruisdael painted in *View of Alkmaar* (1675–80), where Crockett and Tubbs's tiny plane acts as the substitute for Van Ruisdael's minuscule figures on the ground.

In a subterranean nightclub with frightening murals of contorted faces on the walls, Yero agrees to let Crockett and Tubbs venture further into the new frontier and meet with Montoya, the archangel of US drug trafficking. With its painted imagery of screams and death like a Francis Bacon portrait, this underground bar seems haunted with a kind of post-colonial abandonment. The crumbling pillars and dusty floors link

MIAMI VICE AND HI-DEF DAY

Figure 20. Miami Vice

up to a series of places in this middle section of the film – places such as Crockett and Tubbs's Haitian apartment, the deserted town square where the duo meet Montoya, the stash house in Overtown, Isabella's Bauhaus property opposite the Rex Hotel in Havana – that are stunning in their hi-resolution decay. Peeling paint, broken concrete and cobbled streets mingle with cobalt blue skies and ivory white clouds; the new, transnational, technocratic frontier emerging from the ruins of old empires.

This method of shooting the old with the new, of capturing the decay of a physical environment with the highest-resolution, most light-sensitive cameras available, would find its fullest expression in Mann's next film, *Public Enemies*, but its genesis arguably lies here, in *Miami Vice*'s paradoxical look at cutting-edge drug trafficking technology amid old-world decrepitude. When, at the behest of Yero, Trudy, Tubbs's girlfriend, is kidnapped by the Aryan Brotherhood killers from the start of the film, *Miami Vice* launches into its third act, one characterised by gun violence that looks like war reporting. Jean-Baptiste Thoret saw the viewer of *Miami Vice* as a war correspondent and the film as a conflict. At the time of the film's release the disastrous Iraq war was three years into its protracted timeline, and movie-going audiences were more than accustomed to seeing the nightly news's hand-held incursions into the battlefields of Basra and Baghdad. They had internalised the visual and aural conventions of wartime reportage to such a degree – hand-held, shaky images linked elliptically and overlaid with a subjective, localised sound – that the concept of realism on TV and in film was now frequently equated with these characteristics.

When Crockett and Tubbs discover that Trudy is being held in a trailer park near Miami International Airport, they plan a night-time attack to save her that is a marvel of tight framing, tense blocking and jittery camera work. The pre-*Breaking Bad* meth-lab trailer where Trudy is being held captive, blindfolded and wearing a C4 necklace, is a wonder of set-dressing and judicious prop placement that was so accurately created by the film's production team that real law enforcement officials visited it to learn from its look. When the assault on the trailer begins, so does one of the most effective sequences Mann has ever shot. After Crockett chokes out an armed guard, Gina inserts a pinhole camera into the floor of the trailer from underneath – four people, two shooters, she gestures to the others silently. Tubbs then finds a discarded pizza box and masquerades as a delivery man in order to get the trailer door open. In a masterfully edited series of shots Tubbs throws to the ground the first man to answer the door, breaking his neck before swooping into the trailer, followed by Crockett and Gina. He then knocks out a teenage boy armed with a knife and swiftly kills another man who takes aim at him with a baseball bat. Mann now deploys one of his "wobbly close-ups" tight on Tubbs's face, the tension ratcheting up with every additional zoom in. Gina shoots the main Aryan brother, who has been holding the trigger to Trudy's C4 necklace all along, through the medulla at the base of his neck, causing the customary billow of pink mist to emerge as he falls to the ground dead.

Like all war footage, this sequence feels both important and impermanent, formidable but fleeting, like a bystander's mobile phone footage of a natural disaster or market bombing. Thoret writes, "Filming with the camera on the shoulder gives the feeling, new in Mann, of a constant fragility of shots and, therefore, of what they show."[12] As with the flux of camera shots and the narrative fragmentation, this induced fragility, courtesy of the highly mobile, hi-def cameras, was the reason for some of the main criticisms of the film upon its release. Some reviewers felt it cheapened the film experience, reducing it a home-movie version of a serious and muscular police procedural. However, this aesthetic judgement – getting these hi-def cameras off dolly tracks and heavy rigs and on to the shoulder of the camera operator (most likely Mann in this trailer park sequence) – is the absolute key to *Miami Vice*'s success as a zeitgeist-tapping, highly relevant evocation of twenty-first-century image making and storytelling. This fragility in the film that Thoret speaks of is the same fragility that we all now indulge in, through our mobile phones, YouTube and the 280 characters of Twitter. Permanence in storytelling and imagery is now a relative term when cloud storage and online sites have removed the presence of any physical objects in these arenas. Through his jittery imagery, Mann was merely foreshadowing the transience of narrative and visuals that would become more and more apparent with the rise of democratising consumer technologies.

The shootout that caps *Miami Vice*, overlaid with Nonpoint's cover of "In the Air Tonight" by Phil Collins, gathers together the film's hat-trick of multiple camera shots, narrative fragmentation and induced fragility into a kind of love-it-or-leave-it finale. Once Crockett and Tubbs receive the location of the meet with Yero and his gangsters, the two reaffirm their cop buddy relationship by knocking their clenched fists together before heading into potentially mortal conflict. This gesture reinforces the virility and legitimacy of the police partner relationship in US crime fiction, something Christopher Sharrett saw as under threat in *Miami Vice* and perhaps the larger genre in general. He notes of the film's ending: "But most crucial is the threatened status of the male buddy construct basic to American fiction."[13] While Tubbs questions the point of what he refers to as "this bullshit life" after Trudy is severely injured at the trailer park (the trailer explodes after her daring rescue by Crockett and Tubbs), we know that he will remain, first and foremost, an undercover detective. The fist bump moment included, there are many scenes in the film where Crockett and Tubbs reaffirm their relationship after one particularly gruelling task or another, where they talk of trusting one another 100% and never doubting one another's judgement. Despite the film's insistence on charting the romantic entanglements of Crockett or the ongoing relationship of Trudy and Tubbs, the most interesting pairing is Crockett and Tubbs themselves. Frequently blocked together by Mann and cinematographer Dion Beebe, the duo are the film's lodestone, via which everything else is attracted or repelled depending on the polarity involved. Even when Crockett shows signs of losing his bearings in his assumed identity as a smuggler – something Mann refers to as *mentalist syndrome* – Tubbs still publicly backs him without hesitation in front of his own boss and the FBI SAC Fujima.

At the shootout's end Yero is dead along with several of his Aryan Brotherhood cronies, and Isabella now knows Crockett's true identity. Tubbs returns to be with Trudy at the hospital while Crockett takes Isabella to a safe house on the coast where she can await a boat back to Cuba. The wrenching departure of Isabella from Crockett's life is a rarity in Mann's oeuvre and adds a new and unexpected pathos to *Miami Vice*'s ending. Typically, the endings of Mann's films revolve around either the man departing from the woman (*Thief, Heat*), the woman being absent from the male's resolution of events (*The Insider, Ali*), the couple being reunited (the original cut of *Manhunter*) or properly forming for the first time (*The Last of the Mohicans, Collateral* and *Blackhat*). Although the bleakness of Crockett and Isabella being torn asunder is balanced out as Trudy shows signs of emerging from her coma and coming back to life, the ending of *Miami Vice* remains anomalous. It's certainly not as bleak an ending as, say, *Thief*'s but neither is it as affirmative as *Manhunter*'s (original cut) or as cathartic as *Ali*'s. The final shot of Crockett walking back into the Miami hospital where Trudy is recovering, after having said goodbye to Isabella forever, seems to tell us that nothing has really changed. Minutes earlier it was also made clear that Montoya had escaped arrest by local authorities in his country, therefore denying both the viewer and Crockett and Tubbs any sense of conventional closure. The ending remains, however, powerfully authentic and adopts a similar strategy to the endings of most of Christopher Nolan's films, where a musical cue overlaps multiple images and narrative threads, generating a grand and satisfying summation of events.

Holistically, *Miami Vice* was the most radical shift yet away from the visual and narrative strategies of Mann's early work such as *The Last of the Mohicans* and *Heat*. While all these films are loaded with certain determinants that should be obvious to the reader by this stage, *Miami Vice* moved far ahead of the pack in new ways and placed fresh demands on the audience in terms of their involvement with the film's narrative structuring and its visual grammar. Lensing all this through the searing chroma of the Viper hi-def video camera produced a film that appropriated the look and feel of war footage one moment and an opiated dream world the next. The film has its cumbersome moments – the long middle section that charts the romance between Crockett and Isabella, for all its architectural beauty, saps the energy that the opening 45 minutes worked so hard to create – and seems unrelenting in its doom-laden view of modern times and criminal fraternities. Yet, coming from a director who was 63 at the time, it is also a film of incredible experimentation and dexterity and one that pointed, with the clearest signposting yet, towards an ongoing commitment to creative and technological reinvention.

Miami Vice must be viewed and understood from the vantage of its proper place in Mann's oeuvre. Just as in Darwinian evolution, where a series of small permutations and adjustments lead to big differences over time, Mann's tenth film is best understood as a series of further adjustments within a larger lineage of creative evolution. Taken on its own, it is a film whose narrative radicalism and hi-def aesthetic could be (and, indeed, was) misunderstood as directorial weakness and production cheapness respectively. Its trail-blazing must be contextualised by the foreshadowing that came before it in *Collateral* and the finessing that followed it in *Public Enemies*.

If this strategy is adopted, just like watching a trilogy in the correct order, *Miami Vice* appears as a radical but recognisable entry in Mann's career where the established determinants of crime, framing and cinematic space meet with new innovations in story structure and shot choices.

> Key scene suggestion for hi-def day – any of the daytime flying sequences in the film, where aircraft are positioned against towering, brilliant white clouds or approaching storms.

Notes

1 It should be noted that this chapter is based upon the US Unrated Director's Edition of *Miami Vice* and not the version more readily available in the UK.
2 Richard Zoglin, "Cool Cops, Hot Show", *Time Magazine*, 16 September 1985, https://content.time.com/time/subscriber/article/0,33009,959822,00.html (accessed 23 February 2023).
3 The film does, however, manage to shoehorn in some of the famous pastel-coloured Art Deco architecture of Miami during the opening powerboat race.
4 Manohla Dargis, "Not for the Faint of Heart or Lazy of Thought", *New York Times*, December 2006, https://www.nytimes.com/2006/12/24/movies/not-for-the-faint-of-heart-or-lazy-of-thought.html (accessed 23 February 2023).
5 Graham Fuller, "Which Way is Up?", *Sight & Sound* 16, no. 9 (September 2006): 16.
6 Robert Kolker, *A Cinema of Loneliness: Penn, Stone, Kubrick, Scorsese, Spielberg, Altman*, 3rd edn, Oxford University Press, 2000, 65.
7 Ibid., 75.
8 http://sensesofcinema.com/2007/feature-articles/miami-vice/ (accessed 26 December 2022).
9 Edward W. Soja and Costis Hadjimichalis, "Between Geographical Materialism and Spatial Fetishism: Some Observations on the Development of Marxist Spatial Analysis", *Antipode* 11, no. 3 (1979): 60.
10 Ibid.
11 In an essay on Mann, Christopher Sharrett saw this demise of US superiority appearing as early as *Collateral*, when he wrote that "the world through which they [Max and Vincent] travel is again Los Angeles, a

grim cityscape suggesting the frontier at trail's end (we see coyotes in the street)". See Christopher Sharrett, "Michael Mann: Elegies on the Post-industrial Landscape", in Yvonne Tasker (ed.), *Fifty Contemporary Filmmakers*, Routledge, 2010, 275.
12 http://sensesofcinema.com/2007/feature-articles/miami-vice/ (accessed 26 December 2022).
13 Sharrett, "Michael Mann", 277.

CHAPTER THIRTEEN

Public Enemies and the Driven Detective

> The FBI was totally cooperative with us; they had no sensitivity about Hoover at all, zero. And in Washington they said, "Is there anything else you'd like?" And I said, yeah, pull out the Melvin Purvis file. They said sure, and they went to get the file. There's one sheet of paper in it. One sheet of paper. His employment application. That was it. And they were stunned. And it was like Stalin erasing all these pictures of the politburo with Trotsky before Stalin and Trotsky had been erased. So, same thing. Hoover erased Melvin Purvis.
>
> Michael Mann

Public Enemies is a very interesting film, partly because the central protagonist, the FBI lawman Melvin Purvis (Christian Bale), isn't particularly good at what he does, a heinous crime in Mann's worldview up to this point. The tale of John Dillinger's (Johnny Depp) momentous twelve-month crime spree, from his release from prison in 1933 to his death outside the Biograph Theatre in Chicago in 1934, *Public Enemies* continues, in many ways, the creative reinvention of director Michael Mann in the twenty-first century. Up until 2004's *Collateral*, the detective characters in Mann's work were always competent and, sometimes, highly skilled individuals for whom police work was the "elevated experience" of their lives, as Mann terms it. Even in *Thief,* Mann's first big-screen outing, the cops are sketched out as being at least reasonably competent at what they do, managing to apprehend Frank and cause him numerous problems, however corrupt they are shown to be. But it was 1986's *Manhunter* that introduced audiences to the upscale revision of *Thief*'s police officers, the archetype of the driven detective. Highly motivated, extremely skilled and not dissimilar from his quarry, the driven detective in this film was

FBI Agent Will Graham who apprehended and killed Dollarhyde before reappearing in 1995 in the guise of *Heat*'s Vincent Hanna. Hanna, like Graham before him, possessed incredible intuitive abilities and was shown as willing to sacrifice the stability of his own family in order to tail and eliminate his foe. *Manhunter* and *Heat* are films that acknowledge the selfless (or selfish?) skill of the high-order lawman. They validate the work of detection, whatever the cost to sanity, as in *Manhunter*, or family, as in *Heat*, because ultimately the detectives are successful and the films end with the restoration of a moral order.

But 2004's *Collateral* seemed to change things. It signalled an emergent cynicism about law enforcement in general and the character of the detective in particular. Despite Fanning's consummate skill, he is killed by Vincent in the most pathetic of ways, arbitrarily removed from the remaining events of the film, leaving a taxi driver to do his work for him. Other detectives, police officers and FBI agents in the film are shown to be unmotivated (Detective Weidner), incompetent (the police officer who arrives at Max's crashed taxi) or simply unwilling to cooperate by sharing information (Agent Pedrosa). *Miami Vice*, in spite of surface appearances, continued many of these trends in its exploration of undercover work and the attendant risks involved to personal identity and family security. As well as the fact that the arch villain of the film, the drug lord Montoya, escapes long before law enforcement arrives at his door, the film is replete with other criticisms of police operating procedures and safety protocols: a mole leaks information to the Aryan Brotherhood that an undercover FBI man is posing as a drugs buyer, Trudy is kidnapped because Crockett and Tubbs vastly underestimate Yero and his crew, Crockett becomes romantically involved with a criminal (Isabella). The driven detective remains in these works but in a heavily attenuated form, perhaps more realistic as a human being but also more indicative of Mann's fledgling scepticism about the function of law enforcement in the twenty-first century when set against the behemoth of transnational organised crime.

Public Enemies did little to change this emerging scepticism about new-millennial policing despite the fact that it takes place in 1933. Set during Modernism's great expansion into politics and the artistic establishment and captured, once again, with hi-def video cameras, *Public Enemies* amalgamates detectives Fanning, Crockett and Tubbs with the real historical figure of FBI lawman Melvin Purvis, producing Mann's most tormented and ultimately ineffectual detective yet. In the film Agent Purvis is a lawman who is constantly shown as being plagued by doubt and inner turmoil with regard to what he does and what he is asked to do by his superiors. Irrespective of the fact that he was only in his early

Public Enemies and the Driven Detective

Figure 21. Public Enemies

thirties when he led the investigation into Dillinger and his gang, Purvis was an old Southern gent in his outlook and philosophical approach to policing. He was the vanguard of J. Edgar Hoover's newly inaugurated Federal Bureau of Investigation, the epitome of modernism at the time, but also upheld the notion of chivalry and adhered to a strict code of conduct that grated against the expediency, use of torture and suspension of habeas corpus that Hoover advocated in the FBI's infancy. Ultimately, this conflict within Purvis between the old, treasured traits of the landed gentry and the new, gloves-off approach to crime fighting would lead to him being largely erased by Hoover from FBI records in later years.

Based on the excellent book of the same name by Bryan Burrough, *Public Enemies* foregrounds Mann's burgeoning cynicism of law and order with an opening rebuke of the penal system in America in the 1930s. After some title cards inform us that this is 1933 and the fourth year of the Great Depression (in a font specifically designed for the film), Mann begins with the diegetic sound of marching feet. The first image of the film is a line of prison convicts in white and black striped overalls marching in a single line through the sandy yard of Indiana State Penitentiary. A series of cuts to different shots with varying depths of field and framing remind us of Mann's now customary approach to the use of cinematic space. These are glimpses, fragments or fractals of the whole, slices of an activity that build to what could be termed a master shot of the prison yard and this group of men – leave it to Mann to *end* an opening sequence with the establishing shot. In among these glimpses is the unsettling image of a convict lying motionless in the sand of the yard, at the very least unconscious but, in all likelihood, dead. The others do not acknowledge the body. This was an era when the reckless eyeballing of a prison guard would result in a brutal beating. Thanks to the Sony

205

F23 camera, the long shot that caps this intro is pin sharp in its resolution and we can see small piles of snow at the very back of this space and a hyper-real scattering of clouds in the blue sky that further augments the Y axis.[1] The startling immediacy of these images instantly banishes any idea of nostalgia for the past or the sense that we are passively watching recreated events. It replaces them, instead, with a real-time, real-world sensibility that this is *now*.

The sentiment at work here, something more crucial to this chapter, is the polar opposite of, say, *The Jericho Mile*'s view of prison life or even that of *Thief*, where Frank's negative view of penal life was derived from his need to protect himself from other convicts, not the guards. Dillinger is introduced in the next shot being brought to jail by a marshal, but it's a ruse, some clever ex-con trickery designed to bust the rest of Dillinger's crew out of detention. Dillinger's crew regroup in the prison sally port, change into guards' outfits and then shoot their way out to the getaway car. Dillinger's mentor, Walter Dietrich, is shot in the back by one of the prison guards standing atop the prison wall, an act that seems absolutely cowardly from our point of view because Mann tightly tethers his camera to the dying Walter and his grimacing face. A summation of this opening scene would have to conclude that Dillinger's introduction and characterisation is extremely favourable, portrayed as he is as being highly competent but also compassionate and pragmatic, when measured against the harsh brutality of the prison system. When the film moves to the next sequence and the introduction of Purvis, the tack changes back again and the film's negative rendering of law enforcement in 1933 and, by extension, today is further developed.

Purvis is introduced chasing the outlaw Pretty Boy Floyd through an apple orchard to the tune of "Ten Million Slaves" by Otis Taylor, a strident condemnation of America's slave trade used here to allude to Purvis's Southern roots and the tyrannical government he represents. Mann blocks this sequence so that Floyd is very much the outgunned fox to Purvis's rabid hounds. After yelling a cursory "Halt" at Floyd, Purvis takes careful aim and, from some distance away, shoots him with a Mauser rifle. Like the killing of Walter Dietrich in the opening sequence, Floyd is shot in the back, a cowardly act that smacks of the newly formed federal government's desperation in the face of these skilled, de facto nineteenth-century bandits. This account of Floyd's killing (something Sharrett refers to as "Purvis' murder of Pretty Boy Floyd") is debatable but what is made clear in Mann's interpretation is Purvis's seeming indifference to the demands of his profession.[2] His blank demeanour here, even in the face of Floyd telling him he can "rot in hell" as he bleeds to death, points to what Sharrett later terms Purvis's "essential barbarism, which exceeds Dillinger's".[3]

The binary opposition that links Dillinger and Purvis here may recall *Heat* and the relationship between Hanna and McCauley, but *Public Enemies* is not *Heat 2*. Both are chase narratives in the sense of a cop pursuing a robber and both deal with modernism – one explores its infancy in the 1930s while the other explores its senility in the 1990s – but that is the point where the two diverge.[4] If there's cynicism about the justice system in *Heat* it is marginal and directed exclusively at the supposed opportunities available to ex-cons trying to re-enter mainstream life, as exemplified by the character of Breedan. *Heat* parades its master detective (Hanna) like a prize steer, revelling in his policing prowess and emotional attachment to victims even at the expense of his family. *Public Enemies*, by contrast, comes three films into Mann's twenty-first-century revisionism of his 1990s ideas and is, therefore, far more critical not only of the same detective archetype (as we saw in *Collateral* and *Miami Vice*) but also policing and the prison system in general. Mann's post-millennial crime quartet (*Collateral*, *Miami Vice*, *Public Enemies* and 2015's *Blackhat*) marginalises law and order systems through its open critique of their practices and the detailing of their failures. It is highly interesting and no accident that in this quartet the key detective figures have no hand in the capture and/or elimination of the films' primary villains: Max kills Vincent and not Detective Fanning in *Collateral*; Montoya escapes justice long before Crockett and Tubbs provide the authorities with information about his jungle mansion in *Miami Vice*; Purvis, as we shall see, fails to get Dillinger himself in *Public Enemies* and is emasculated in the process; and in *Blackhat*, Hathaway the hacker eliminates the cyberterrorist Sadak, and not the professional Department of Justice officials or US marshalls assigned to the task.

In place of any positive appraisal of the justice system in 1933, *Public Enemies* idealises the acme of the American bandit while all but ignoring the crushing impact of the Great Depression, a dichotomy summarised by Michael Atkinson when he was discussing *Miller's Crossing* (1990) and *Bonnie and Clyde* (1967): "[They] represent the Depression not as an economic cataclysm but as a romanticised cultural childhood."[5] Although *Public Enemies* is more about the death throes of that cultural experience, as organised crime disavowed criminals such as Dillinger in favour of safer, commodity-free enterprises such as corporate capitalism and gambling, the film still romanticises it, fixing its gaze as it does on Dillinger and his crew for most of the time. Critic Christopher Sharrett refers very aptly to these longing gazes as Mann's "arias" that are "centred on homage for the male group and male beauty", in this instance the beauty of the criminals.⁶

In one of Dillinger's next scenes in *Public Enemies* he and his handsome crew are stocking up on supplies at a dust-bowl farmhouse. The peeling paint on the walls and the one or two tattered laundry items fluttering on the line speak of the Depression's pernicious effects on ordinary people at the time. But the most lingering image here is not of the kind captured by Walker Evans or Dorothea Lange in their sharp, black and white photography but a left-to-right tracking shot of first the distant horizon and then the back of Dillinger's head as he scans the landscape. Yes, it's a variation of Crockett's gaze towards the sea near the beginning of *Miami Vice* or Hawkeye looking to the future at the end of *Mohicans*, but this shot is also a vindication of both Atkinson's and Sharrett's observations about romanticism and longing respectively.

In its alignment with the criminals and not the police, *Public Enemies* recalls one of the Hays Office's original codes that was specifically aimed at gangster pictures of the early 1930s: films could no longer present criminal activity "in such a way as to throw sympathy with the crime as against the law and justice or to inspire others with a desire for imitation".⁷ Introduced to try and tone down future gangster films that might have wished to ape the likes of *Little Caesar* (1930), *The Public Enemy* (1931) and *Scarface* (1932), the Hays' Codes remind us of the genuine fear that existed in certain moral circles with regard to crime films that dared to suggest a parity between the criminals and the audience.

As the film progresses Mann takes pains to establish Dillinger as a man of the people – which he was – while rendering Purvis in effete hues, even at this early stage of his ascension to SAC of the Chicago Field Office of the new FBI. Purvis's suits, immaculately made by occasional Mann costume designer Colleen Atwood, his carriage and his demeanour reveal the heavily codified, gentrified, old-time Southern upbringing that will soon bring him so much turmoil, even as Hoover is dropping him right into the centre of his modern, unregulated war on crime. While Dillinger casts himself as a hero for the poor by regurgitating Neil McCauley's line from *Heat* about being here for the bank's money and not yours (the public's), Purvis is, quite literally, dressing to kill. Despite the trappings of his background, Purvis throws himself into the search for Dillinger. Via data analysis of where Dillinger bought a coat and pioneering innovations in voice recording, the FBI begins to narrow its search and close the noose around Dillinger's neck. Vincent Hanna or Will Graham might have used the same technologies decades later, but they did so without any real sense of a higher power monitoring their moves and riding their coat-tails. Jack

PUBLIC ENEMIES AND THE DRIVEN DETECTIVE

Crawford puts Will up to finding Dollarhyde but Will answers to no one because of his exceptionalism. The same can be said of Hanna, who acts as detective and boss at the same time and whose successes are his own.[8] Purvis, by contrast, is a detective who appears constantly under the aegis of another, in this case a highly unscrupulous machine politician who would eventually destroy him.

Dillinger meets Billie Frechette, a half-French, half-Menominee Indigenous woman, and a short time later they spend the night together, an event that Mann deconstructs with editing so that the act of lovemaking is intercut with the following discussion about who Billie is and her experiences of racism. Elsewhere, Mann has explained that the deconstruction was an attempt to arrive at a kind of Morphean sensibility or state of dreaminess in the scene, a timeout for two people who are normally always on the lookout. If viewed, however, in the light of Mann's twenty-first-century project, something that he experimented with in *Collateral* before fully venting it in *Miami Vice*, this scene is yet a further blow to the conventional narrative organisation we would expect to see elsewhere or, indeed, that usually appeared in Mann's films of the 1980s and 1990s. The state of flux here, with its fragmentation and paradoxical sense of unity, is part of Mann's discordant recording of how real dramatic moments such as these unfold. It's also a form of experimentation that he must have deemed successful, as he captures a scene between Hathaway and Chen in *Blackhat* in a very similar way, mixing up the present – Chen asleep and Hathaway staring blankly – with earlier moments – Hathaway talking about his father while he thinks about his time in jail – so that the scene becomes diffuse and elastic, like the movie itself.

Although Mann was not part of the New Hollywood cinematic movement of the late 1960s and 1970s, scenes such as this one in *Public Enemies* nevertheless recall that period's zeal for temporal experimentation and, obviously, the specifics of Arthur Penn's *Bonnie and Clyde* (1967). Alongside this sequence with Dillinger and Billie, *Public Enemies* and *Bonnie and Clyde* feature other key scenes that are edited in oblique forms which call the audience's attention to the form of cinema itself. The invisible harmony of the traditional Hollywood continuity style is broken by a desire to make audiences work for the meaning of the imagery. In the climactic shootout of *Bonnie and Clyde*, time is not conflated, as in this sequence in *Public Enemies*, but dilated. Where Mann is mixing up his tenses in order to make a candid statement about the evolving bond between Dillinger and his moll, Penn uses editing to stretch out a single, longing glance between Clyde Barrow and Bonnie Parker (as they realise they are about to be shot dead) into a series of disjointed and rapid-fire

Figure 22. Public Enemies

images that mimic the panicked synapses firing in their brains. Despite the differing use of editing, the objective is the same in each case – to highlight the bond between two people (its beginning in *Public Enemies* and its end in *Bonnie and Clyde*) through a disjointed montage loaded with meaning.

Purvis next appears at a rented apartment that his team thinks belongs to Dillinger. Massing outside, Purvis asks about line of sight and which members of the team are in position, to which questions he gets an embarrassed and silent response. Once again Mann is counterposing the proficiency of Dillinger's criminal crew against the general ineptitude of Purvis's law-enforcement team. While it is historically accurate to display the two sides of this crime war in these ways, Mann is also perpetuating a theme here, developing a change in his representation of investigative law officials of which there were signs in *Collateral*. One of Purvis's deputies is shot dead by the man – Baby Face Nelson and not Dillinger – who lives in the apartment, an act that, in turn, prompts a larger shootout on the street. Purvis kneels at the head of the dying man and internalises the angst of the moment (much as Hanna does in *Heat* when he sees Bosko being shot) before recomposing himself and heading down the corridor. Bale is particularly good here as Purvis, moving as he does with sleek efficiency from door to door with his rifle drawn and his gold ring twinkling in the darkness. The percussive power of the weaponry being used here is made clear through the film's sound design, as round after round hits the plaster of exterior walls and the soil of street flowerbeds. Nelson and his crew flee in a light show of muzzle flashes and screeching tyres while Purvis is once again frustrated by the failure of his men to act professionally. Purvis's pursuit team, two agents in a car who should have stood ready to chase down Nelson, instead come running to the commotion of the shootout in the street and let Nelson escape in the process. It should be remembered that, although Hanna suffers from similar ineptitude in *Heat* when the officer bangs against the side of the trailer, thus alerting McCauley to the police's presence, *Heat* reaffirms the sanctity of the police as an institution by having Hanna kill McCauley at the film's climax. No such affirmation will be present at the end of *Public Enemies*.

In the next scene Dillinger and his team successfully rob another bank, this time of $74,000, a huge sum in 1933. This is followed by Hoover haranguing Purvis for his failure to apprehend Nelson. Purvis stands by his FBI office window in Chicago, pleading with Hoover to let him bring up some Texas lawmen – cowboys in essence and murderous ones at that – to assist in the hunt for Dillinger. Hoover repeats his founding intentions for the FBI, which was to build a modern police force, not one staffed by old-timers from the Wild West. Purvis offers a line in response that is not intended as an excuse for his failures but more as a poignant moment of self-realisation – "Our type cannot get the job done." Purvis, the previously driven detective, is acknowledging that the modern and effete lawmen that Hoover has been busy recruiting (of whom he is one) are completely ineffectual against these foes.

The easy escape of Nelson brought it home to Purvis that to kill nineteenth-century bandits you need nineteenth-century killers, adherents of a violent philosophy, men of true grit. For Mann, Charles Winstead represents exactly the kind of new brutality that is required to take down his twenty-first-century incarnation of criminals. Purvis, like Detective Fanning in *Collateral* or the Department of Justice officials in *Blackhat*, wields an array of modern tools in his war on crime but lacks the single-minded sensibility to simply walk up behind the bad guy and pull the trigger. In *Collateral* it takes the simple-minded but chaotic approach of Max to stop Vincent, the willingness just to stand up and shoot at him through the door of the train. In *Blackhat* it falls to Hathaway and his *Taxi Driver*-inspired cache of sharpened screwdrivers and semi-bionic magazine appendages to kill Kassar and Sadak (which he does with some of the most brutal violence Mann has ever filmed). The notion of the successful detective of *Manhunter* or *Heat* has been replaced by more extreme variants in Mann's post-millennial cinema, as if in acknowledgement of these new patterns of globalised crime and the new threats they pose.

Winstead and his Texas lawmen arrive at Union Station in Chicago (the stairs on which the famous climax to Brian De Palma's *The Untouchables* (1987) was shot are visible to the right of the frame) and ready themselves to work with Purvis's FBI office and their modern methods. Dillinger is unexpectedly arrested in Tucson, Arizona, where he was holidaying with Billie and the rest of his gang. In his holding cell Dillinger comes face to face with Purvis, who has travelled to meet him during this interim period before he goes to court. This meeting between the two men never took place and is instead a relatively rare example of dramatic licence on Mann's part, intended to convey a number of things. The first is to reinforce the men-of-the-West mentality that was earlier introduced through the arrival of Winstead, and the second is to clarify, for the last time, the difference between Purvis and Dillinger. The older generation lawmen whom Dillinger was arrested by in Tucson, while happy to use violence in their apprehension of suspects, also possess a chivalry and honour that Hoover was attempting to completely expunge in his maniacal drive for arrests. While Hoover was suspending habeas corpus, these older lawmen were giving Billie a few dollars and seeing her on to a bus back to Chicago even as they were arresting Dillinger. These men represent an inversion of the *fin-de-siècle* sensibility of Sam Peckinpah's *The Wild Bunch*, where the cowboys were at the end of their usefulness but didn't know it. Here, in *Public Enemies*, the old law men, previously outdated, become relevant again as they succeed in getting Dillinger when Purvis and the FBI fail.

The other function this fictional scene serves is to allow Dillinger to penetrate the surface of Purvis's carapace and verbalise an insight, the core of which Purvis has secretly been wrestling with for some time – that Purvis lacks the mettle for this work. Having been told by Purvis that the only way he'll leave a jail cell is when they take him out to execute him, Dillinger waits a second before saying, "Gotta get yourself another line of work, Melvin." On the surface a glib line, this recommendation by Dillinger cuts to the heart of Purvis, who stands at the door for a few seconds before leaving. The bank robber is calling into question the potency of Purvis's piss and vinegar, his confidence and his ability to go toe-to-toe with someone who is used to death and dying. Purvis is a tragic figure from here on, still capable in certain scenes but ultimately redundant without accepting it. Dillinger may be the anachronism but Purvis is simply impotent.

Dillinger is taken to the jail in Crown Point, Indiana, from which, a short while from now, he will mount an audacious and thrilling escape, something that will only give further ballast to his recommendation to Purvis in the earlier scene. Hoover despairs as he learns of the escape and provides Purvis with even more state powers to use in recapturing or killing Dillinger. So paranoid was Hoover that Dillinger would escape

PUBLIC ENEMIES AND THE DRIVEN DETECTIVE

from the jail at Crown Point that he stationed a number of former WWI soldiers outside the building to keep guard on the comings and goings. This move, too, proves inadequate. Using a carved wooden replica of a handgun, Dillinger busts out of Crown Point and, stealing the Sheriff's new Ford V8, flees once again into the landscape. Dillinger phones Billie in Chicago to inform her of his release and that he intends to come and get her. She pleads with him to stay away, but his nineteenth-century notions of chivalry and honour prevent him from abandoning her in such a time of need. Mann captures Billie's plight here, her growing sense of entrapment and paranoia that government agencies were closing in (which they were by this point with wire taps and other methods) via some very deliberate, Hopper-esque framing and shot compositions, particularly at 1:05:02 into the film.

The use of negative space (also to be found in *The Insider*) to the right of Billie recalls the fragility in Hopper works such as *Hotel Room* (1931) and *Room in Brooklyn* (1932), images that brilliantly evoke the bleak isolation and vulnerability of individuals in Depression-era America. The 1930s may have seen modernism really take root, but it happened in the dark shadow of loneliness and poverty. Dillinger hits another bank not long after his escape, but he does so with much more amateurish men, given that his old crew remain in jail elsewhere. Coming out of the bank after the robbery, Dillinger is shot in the arm, one of his crew members, Tommy Carroll, takes a round in the head and Baby Face Nelson shoots several innocent bystanders and at least one police officer. This sets off a chain of events that will lead to the infamous Little Bohemia Lodge shootout, a major embarrassment for the fledgling FBI that resulted in calls for Purvis's suspension and Hoover's resignation.

When Mann returns to Purvis it is during the vigorous and brutal torture of the seriously injured Tommy Carroll, whom the FBI have apprehended after the botched robbery. In the film's ongoing indictment of Purvis and the FBI, Purvis has one of his deputies do the torturing, which involves denying Carroll the pain relief he desperately needs for the bullet that is lodged behind one of his eyes and then pushing down on Carroll's face when he tries to resist. The deputy finally extracts the information he needs – Dillinger's hideout location at the Bohemia Lodge – but Carroll then spits in his face. Even Carroll, the criminal, cannot fathom this abhorrent treatment by the authorities. The deputy turns and looks up at Purvis with a mixture of disgust and anger at having to stoop to this base level in order to do police work. In a tight and wobbly close-up from across the room, Mann then captures Purvis's face with the deputy and Carroll out of focus and in the background. Purvis is facing away from the horrors being inflicted on Carroll and has an expression on his face that seems to bespeak a mix of revulsion at his adopted methods and resignation at having failed himself and his Southern principles. Although Purvis came from the landed gentry, where violent retribution was advocated, torture was deemed abhorrent and deeply unfair, and would, therefore, have been firmly excluded from methods of conflict resolution. Mann's close-up here renders a devastating judgement on Purvis, however much he is himself in conflict with what Hoover is now insisting his G-Men do.

Purvis, Winstead and the rest of the FBI team arrive at Bohemia Lodge in the dark after having learned of Dillinger's whereabouts from Carroll. Ignoring the advice of the learned Winstead, who cautions against trying to take Dillinger and his crew by themselves, Purvis assigns each man a position and begins his assault. The shooting then begins with Purvis accidentally murdering three innocent workers who happened to be drinking in the lodge's bar and tried to leave the area in their car. It's made clear that Purvis thought the men were part of Dillinger's crew, but nonetheless, his shooting of them represents another savage condemnation of the agent and a further illustration of his ineptitude. Hearing the shots, Dillinger awakes from sleep with lightning-fast reactions (like Hanna's instinctive reaction when he hears Toreno use the word "slick" in the underground nightclub scene from *Heat*) and heads to the window with his gun. The shootout is staged much more along the lines of *Miami Vice*'s war reportage approach than *Heat*'s Wild West in the canyons of LA. The hyperactivity of Mann's hand-held camera, as it runs, ducks and crashes amid the gunfire, brings back that ephemeral feeling that the imagery had in *Vice*, that fleeting sensibility of up-to-the-minute, ultra-modern news footage, irrespective of the fact that *Public Enemies* is set in 1933.

Dillinger and Red Hamilton escape from the lodge and run off into the woods, pursued by Winstead, who really is the most sensible and capable agent in this sequence. Tossing his hat into the dirt so that he can aim more effectively, Winstead somersaults around, completely avoiding Dillinger's spray of bullets while laying down some devastating rifle fire into the trees that Dillinger is using for cover. At one point he even seems to disappear into thin air, properly becoming the haunting spectre in the woods like Pacino did among the storage containers during the airport shootout at the end of *Heat*. Minutes later Purvis is seen shooting dead both Homer Van Meter and Baby Face Nelson in a clearing, although this scene never took place in real life. While, from a narrative point of view, the decision by Mann and his screenwriters to invent this moment is clever and economical, a way of conflating events and providing closure for the audience with regard to the psychotic Nelson, it also smacks of an attempt to provide Purvis with at least a modicum of redemption in the face of all his failures in the film. Finally, after months of searching, thousands and thousands of taxpayers' dollars and the deaths of several of his deputy agents, Purvis gets two of his public enemies – just not the one he really wants.

From this point on, Purvis's outfit of FBI deputies descend further into the savage thuggery of the police state they have helped create. Billie Frechette, Dillinger's great love, is apprehended and subjected to a series of brutal beatings by the FBI in an attempt to learn the whereabouts of Dillinger, now that he is completely isolated. Although Purvis is absent from the Chicago office while these beatings are taking place, he has nevertheless validated this behaviour by not contesting Hoover's abolition of habeas corpus. In showing Billie's brutal treatment from a low vantage, with her shackled to a chair and thoroughly broken, the film recalls the similar moment in *Miami Vice* when Trudy is kidnapped and held in a meth trailer by white supremacists. Mann's films may be arias to the male group but they are also now, in the twenty-first century, strong criticisms of misogyny and the largely intractable systems of patriarchy that remain in place in our society, from drug running to federalised police forces.

All this vitriol and hatred takes place alongside the burnishing of Dillinger's mythology as an insuperable robber extraordinaire. Forces are aligning themselves against him from all sides, including former associates and sex workers who inform on him to Purvis and his Chicago office. This, however, does not prevent him from walking into a police station and parading around the Dillinger squad room in an insane and brilliantly brazen bout of curiosity and arrogance. Dillinger finds the room empty aside from a small group of agents crowded around a radio listening to a baseball game; such imagery would be unthinkable in Mann's policing magnum opus *Heat*. Yet, despite gaining access to this room and scouring the bulletin boards for information, Dillinger fails to foresee the operation to kill him later that night outside the Biograph Theatre on Lincoln Avenue, an event that forms the film's final condemnation of Purvis's driven detective and Hoover's machine politics.

As history knows, Charles Winstead was the man who killed Dillinger after he exited the gangster movie *Manhattan Melodrama* (1934) and started to walk off down Lincoln Avenue. In attempting to resolve the question of why it was Winstead and not the FBI's Purvis who pulled the trigger, Mann blocks this climactic sequence so that Purvis appears encumbered by the throngs of cinemagoers on the street, his gentrified Southern ways prohibiting him from simply pushing people aside in his pursuit. By contrast, Winstead is shown to aggressively shove those same people to the ground in his single-mindedness to kill Dillinger. In his failure to validate Hoover's extreme methods and show that the FBI could get the job done, Purvis joins Mann's recent rank of detectives who appear greatly weakened by their experiences of the global forces at work around them. This is a detective archetype whose intuitions are ignored by partners and senior members (*Collateral*), whose ignorance of criminal organisations results in the true villain slipping away (*Miami Vice*), whose slavish following of orders that he disagrees with puts him in a state of conflict that greatly reduces his effectiveness (*Public Enemies*) and whose authority is undermined by the upper echelons of government, resulting in a convicted felon doing his job for him (*Blackhat*). While four films hardly constitutes a definitive shift in Mann's conception of the police and the processes of law enforcement, his twenty-first-century work, with all its edge, flux and fragmentation, does seem to be at least reinterpreting the function of these institutions. As has hopefully become clear, *Public Enemies* forms the most critical and angry of these reinterpretations. It is a period film about modernism, in which lies a version of the detective archetype whose competency is at its weakest yet. Purvis is an intriguing character, particularly in his dress sense and the way he carries himself, but place him next to Graham from *Manhunter* or Hanna from *Heat* and that Mannian sense of the detective as an almost supernaturally gifted investigator very quickly dissipates.

Public Enemies confirmed Mann's love of digital cinema and demonstrated that period films shot with hi-def video offered a new experience for the viewer, a hyper-reality that stripped away the artifice normally required for the recreation of history and made things seem tangible, palpable and veritable. Although it lacks the epic trappings of our other cops and robbers film *Heat*, *Public Enemies* is not a minor work by any means. Several of its bravura sequences show that Mann's ability to stage complex camera moves and orchestrate a now digitised cinematic space had not diminished. However, the film's rooting in the real-life stories of Dillinger and Purvis, with their compressed time periods, complex social dynamics and period psychologies, seems to have limited the potential of this eleventh film. The previously impervious determinant of the driven detective finds itself, here, in an altered state far away from Graham's intuitions or Hanna's obsession. In 2009 the detective became for Mann a weary and institutionalised figure, immaculately dressed but stripped of the drive or mania that made the detectives in *Manhunter* and *Heat* so successful. Of course, those characters had failings too, but in those films these failings were, by-and-large, related to their families and not the cases they worked on. For Purvis, neither a husband nor a father in the context of the film, all he has to fail at is his police work, and it is this anomaly that pushes his role in *Public Enemies* from that of elite detective to that of police officer.

> **Key scene suggestion for the driven detective – the night-time car chase in the woods of Wisconsin when Purvis is hunting down Baby Face Nelson and Homer van Meter.**

Notes

1 In *Sight & Sound* Nick James likens the opening of the film to the sunshine and brightness of Polanski's *Chinatown*. Nick James, "Jonny Too Bad", *Sight & Sound* 19, no. 8 (August 2009): 24.
2 Christopher Sharrett, "Michael Mann: Elegies on the Post-industrial Landscape", in Yvonne Tasker (ed.), *Fifty Contemporary Filmmakers*, Routledge, 2010, 277.
3 Ibid.
4 Although both films make similar statements about recidivism.
5 Michael Atkinson, "Thunder Roads", *Sight & Sound* 19, no. 8 (August 2009): 32.
6 Sharrett, "Michael Mann", 277.
7 David Hayes, *The Motion Picture Production Code*, https://productioncode.dhwritings.com/multipleframes_productioncode.php (accessed 23 February 2023).
8 Something elaborated on in Mann's novel, *Heat 2*. Hanna's single-minded determination, work ethic and intuitive, empathetic abilities help him rise above the rigid hierarchy of law enforcement. These qualities do, however, take their toll on him.

CHAPTER FOURTEEN

Blackhat and Fragmentation Cinema

It's not what a movie is about, it's how it's about it.

Roger Ebert

Six years after *Public Enemies* was released Mann returned to the cinema screen with *Blackhat*, the story of an imprisoned hacker who is furloughed in order to help government agents track down the individual responsible for a series of serious cybercrimes. In the interim Mann was heavily involved with *Luck*, the horseracing drama for HBO that opened this book, and with producing other people's films, including his daughter Ami Canaan Mann's *Texas Killing Fields* (2011). In his customary style Mann also spent three of those years researching the background to *Blackhat*, something that involved visiting government agencies such as the House Intelligence Committee in Washington and holding detailed discussions with real hackers such as Kevin Poulsen, now senior editor of *Wired News*.

When released, *Blackhat* did not do well, either critically or commercially, grossing only $17.8 million against a $70 million budget. Some reviews asked whether Mann had spent too long away from the cinema and if his skills had begun to wane as a result. Others took issue with the casting of Chris Hemsworth as the hacker Hathaway or the seeming lack of suspense in many key scenes. Commentators found fault with the story too and its pacing; the film felt weirdly rushed in places and far too tranquil in others. The drama didn't seem to gel either, particularly the romance between Hathaway and Lien, but also the climax, which came across as overly violent but redundant. These same critical commentaries did concede some of the film's strengths – there were some excellent individual sequences, including a riveting foot chase through a residential area outside Hong Kong that ends in a storm drain shootout with echoes of the chase in Kathryn Bigelow's *Point Break* (1991); and the film was as timely and opportune as a filmmaker could hope for (Stuxnet had already waged war on Iran's nuclear centrifuges and the Sony email hack was still

219

causing tidal waves around Hollywood) – but these aspects were drowned out by the overall pejorative clamour deriding the experience.

Staying truthful to the central tenet of this book demands that we carve out an honest account of *Blackhat* and both its relevance to understanding its director and the place the film occupies in his lineage of work. This means first acknowledging that it remains a deeply frustrating film and one that bears the scars of studio mismanagement, marketing failure and too much editorialising on the part of its director. Reconfigured tropes, themes and lines of dialogue that played well across multiple films in Mann's back catalogue fall flat in *Blackhat*. They seem old-fashioned now, anachronistic and trite when set against the film's bolder aspirations to examine the absolute forward edge of tech, crime and the human body. So, how best then to approach a discussion of *Blackhat*? In the spirit of the film's language of computer code, perhaps a type of conceptual algorithm is best for unlocking its complexities and ambiguities, a codified tool that helps to reframe what the film is about by looking at *how* it's about it.

Ebert's quote provides immediate dividends. Exploring *how* Mann made *Blackhat* is so much more rewarding for our purposes here than any assessment of *what* it's about. If this seems like a slippery way of sidestepping the film's arguable failings, that is not the primary intention. Those failings have been detailed accurately in other writings and this book, to a large extent, stands by them. As a piece of dramatic storytelling, *Blackhat* is an inferior product when set against Mann's earlier titans of the 1990s and even early 2000s. In large part, this is due to the inherently poor structure of the film in key places and lesser issues such as the weak antagonist. But if we allow ourselves the indulgence of situating *Blackhat* within the broader framework of an ongoing creative experiment, something that is likely to continue in Mann's upcoming *Ferrari*, then other, more rewarding ideas begin to present themselves.

As we now know, since 2001's *Ali*, Mann has been on a steady and incremental quest to denude, attenuate, modify and augment the dramatic requirements of film storytelling. If *Blackhat* is the most recent entry in that quest, we must assume that this film will represent the most radical iteration of that experiment to date and receive it as such. Where *Collateral*, *Miami Vice* and *Public Enemies* are 1st, 2nd and 3rd on the gearbox of Mann's twenty-first-century cinematic vehicle, *Blackhat* jumps way ahead, to both 5th gear and cruise control in one. It's a work so enthralled by its own innovation and self-confidence, so intent on the *how* of the thing, that too much attention to the *what*, to the relationship between Hathaway and Lien or the climax set in the middle of an Indonesian parade, can be detrimental to recognising the maturation of

Blackhat and Fragmentation Cinema

Figure 23. Blackhat

Mann's fragmentation cinema when you see it. Writing in the *New York Times* in 2015, Manohla Dargis was savvy enough to see *Blackhat*'s futuristic vintage, its potent distillation of *Collateral*, *Miami Vice* and *Public Enemies*, when, in her review of the film, she acknowledged the presence of "Mr. Mann's singular hybrid approach, which exists at the crossroads of the classical Hollywood cinema and the European art film and is evident in his oscillation between action and introspection, transformation and stasis, exterior and interior realms."[1] To highlight just how far Mann has come in his "oscillation between", for example, the "exterior and interior realms", one need only consider the opening 20 minutes of *Blackhat*.

Beginning with the ghostly, exterior image of an Earth blanketed in a haze of data transmission and cyber communications (the invisible exoskeleton of data, as Mann refers to it), Mann hovers over the macro realm for a few quiet seconds until a series of dissolves takes us past the outside of a Chinese nuclear power station, into the reactor control room and through the pixels of a computer screen before ending up in the interior realm of computer circuitry, quantum physics and electrons carrying packets of information.[2] A virulent piece of code appears and proceeds to spin the nuclear plant's cooling turbines out of control. The plant explodes, precipitating an international manhunt for the hacker. Hathaway (Chris Hemsworth) is quickly furloughed from prison, having been convinced to help the US Department of Justice in its joint investigation with the Chinese.

Outside the prison, we see Hathaway embracing his long-lost friend, Dawai, for the first time in many years. Mann brings in composer Harry Gregson-Williams' cue *Leaving Prison*, a heavy strings and piano piece, the beginning of which recalls the best Elliot Goldenthal moments from *Heat* and *Public Enemies*. As a result of the music this reuniting of two hackers becomes the kind of male buddy aria that Christopher Sharrett mentioned earlier. Hathaway's girlfriend-to-be (Dawai's sister Lien) looks on in the background, present but marginalised in favour of the real relationship at this point. There's a cut and Hathaway is now at an airport, about to board the DOJ flight to Los Angeles with the rest of the newly assembled team. Gregson-Williams' cue continues over the cut but shifts in tone. A piano is introduced and the mood transitions to something mournful and elegiac. Hathaway should be ecstatic to be free (even temporarily) but the moment is loaded with portent. The distant hills merge with a pin-sharp, azure sky. The wonderfully green and yellow taxiway of the airport runway complements the tones of Hathaway's shirt and it feels as though we're back in the zesty locales of *Miami Vice*. Only here, the image is not one of opiated paradise but stark realisation. Hathaway stops near the steps of the plane and stares into the distance, in all likelihood perceiving the struggle to come and how the manhunt will soon be for him.

Through the careful placement and timing of the music, the jerky close-ups of Hathaway's face and the slow left-to-right panning shot of the horizon (like the one in *Public Enemies*) Mann almost imperceptibly transitions from a moment of action – the completion of the team and the start of the hunt – to a pause for introspection. Rarely do these pauses serve any narrative purpose in Mann's cinema but, as Roger Ebert verbalised, they are about the *how* rather than the *what*. How Mann creates these impressions of introspection is of much more importance in the understanding of his craft at this point in his career than what the moments are about. Although we can divine what Hathaway is likely thinking here, the real point in the scene is to soak up the feel and acknowledge the foregrounding of technique.

The Los Angeles sequence is carefully staged by Mann to avoid his earlier representations in other films. In some respects, the LA scenes here embrace the flat interiority, shallow depth of field and close-quarter confines of those films he actively railed against in *Heat* and *Collateral*. Hathaway and the team manage to work out that a low-level hacker by the name of Alonzo Reyes was involved in helping to facilitate the attack in Hong Kong. During this period of detection, there's a moment when Hathaway channels an empathetic and intuitive ability much like that of Vincent Hanna or, more accurately, Will Graham in *Manhunter*. Rising from his computer, Hathaway enters into a mock dialogue with the hacker they are after. The other team members and the rest of the world slip away as Hathaway concludes to himself that "the real hit is still to come". Soon after, Hathaway and Lien arrive at Reyes's apartment only to find him dead from a suspected drug overdose. Hathaway searches through the dead man's laptop and discovers that a meet was due to take place at a restaurant in Koreatown later that night.

Posing as Reyes, Hathaway takes Lien to dinner in the hope of gaining his next clue in the cybernetic puzzle. After a dreamy cab ride to the restaurant, Hathaway and Lien order food and exchange the kind of honest life stories that only relative strangers can do. Mann frames these exchanges amid the gorgeously deep red walls of the restaurant and, at one point, even captures a profile shot of the left-hand side of Hathaway's face with an extreme amount of negative space to the left of the screen. We know Hathaway is looking at Lien but this startling cutaway profile shot also reminds us of how Mann is intent on breaking into these conventional dramatic spaces with camera and editing and smashing them apart. In this moment, he captures the abandonment and desolation of the part of Hathaway's psyche still affected by his imprisonment, as he listens to Lien's assessment of their current situation. This is exactly the kind of "oscillation between action and introspection" that Dargis spoke of in her review of the film. For the significant shots that follow in this part of the sequence, Mann completely abstracts the restaurant setting into an amorphous red limbo in order to underscore the growing feelings between these two people. This abstraction also works to reinforce the frenetic brutality of what comes next.

Hathaway soon notices the security camera on the rear wall and, when the waiter is distracted, slips into the back office to access the restaurant computer. A flurried exchange of coded messages allows Hathaway to quickly uncover the online persona of the über hacker, a figure with the username *sdksdk* who is based in Ukraine. Hathaway leaves the back office to rejoin Lien and leave, but the pair are instantly confronted by a group of men, who have clearly been alerted by the restaurant. What follows is Mann's best, most unhinged and vicious hand-to-hand combat scene to date and a sequence hugely elevated by the somnambulism and oscillations of the previous minutes. Despite being outnumbered 3 to 1, Hathaway grabs, punches, slices with a broken bottle and stomps his way to safety, at one moment even using one of the restaurant tables to bat away an assailant. As the camera thrusts, swipes, rises and falls with the fighting men, the moment recalls Mann's use of the pioneering Elmocam in the boxing bouts in *Ali*, that tiny, box-shaped camera that permitted Mann and cinematographer Emmanuel Lubezki to interrogate those tight spaces between the bodies of the fighters. This approach to the staging and filming of combat was then reconfigured in *Miami Vice*'s trailer park sequence before turning up here in *Blackhat*, in its most extreme variation. The moment plays like something closer to Paul Greengrass's work on

Figure 24. Blackhat

the fight scenes in the *Bourne* trilogy, where there is the very effective combination of tightly controlled fight choreography with the sense of a completely unplanned series of camera shots. The effect is the kind of induced documentary feel that William Friedkin always talked about wanting to capture in *The French Connection*.

The ability of Mann to move between these spaces, between the binary code of a computer circuit board and the bodies of fighting men, is perhaps the key to enjoying *Blackhat*. Returning to her *New York Times* review of *Blackhat*, Dargis referred to this technique as a "hybrid approach".[3] Hybrid is an interesting choice of word. Although the literal definition is something composed of incongruous elements, it also has connotations of the future, of a forward-looking innovation that seeks to improve on the past by reconfiguring its components. If Michael Mann's current approach to movies can be summed up at all, it's via this notion of hybridity, of works that are forward-looking innovations into the frontier of story, image and the global experience.

Hinted at in *Heat* and *The Insider* and explored more determinedly in *Collateral* and *Miami Vice*, the idea of the frontier of human experience in the twenty-first century is adrenalised to near breaking point in *Blackhat*'s frantic travelogue of the world. In its exploration of this boundary line, *Blackhat* pushes it to its furthest point yet, with a story of global cybercrime that opens with a shot from the distant vantage of outer space. How far we have come, both figuratively and literally, since the confines of Murphy's prison cell in *The Jericho Mile*. The film offers the viewer many memorable moments and fresh ideas, none more so than when it shifts its focus to Hong Kong. In an elision that is quite destabilising, the story abruptly moves from Hathaway and Lien's sleepy lovemaking, shot and edited in a manner very similar to the scene in *Public Enemies*, to images of Hong Kong that more closely resemble the vertical panels and circuitry of a PC interior than a Far Eastern megalopolis. Of course, this is entirely the point. After a quick stop-off at the stricken nuclear power plant, where Hathaway runs around in a ridiculous manner with his shirt partially unbuttoned while emergency responders are suited in full HazMat outfits, the team arrive at their accommodation in the city. They meet their counterparts in Chinese intelligence and law enforcement and begin to plan their next moves. On discovering another man in the master hacker's crew, a former member of the right-wing Christian Phalangists called Elias, Hathaway and the expanded team chopper out to Shek O in the south-east of Hong Kong island in an attempt to re-establish contact with the team tasked with surveilling him. What follows is a brilliantly deranged foot chase through the alleyways and residences of a Shek O neighbourhood that stands as our penultimate example of Mann's fascination with the *how* as much as the *what*.

Like the fist-fight in Koreatown, this chase to the location of the surveillance team marries tight choreography with hand-held visuals, while also adding in a complex point of view that can easily be missed on first viewing. A high-pitched electronic pulse scores the team's run between the houses. The SWAT team break away and arrive at the surveillance team's hideout to find the men shot dead. We cut back to Hathaway and his group en route to Elias's rented apartment, in the hope of apprehending him there. Mann cuts to a wide shot from the right, as the team run into the frame from screen left. Then, instead of placing the viewer back with the group by cutting, Mann decides to move his camera into the line of running men, as if we the audience have just assumed the role of a new SWAT team member. It's a bizarre and brilliant shot choice that somehow fits with the film's overall ambition to break with convention and fragment the audience's place within events. As if once wasn't enough, Mann repeats this approach minutes later and then again for a third time, as Hathaway's team run and shoot guns between the bulk of shipping containers. Before Lien's brother Dawai even corners a green shipping container and runs to the right of frame, Mann's camera is running left to right and we become that same new SWAT team member, rejoining the chase with these other men as they make their approach to the water's edge.

The airport runway introspection, the somnambulistic restaurant conversation, the vicious fistfight, the foot chase with its bizarre point-of-view switches; these moments and the others like them in what's left of *Blackhat* are the key to appreciating the film's textures and ambition. The unholy alliance between these innovations and the outmoded lines

225

of dialogue and well-worn themes is where the dissonance comes from and what reviews were really referencing when they talked about the film being dramatically inert or a dud. Although *Blackhat* is undeniably a film about the future of its director's creative ambitions, what we have been calling the *how* in this chapter, the *what* – those same lines of dialogue and well-worn themes – still holds sway, perhaps to too great a degree. As *Blackhat* searches for the future potential of those "oscillations between action and introspection", it's a film incapable of dispensing with a large part of the story template Mann has been repurposing since the running track of Folsom Prison.

Hathaway and what's left of his team after the folly of the harbour shootout, with its abstract imagery of storm drains that look like computer terminals, return again to the stricken nuclear power plant in an attempt to retrieve data files from the control room before a complete meltdown occurs. We get another interrogation into cinematic space here as Mann presents Hathaway swinging his axe at the control room computer in the style of John Woo's Hong Kong cinema, specifically the tea house shootout on the stairs in *Hard Boiled*, where Woo dilates the time it takes Chow Yun-Fat's Inspector Yuen to slide down the banister while shooting at multiple enemies.[4] As well as serving as a nice homage to the cinematic style of the city he's shooting in, Mann also offers up this shot repetition as part of *Blackhat*'s ongoing wish to investigate the time and space within individual moments.

In order to reconstruct the remnants of the hacker's code that he finds on the power plant's computer drive, Hathaway hacks into the NSA's secretive and powerful Black Widow programme, a programme that can reassemble corrupted, fragmented and deleted files. It is at this point that Hathaway both learns the location and identity of the master hacker, named Sadak, and becomes himself a fugitive, wanted by the FBI and DOJ for the hack. Rather than hand his friend over to the American authorities, Dawai alerts Hathaway to this and is then killed while helping him escape Hong Kong with Lien on a private plane. The departure of the plane is a gorgeous moment in the enjoyment of *Blackhat*'s aesthetic, as is the sequence in a dried-up river bed in Malaysia and Lien's USB trickery in a bank in Jakarta. The biological and the mechanical then fuse during the film's climax as Hathaway invokes *Taxi Driver*'s Travis Bickle before entering into combat with Sadak, played by Yorick van Wageningen, at a parade in Banteng Square in Jakarta. Hathaway's lo-fi approach here, torso padded with magazines, sharpened screwdrivers sutured to his forearms and thick scarves for neck protection, helps provide the paragon of Dargis's "oscillation", in this instance between the high-tech, digitised realm of the preceding 120 minutes and the real-world physics of fighting another human being. In the end, *Blackhat*'s oscillation back to the simple brutality and ingenuity of combat, of the danger of seemingly incongruous items such as screwdrivers and magazines, recalls the similar aura of homemade threat that pervades Mann's first work, *The Jericho Mile*, a film worth briefly revisiting now, along with the rest of the back catalogue.

> **Key scene suggestion for the fragmentation cinema of *Blackhat* – the Hong Kong foot chase and shootout with its destabilising point-of-view computerised filming locations.**

Notes

1 http://www.nytimes.com/2015/01/16/movies/blackhat-a-cyberthriller-starring-chris-hemsworth.html?_r=0 (accessed 26 December 2022).
2 Witnessing this imagery during a first viewing of the film recalled *Thief*'s similar transition between the big and the small, between street and safe and the notion of the omniscient eye, but thoroughly revolutionised it for the twenty-first century, a time fraught with concerns about surveillance and cyber terrorism.
3 http://www.nytimes.com/2015/01/16/movies/blackhat-a-cyberthriller-starring-chris-hemsworth.html?_r=0 (accessed 26 December 2022).
4 As already noted earlier, Mann also does this in *Heat*, repeating the shot of Hanna shouldering his rifle before killing Cheritto.

Afterword

The Jericho Mile introduced Mann's fascination with the prison environment, but it stands alone in its rather optimistic take on this world. *Thief* brought to the stage Mann's abiding and ambiguous love of the criminal and remains a reference point for most of his crime fiction to date. *The Keep*'s horribly divergent dreamworld of stylisation has minimal standing in Mann's canon, yet still has flourishes that he would revisit in *Public Enemies* and *Blackhat*. *Manhunter*'s modernism is an integral determinant that continues to catalyse everything he does. *The Last of the Mohicans* foregrounds an indispensable idea of professionalism that extends through the majority of Mann's principal characters to the man himself. *Heat* crystallised his feelings about modern conceptions of the city, using Los Angeles in a way rarely done before or since – this work remains the quintessential Mann experience. *The Insider* brought negative space and yawning framing to Mann's filming style, something that has never left him even with his uptake of digital video. In its singular embrace of history as a haze of time and memory, *Ali* bridged the gap between the analogue and digital Mann, but its epic scope perhaps limits its pertinence as a key work. 2004's *Collateral* is another touchstone that revisited Mann's conception of the city while energising it with a mobile, all-seeing eye that pierced the postmodern night in high-definition. *Miami Vice* stepped way ahead of the pack, using that same hi-def eye to paint a lurid picture of the new American frontier caught in the flux and fragmentation of transnational crime. *Public Enemies* applied these lessons to modernist concepts of the 1930s while also introducing us to a new, far less successful model of the driven detective. Then, after a six-year hiatus from cinema, came *Blackhat*, a work that was perhaps too radical for even ardent Mann fans. The marketing of the film failed to capture its nuance or target its intended audience. The studio eventually pulled it from distribution in countries such as Belgium. It is a work that demands to be revisited and re-evaluated more broadly than there is scope for here.

It is worth recapping Mann's filmography like this as it allows us to be concise about his key concerns and view, in shorthand, where his auteurism lies. In its introduction this book stressed that it would not fall into the familiar trap of forcing the work of the filmmaker through a single, explanatory lens in the hope of arriving at a tidy conclusion. Hopefully it has become clear that, like directors such as Robert Altman, Michael Mann deserves his status as *auteur terrible*, but not because of his entire body of work. Some of the films that he has crafted – *The Jericho Mile*, *The Keep*, *Ali*, *Public Enemies* – are either too different in their sensibility or too divergent in their experimentation to qualify them as supremely relevant to Mann's status as an auteur. But once again, like Altman's best work, Mann's key cinematic entries more than make up for his ideological dalliances elsewhere. Films such as *Thief*, *Manhunter*, *The Last of the Mohicans* and *Heat* have secured his love of the empathetic criminal, the investigative process, the consummate professional and the modern city respectively, while *The Insider*, *Collateral* and *Miami Vice* cement his fascination with space, light and the future. The jury is likely to stay out on *Blackhat*, but it is a film that, at the very least, deserves a holding place alongside those other, beloved stylistic rebels *The Jericho Mile*, *The Keep*, *Ali* and *Public Enemies* for its maddening foray into worn-out themes with cutting-edge methods.

In the intervening years between the arguable failure of *Blackhat* and the devastating Covid-19 pandemic, Mann has enjoyed a resurgent critical appreciation that included a series of highly commemorative public speaking engagements, new 4K presentations of favourites such as *Heat* and *Collateral*, in-depth interviews by Mann of other directors including Alejandro González Iñárritu and Ridley Scott, and being awarded the DEA's Educational Foundation Lifetime Achievement Award in October 2017. He appeared at the Toronto International Film Festival in 2015, at 2017's Lumiere Film Festival in Lyon and, at the Samuel Goldwyn Theatre in Los Angeles in 2016, subjected himself, along with Al Pacino, Robert De Niro and the other major cast members, to an intensive, borderline forensic examination of *Heat* by fellow director and devotee Christopher Nolan, whose own film *The Dark Knight* is heavily influenced by Mann's LA epic. Combine all this with the ongoing digitisation and high-resolution restoration of most of the rest of his back catalogue and you have an auteur who seems far from being put out to pasture.

Afterword

When we consider Mann being awarded the Lifetime Achievement Award by the DEA, do films such as *Blackhat* acquire a new resonance? In his acceptance speech at the DEA ceremony, Mann talked for several minutes about that other side of his career, the one spent with law-enforcement officials, FBI agents and, here, the professionals of the Drug Enforcement Agency. He detailed his experiences developing and producing the TV miniseries about DEA agent Enrique Camarena and his discovery of the massive marijuana operation in northern Mexico, his fairly well-developed layman's understanding of transnational drug trafficking ("the multiplication of value, from the farm to the arm") and his time spent with the DEA in the border regions of Thailand in the 1980s. He elaborated on his friendship with one of the agents directly responsible for bringing down Pablo Escobar and the Medellin cartel before finally moving on to his exposure to the post-9/11 convergence of drug trafficking, terrorism and cybercrime, unholy alliances that utilise the dark web to generate wealth and effect often violent chaos as a result. When viewed from this perspective, *Blackhat* offers a radical, if slightly attenuated, demonstration of the years' worth of learning and data Mann has gleaned from the field. The regional and national alliances may be more tenuous in the post-9/11 world, the villains more opaque (think of how Sadak is filmed in *Blackhat*), but nevertheless, the function of the film as a celebration of US strategic dominance, here cyber dominance, is a tenable one.

Continuing to search for real-life analogues, are we meant to see, for instance, Hathaway as an Edward Snowden-type, on the run for exposing the intelligence community's terrifying infiltration of our private lives through programmes such as the NSA's Black Widow? Is the film's roving camera really a modern-day Athena's Shield, held aloft by Mann to reflect back on itself the US-controlled cyber exoskeleton that envelops the world? While in interviews surrounding the release of *Blackhat* Mann revealed himself as a critic of US cyber security and its overreach – when discussing the Stuxnet hack he conceded that it was likely an American/Israeli-built weapon and offered no further comment – the movie's closing scenes, with their affirmation of real, physical bodies, actual environments and the promise of human contact, point to a scepticism about cyber security, the inherent limitations it places on human interaction and the dangers it poses to public utilities. For all its narrative and editorial foibles, *Blackhat* does signpost Mann's other professional life, the one spent in the intelligence communities and cross-border law enforcement agencies of the world. Like Oliver Stone, Mann uses the dramatic form of cinema to explore these communities and agencies, foregrounding his discoveries and laying bare his thoughts about the global, geopolitical arena.

The Films of Michael Mann

Tokyo Vice, Mann's 2022 return to television courtesy of HBO and based on Jake Adelstein's non-fiction book of the same name about the investigation of corruption in a Japanese vice squad, continues his parlay of the years spent working alongside the world of law enforcement into popular entertainment. Renewed for a second season, the visual template laid down by Mann in his direction of the pilot episode of *Tokyo Vice* remains fixed firmly in place, an authorial stamp that harkens back to his influence on *Miami Vice* and *Luck*. *Heat 2*, a concurrent project and novelisation prequel/sequel to his 1995 film, saw Mann turn writer alongside crime novelist Meg Gardiner to a spectacular degree. Topping the bestseller lists, the epic crime follow-up pulls in multiple strands and references from Mann's filmography, including *Miami Vice*'s economic playground Ciudad del Este and the psychotic Chicago home invaders that formed the basis of *Thief*. There are some particularly fine sequences in *Heat 2*, and Mann's writing benefits from the assistance of Gardiner, who brings her experience in the crime genre to bear. Most exciting of all is the suggestion that Mann intends to turn the events of the book into a film, although who will play the young De Niro, Pacino and Kilmer remains to be seen.

Ferrari, the elusive project that Mann has chased for over twenty years and prefaced with his production of James Mangold's highly successful *Ford vs. Ferrari* (2019), is, at the time of writing, in production in Modena, Italy, and is due to be released in 2023. An adaptation of Brock Yates's *Enzo Ferrari – the Man and the Machine* (an apt title, given the ferocious climax of *Blackhat*), *Ferrari* will tell the story of the formative six-month period in 1957 when Enzo Ferrari was desperately trying to save both his marriage and the future of his company. The centre point of the film will likely be its recreation of the Mille Miglia, the infamous 1000-mile motorsport endurance race across Italy that Ferrari used to try and reinvigorate his failing prospects. It's tantalising to consider how good this film could be, if Mann is successful in blending the stylistic innovations he has been pushing since *Ali* with the quality of writing that made, say, *The Insider* so rewarding.

The Insider is a deliberate choice to end on here. Aside from being the source for this book's cover image, it is a film that ably sidestepped the kind of dialogue tropes and tired themes that have blighted some of Mann's work since then, while still revisiting and updating the other ideas we have come to love and expect from this most interesting and exciting of contemporary filmmakers.

Bibliography

Adorno, Theodor, *Prisms*, MIT Press, 1981

Aitken, Ian, *European Film Theory and Cinema: A Critical Introduction*, Indiana University Press, 2002

Anderson, Michael J., "Before Sunrise, or Los Angeles Plays itself in a Lonely Place", *Senses of Cinema*, October 2004, sensesofcinema.com/2004/feature-articles/collateral/ (accessed 23 February 2023)

Atkinson, Michael, "Thunder Roads", *Sight & Sound* 19, no. 8 (August 2009): 32–34

Banham, Reyner, *Los Angeles: The Architecture of Four Ecologies*, University of California Press, 1971

Barton Palmer, R., and Sanders Steven (eds), *Michael Mann: Cinema and Television Interviews, 1980–2012*, Edinburgh University Press, 2014

Bevan Joseph, "Christopher Nolan: Escape Artist", *Sight & Sound* 22, no. 8 (August 2012): 14–18

Cousins, Mark, "The Inexpressible", *Sight & Sound* 23, no. 3 (March 2013): 41–43

Crockett, Dennis, *German Post-Expressionism: The Art of the Great Disorder 1918–1924*, Pennsylvania State University Press, 1999

Dargis, Manohla, "Not for the Faint of Heart or Lazy of Thought", *New York Times*, December 2006, https://www.nytimes.com/2006/12/24/movies/not-for-the-faint-of-heart-or-lazy-of-thought.html (accessed 23 February 2023)

Davis, Mike, *City of Quartz: Excavating the Future in Los Angeles*, Verso, 2006

Du Bois, W.E.B., *The Souls of Black Folk* (1903), Gramercy Books, 1994

Erickson, Steve, "The Reality of Film; Thom Andersen on 'Los Angeles Plays Itself'", *Indiewire*, 2004, https://www.indiewire.com/2004/07/the-reality-of-film-thom-anderson-on-los-angeles-plays-itself-78765/ (accessed 23 February 2023)

Feeney, Duncan, *Michael Mann*, Taschen, 2006

Fuller, Graham, "Which Way is Up?", *Sight & Sound* 16, no. 9 (September 2006): 14–18

Gaine, Vincent, *Existentialism and Social Engagement in the Films of Michael Mann*, Palgrave Macmillan, 2011

Harkness, John, "White Noise", *Sight & Sound* 7, no. 2 (November 1992): 15

Haut, Woody, *Neon Noir: Contemporary American Crime Fiction*, Serpent's Tail, 1999

Hayes, David, *The Motion Picture Production Code*, https://productioncode.dhwritings.com/multipleframes_productioncode.php (accessed 23 February 2023)

James, Nick, *Heat*, BFI Publishing, 2002

James, Nick, "No Smoking Gun", *Sight & Sound* 10, no. 3 (March 2000): 14–17

James, Nick, "*Miami Vice* review", *Sight & Sound* 16, no. 10 (October 2006): 68–70

James, Nick, "Jonny Too Bad", *Sight & Sound* 19, no. 8 (August 2009): 24–27

Jay, Martin, *The Dialectical Imagination: A History of the Frankfurt School and the Institute of Social Research, 1923–1950*, University of California Press, 1996

Kael, Pauline, "Circles and Squares", *Film Quarterly* 16, no. 3 (1963): 12–26

Kael, Pauline, *Taking It All In*, Marion Boyars, 1986

Kagan, Jeffrey, *Directors Close Up*, Scarecrow Press, 2006

Kolker, Robert, *A Cinema of Loneliness: Penn, Stone, Kubrick, Scorsese, Spielberg, Altman*, 3rd edn, Oxford University Press, 2000

Leader article, "The Shock of the Old", *The Guardian*, 25 August 2007, https://www.theguardian.com/commentisfree/2007/aug/25/comment.comment2 (accessed 22 February 2023)

McCoppin, Robert and Glenn Wall, "Newly Disclosed Account Surfaces in 1966 Valerie Percy Murder Case", *Chicago Tribune*, 14 June 2011, https://www.chicagotribune.com/news/ct-xpm-2011-06-14-ct-met-percy-murder-20110614-story.html (accessed 23 February 2023)

Mann, Michael, and Meg Gardiner, *Heat 2*, HarperCollins, 2022

Merton, Robert, *Social Theory and Social Structure*, Free Press, 1957

Müller, Jürgen, and Steffen Haubner, "Aesthetics of Film in the Eighties", in *Best Movies of the 80s*, Taschen, 2006

Murray, Christopher John, *Encyclopedia of the Romantic Era, 1760–1850*, Taylor & Francis, 2004

Olsen, Mark, "It Happened One Night", *Sight & Sound* 14, no. 10 (October 2004): 14–16

Osborne, D.M., "Real to Reel", *Brill's Content* (July/August 1999): 75–80

Robey, Tim, "Kubrick's Neglected Masterpiece", *Daily Telegraph*, 31 January 2009

Rybin, Steven, *The Cinema of Michael Mann*, Lexington Books, 2007

Sarris, Andrew, "Notes on the Auteur Theory" (1962), in Leo Braudy and Marshall Cohen (eds), *Film Theory and Criticism*, Oxford University Press, 2004

Sharrett, Christopher, "Michael Mann: Elegies on the Post-industrial Landscape", in Yvonne Tasker (ed.), *Fifty Contemporary Filmmakers*, Routledge, 2010, 253–62

Soja, Edward W., and Costis Hadjimichalis, "Between Geographical Materialism and Spatial Fetishism: Some Observations on the Development of Marxist Spatial Analysis", *Antipode* 11, no. 3 (1979): 3–11

Starbuck, David, *Massacre at Fort William Henry*, University Press of New England, 2002

Swan, Deryck, "*Heat*: An Appraisal", *Media Education Journal* 50 (2011): 21–28

Truffaut, François, "A Certain Tendency of the French Cinema", in Scott MacKenzie (ed.), *Film Manifestos and Global Cinema Cultures: A Critical Anthology*, University of California Press, 2014

Youngkin, Stephen D., *The Lost One: A Life of Peter Lorre*, University Press of Kentucky, 2005

Zoglin, Richard, "Cool Cops, Hot Show", *Time Magazine*, 16 September 1985, https://content.time.com/time/subscriber/article/0,33009,959822,00.html (accessed 23 February 2023)

Index

17 Days Down the Line (1972) 16, 168, 171
2001: A Space Odyssey (1968) 66, 70

A Better Tomorrow (1986) 59
Adorno, Theodore 86
A.I. (2001) 187–88
Ali, Muhammad 22, 155–70
Alighieri, Dante 68
All the President's Men (1976) 142, 146
Altman, Robert 1–2, 4, 9, 63, 230
American Dream 40, 48
An American Werewolf in London (1981) 53
Andersen, Thom 119, 124, 127, 188
Antonioni, Michelangelo 119
Art Deco 116, 190–91, 201
Aryan Brotherhood 197, 199, 204
Aspects of Negro Life (1934) 159
Atkinson, Michael 207
Auditorium Building, Chicago xiii, 12
    see also modernist architecture
Audubon Ballroom 157, 164, 196

Bale, Christian 203
Bardem, Javier 180
Barry Lyndon (1975) 101
Batman Begins (2005) 9
Bauhaus 197

Beebe, Dion 173, 199
Beelman, Claude 116
    see also Art Deco
Beineix, Jean-Jacques 52–53
Beresford, Bruce 104
Berg, Peter 3
Besson, Luc 52–53
    see also Beineix, Jean-Jacques; Carax, Leo
Bevan, Joseph 9,
Bigelow, Kathryn 219
Biograph Theatre 11, 101, 157, 203, 215
Black Robe (1991) 104, 108
Blade Runner (1982) 53, 62, 83, 92, 117, 129–30, 133, 174, 180
Blake, William 84
Boele, Vincent 149
Bogdanovich, Peter 15
Bonnie and Clyde (1967) 15, 207, 209–10
Boone, David 100
Boot, Das (1981) 53
Bottin, Rob 71
Bougainville, Louis Antoine de 102
Bourke, Pieter 30, 151
Braveheart (1995) 108
Breakout (1975) 26
Bremner, Marie 152
Bresson, Robert 58
    see also Bressonianism
Bressonianism 54
Bronk (1976) 62
Bronson, Charles xiii, 26
Brown & Williamson 137–38, 143–44, 150, 152, 154, 164

237

Bunker, Eddie 17
Bunker Hill 116–17, 175
Burrough, Bryan 205

Caan, James 14, 37, 40, 46–47, 54, 99
Camarena, Enrique 231
Cameron, James 91
Canby, Vincent 39
Carax, Leo 52–53
Carpenter, John 56, 68, 78
Cassavetes, John 15
CBS 135–37, 139, 148, 150, 152
CBS News 17, 152
    see also CBS
Cesaretti, Gusmano 119
Chapman, Michael 161
Chavez, Cesar 142, 170, 188
    see also Portrait of La Causa
China Syndrome, The (1979) 142, 146
Chinatown (1974) 115–16, 174
Chomette, Henri 65
Christine (1983) 56
cinema du look 52–55, 57, 61, 64
Cinema of Michael Mann, The 13, 37, 84, 103, 139
cinematic space 6, 9, 135, 142, 145–47, 201, 205, 216, 226
Citizen Kane (1941) 82
City of Quartz 117, 173
    see also Davis, Mike
Ciudad del Este 190, 195–96, 232
Clash of the Titans (1981) 53
Cold War 37, 173
Collateral (2004) 181, 184–85
Cooke, Sam 158, 160
Cooper, James Fenimore 96–97, 100, 102–04, 108, 111–12
Costner, Kevin 100
Cousins, Mark 66, 88, 106, 115
Crime Scene Investigation (2000–15) 83
Cronkite, Walter 162, 166
Crowe, Russell 135, 143–44, 150
Cubism 87–88, 118, 120, 131

Daley, Richard Mayor xiii, 11, 49
danse macabre 64
Darabont, Frank 34
Dargis, Manohla 190, 221
Dark Knight, The (2008) 41, 184, 230
Dark Knight Rises, The (2012) 184
Dassin, Jules 52, 177
Davis, Mike 117, 129, 173, 180
Davis, Miles 126, 178–79, 188
De Niro, Robert 46–47, 104, 118, 143, 230, 232
de Palma, Brian 145, 211
De Salvo, Albert 76
Deadwood (2004–06) 7
Death of Wolfe, The 102
Delon, Alain 52
Demme, Jonathan 84
Depp, Johnny 48, 203
desert modernism xiii
    see also Collateral
Desperado (1995) 56
determinism 178
Devil in a Blue Dress (1995) 115
Dietrich, Walter 13, 206
digital video 12, 106, 173, 174, 176, 187–88, 229
Dillinger, John 6, 11, 13, 20, 36–37, 43, 46, 48, 57, 69, 84, 111, 156, 157, 203, 205–16
Dirty Harry (1971) 21
Django Unchained (2012) 100
Dore, Gustave 68
Dostoyevsky, Fydor 39, 58
Double Indemnity (1944) 177
Douglas, Aaron 159, 161, 163, 170
    see also Aspects of Negro Life
Dr. Strangelove (1964) 66
Dragnet (1951–59) 129
Drive (2011) 45, 58, 187
Du Bois, W.E.B. 158
Duel (1971) 36
Dundee, Angelo 158, 169
Dungeon East & Wild Peach 163
Dylan, Bob 166–67, 189

INDEX

Eastwood, Clint 26, 100
  see also Dirty Harry
Ebert, Roger 58, 222
Edgerton, David 117
Elmocam 163, 223
Encino Man (1992) 115
Escape from Alcatraz (1979) 26
Escape from Los Angeles (1996) 180
Escher, M.C. 41, 65
Excalibur (1981) 53
Existentialism and Social Engagement in the Films of Michael Mann 3, 27

Fadlallah, Sheikh 136–37, 139, 146
Falling Down (1993) 115, 117
Far East 146, 152, 164, 196, 225, 118, 126, 133
Farina, Dennis 45, 55, 79
Fat Man and Little Boy (1989) 41
F.B.I. 13, 75, 79, 81, 84, 99, 152, 154, 192, 199, 203–05, 208, 211–16, 226, 231
Fermi, Enrico 11
fin-de-siècle 48, 212
Flak Tower, Vienna 70
Folsom State Prison 9, 17–21, 23–27, 29–33, 35–37, 39, 128, 226
Ford, John 108
Foreman, George 34, 155
formalism 18, 79, 92, 157, 191–92
Fort William Henry 100–03, 105, 107
Foxx, Jamie 29, 111, 159, 174, 183
fragmentation cinema 195, 221
Franco, Jesus 61
Frazier, Joe 155, 168
French Connection, The (1971) 58, 224
Friday the 13th (1980) 70
Friedkin, William 23, 63, 70, 224
Friedrich, Caspar David 149
  see also Two Men by the Sea
Fuller, Graham 96, 192–93
futurism 89, 117, 129, 190

Gaine, Vincent 3, 27
Gardiner, Meg 232
Gavras, Costa 23
Gein, Ed 76
German Expressionism 65, 67
Geronimo 142
Gerrard, Lisa 30, 144, 151
giallo genre 81–82, 91
Gingerbread Man, The (1998) 1
Ginsberg, Allen 142, 170, 188
Glass, Philip 71
Glenn, Scott 64
Godard, Jean-Luc 23, 56
Godfather, The (1972) 49, 185
Goldenthal, Elliot 5, 123, 221
golem, the 65, 67
Goodfellas (1990) 56, 66
Gorky Park (1983) 62
Greene, Graham 75
Greengrass, Paul 223
Gries, Tom 26
Grosbard, Ula 17
Guardian, The 10

Hall, Philip Baker 152
Halloween (1978) 56, 70, 78, 123
Hard Boiled (1982) 59, 226
Hardcore (1979) 51
Harkness, John 97, 100
Harris, Thomas 22, 87
Haubner, Steffen 53
Haut, Woody 51,
Hays' Codes 208
Heizer, Michael 130
Hemsworth, Chris 219, 221
Hendrix, Jimi 166–67
Heron III, Willie 24
Hitchcock, Alfred 75–78, 86, 88, 188
Hoenig, Dov 4, 110
Hoffman, Dustin 17, 142
Hohimer, Frank 13–14, 44, 46, 57, 69
Holden, William 48

239

Home Invaders: Confessions of a Cat Burglar, The (1975) 44
Hong Kong cinema 226
Hoover, J. Edgar 203, 205, 208, 211–16
Hopper, Edward 46, 126, 137, 173, 213
Hotel Room (painting) (1931) 213
Howard, James Newton 184
Howling, The (1981) 53
Humboldt Park 11
hybridity 61, 187, 224
hyperlink cinema 195

impressionism 157, 159, 161
Iñárritu, Alejandro González 230
Inception (2010) 62
Into the Void (2009) 145

James, Nick 58, 113, 138, 143
Jarmusch, Jim 177
Jaws (1975) 36
J.F.K. (1991) 194–95
Joffe, Roland 41, 109
Jones, Trevor 98–99
Joyless Street, The (1925) 14

Kaczynski, Ted 44, 152
  see also Unabomber
Kael, Pauline 5, 39
Keita, Salif 161, 168–69
  see also "Tomorrow"
Kennedy, John F. 35, 166, 167
Kennedy, Robert 167
King, Martin Luther 161, 164–65, 167
Kingdom of Heaven (2005) 105
Kirkwood, Gene 62
Klute (1971) 142
Koch, Hawk 62
Kochiyama, Yuri 164
Kolker, Robert 1–2, 45, 63, 76, 194,
Koyaanisqatsi (1982) 71
Kroeger, Wolf 105

Kubrick, Stanley 1, 15, 64, 101, 106, 113, 147, 187–88
Kurosawa, Akira 108

L.A. Confidential (1997) 115
L.A. Takedown (1989) 116
Lamm, Herbert K. 13, 20, 46, 52, 57
Lang, Fritz 75
Lange, Dorothea 208
LAX (Los Angeles airport) 117, 123, 130–31, 174, 188
Leatherstocking Tales 104
  see also Cooper, James Fenimore
Leifer, Neil 163
Lescaze, William 89
Lethal Weapon (1987) 115
Lewis, Daniel Day 97, 99, 102, 109, 111
Lewis, Joseph H. 177
Ligeti, György 70
Liston, Sonny 155, 157, 162, 170
Little Caesar (1930) 208
London International Film School 15, 22
Long Goodbye, The (1973) 2
Lorraine Motel, Memphis 165–66
Lorre, Peter 75
Los Angeles 5, 10–12, 16–17, 24, 45, 48–51, 54, 56–57, 82, 84, 104, 112, 115–32, 173–89, 201, 222, 229, 230
Los Angeles Plays Itself 119, 188
Louis, Morris xiii, 47
Lubezki, Emmanuel 162–63
Luck (2011–12) 5–10, 219, 232

M (1931) 75
Malick, Terrence 156, 181
Mangold, James 3, 232
Manhattan Melodrama (1934) 215
Mann, Ami Canaan 3, 219
mannerism 53, 140, 171
Marathon Man (1976) 142
Marcuse, Herbert 147

Index

Marriot Marquis, Atlanta 82
Martin, Adrian 139
Marvin, Lee 48
M.A.S.H. (1970) 2
McBain, Ed 82
McCabe & Mrs Miller (1971) 2
McKellen, Ian 64
Mean Streets (1973) 23, 47, 58, 106, 161,
Melville, Jean-Pierre 52
memento mori 64–65
Messina, Antonella Da Messina 107
Midnight Express (1978) 26
Mighty Joe Young 47
Milch, David 5, 7
Mille Miglia 232
Miller's Crossing (1990) 207
Mission, The (1986) 109
Moby 30, 171
modernism 12, 78, 84, 86–87, 122–23, 129, 186, 204–05, 207, 213, 216, 229
modernist architecture 52, 69, 77, 82
Monte Walsh (1970) 48
Muhammad, Elijah 163
Mulholland Falls (1996) 115
Müller, Jürgen 53
Murnau, F. W. 65

New Hollywood 209
New Left 16, 141–42
New Objectivity movement 14
New York Times, The 18, 62, 152, 221, 224
Night and the City (1950) 177
Night on Earth (1991) 177, 188
Nightcrawler (2014) 132, 187
Noé, Gaspar 145
Nolan, Christopher 4, 9, 41, 62, 184, 200, 230,
Noonan, Tom 22, 120
North by Northwest (1959) 77
Nouvelle Vague 14

Oasis of the Zombies (1981) 61
Ocampo, Octavio 142
Office in a Small City (painting) (1953) 137
Olsen, Mark 12
Oregon Trail, The 102
Ortiz, John 111
Ozu, Yasujiro 137

Pabst, Georg Wilhelm 14
Pacino, Al 50, 59, 99, 120, 135–36, 138, 143, 147, 152, 179, 214, 230, 232
Pakula, Alan J. 142
Pan's Labyrinth (2006) 61–62
Parallax View, The (1974) 142, 146
Parker, Alan 26
Parkman, Francis 102
  see also Oregon Trail, The
Peckinpah, Sam 212
Peeping Tom (1960) 81
Penn, Arthur 209
Percy, Valerie 44
Petersen, William 83, 99
Pickpocket (1959) 58
Picture of Dorian Gray, The (1891) 76
Plummer, Christopher 139, 146
Point Break (1991) 115–16
Police Story (1976–78) 17, 62
Poliziotteschi movement 82, 91
Popeye (1980) 63
Portman Jr, John Calvin 82
Portrait of La Causa (painting) 142
postmodernism 121, 186, 188
Poulsen, Kevin 219
Powell, Michael 81
Powell and Pressburger 23
Predator (1987) 70
Predator 2 (1990) 115
Prosky, Robert 46, 56, 63–64
Psycho (1960) 75
Public Enemy, The (1931) 208
Purvis, Melvin 157, 203–16

241

Raging Bull (1980) 161, 163–64, 168
Raiders of the Lost Ark (1981) 53
recidivism 20, 217
Red Dragon novel (1981) 22, 87
Red Shoes, The 23
Refn, Nicholas Winding 45
Renaissance art and perspective 77, 106–07, 122, 135, 145, 150, 157, 186–87, 192
see also Messina, Antonella Da Messina; Uccello, Paolo
Return of the Jedi (1983) 61
Rififi (1955) 52, 54
Rivele, Stephen J. 156
Rocky (1976) 62
Rocky Horror Picture Show, The (1975) 66
Rodriguez, Robert 56
Rollin, Jean 61
Room in Brooklyn (painting) (1932) 213
Royko, Mike xiii, 49
Rugendorf, Leo 44
Ruisdael, Jacob van 196
see also *View of Alkmaar*
Running Man, The (1987) 180
Rybin, Steven 3, 13, 37, 72, 84, 103, 139, 171

Samourai, Le (1967) 52
Sant'Elia, Antonio 117
Santucci, John 13, 46, 51
Sarris, Andrew 23, 39, 52
Scanners (1981) 67
Scarface (1932) 208
Scarface (1983) 61
Schindler's List (1993) 36
Scorsese, Martin 3, 15, 23, 56, 66, 68, 161, 163
Scott, Randolph 96, 109
Scott, Ridley 53, 83, 105, 129, 230
Searchers, The (1956) 108, 185
Seitz, George B. 96

Sharrett, Christopher 199, 201, 206–08, 222
Shawshank Redemption, The 34
Shikler, Aaron 35
Shining, The (1980) 64, 106, 147, 188
Siegel, Don 26
Sight & Sound 9, 12, 81, 88, 97, 113, 138, 192, 217
Silence of the Lambs, The (1990) 84–85, 88, 93
Silent Witness (2015–17) 83
Smith, Jada Pinkett 161, 174
Smith, Will 157, 163
Snake Eyes (1998) 145
Snowden, Edward 231
So Dark the Night (1946) 177
Soja, Ed 121, 129
Solomons, Jason 10
Sony Cine Alta camera 157
Sony F23 camera 206
Sony F900 camera 175–76
Sorcerer (1977) 63
Southland (2009–13) 132
Spielberg, Steven 4, 15, 17, 36, 187, 188
Spinotti, Dante 4, 98, 101, 118, 143
Star Wars (1977–) 42, 71, 174
Star Wars Episode I: The Phantom Menace (1999) 174
Starsky & Hutch (1975) 62
Stevenson, Robert Louis 75
Stone, Oliver 194–95, 231
Stowe, Madeleine 101
Straight Time (1978) 17, 19
Strain Theory xiii, 48
Strange Case of Dr Jekyll and Mr Hyde (1886) 75
Studi, Wes 110
Stuxnet 219, 231
Sullivan, Louis 12, 52, 174
Superman (1978) 66
Sv. Trojica Holy Trinity Church, Slovenia 65

Index

Tangerine Dream 30, 40, 42, 50, 63, 66, 70
Tarantino, Quentin 100
Tarzan the Ape Man (1981) 53
Taschen 68, 71, 154
Taxi Driver (1975) 33, 47, 51, 106, 161, 176, 211, 226
Taylor, Otis 6, 206
Terms of Endearment (1983) 61
Texas Killing Fields (2011) 219
Thin Red Line, The (1998) 156, 181
Thing, The (1982) 68, 71
This Gun for Hire (1942) 177
Thoret, Jean-Baptiste 194, 197–98
Three Days of the Condor (1976) 142
Tillman, Martin 164
Time Bandits (1981) 53
Tokyo Vice (2022–) 3, 10, 18, 232
"Tomorrow"161, 169
Tosar, Luis 195
Trading Places (1983) 61
Tree of Life (2011) 156
trompe l'oeil 107, 150
Truffaut, François 1, 23
Tuttle, Frank 177
Two Men by the Sea (painting) 149

Uccello, Paolo 107
Unabomber 44, 152
Unforgiven (1992) 100
Untouchables, The (1987) 211

Vampire of Düsseldorf 75
Veevers, Wally 66
Vega$ (1978–81) 62
Venora, Justine 120, 140
verité 23–24, 47, 58
Vice, Tokyo (2022–) 3, 10, 18, 232
Videodrome (1983) 71
Vietnam War 15–16, 22, 115, 117, 156, 166
View of Alkmaar (painting) (1675–80) 196

Viper Filmstream camera 175, 190
Voight, Jon 162, 58

Wallace, Dennis Wayne 89–90
Wallace, Mike 137, 139, 146, 150, 162
Wambaugh, Joseph 82, 174
Waxman, Michael 4
Webster, Colonel David 99
Wegener, Paul 65
Weld, Tuesday 28, 43
Welles, Orson 82
West, Benjamin 102
  see also *Death of Wolfe, The*
West Coast prison culture xiii, 9, 17, 19, 27, 28, 31, 36–37, 122
Westin Bonaventure Hotel 82
White Men Can't Jump (1992) 115
Who's Afraid of Virginia Woolf (1966) 15
Wild Bunch, The 48, 212
Wilde, Oscar 76
Wilder, Billy 177
Wilkinson, Christopher 156
Williams, Harry Gregson 221
Williams, John 42
Wilson, F. Paul 62–63
Woo, John 56, 59, 226
  see also Hong Kong cinema
Wright, Frank Lloyd 12, 117

X, Malcolm 126, 156–58, 160–61, 163–68, 171, 179
X, Y and Z axes xiii, 65, 124

Yates, Brock 232
Yerkovich, Anthony 189

Zabriskie Point (1970) 119
Zinneman, Tim 16–17
Zombie Lake (1981) 61